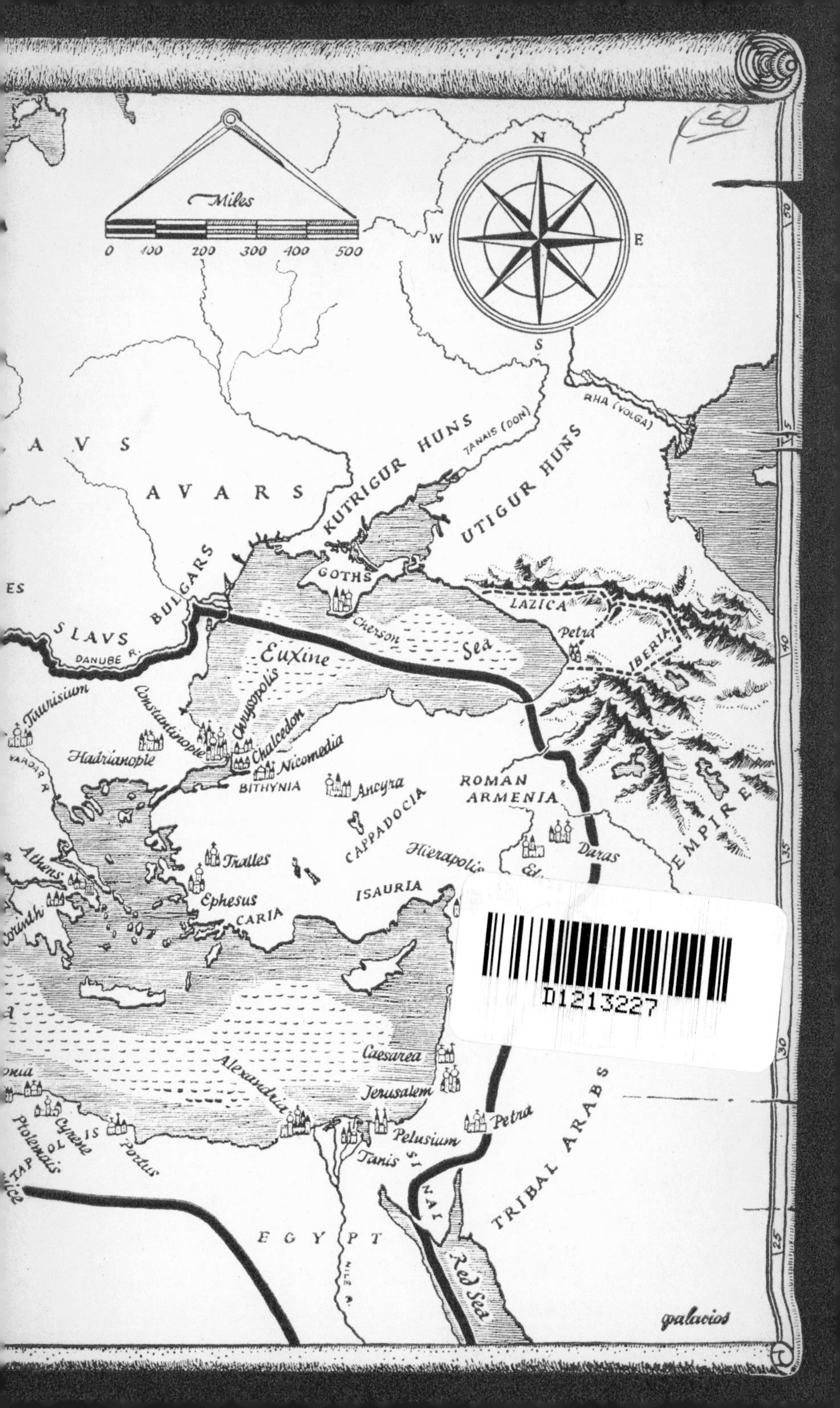

Miles
0 100 200 300 400 500
N
W
E
S
RHA (VOLGA)
TANAIS (DON)
KUTRIGUR HUNS
UTIGUR HUNS
A V S
AVARS
BULGARS
SLAVS
DANUBE R.
GOTHS
Cherson
Euxine
Sea
LAZICA
Petra
IBERIA
Chrysopolis
Constantinople
Chalcedon
Nicomedia
BITHYNIA
Hadrianople
VARDAR R.
Ancyra
CAPPADOCIA
ROMAN
ARMENIA
Daras
EMPIRE
Hierapolis
Tralles
Athens
Ephesus
CARIA
ISAURIA
Corinth
Caesarea
Alexandria
Jerusalem
Petra
Pelusium
Tanis
SINAI
TRIBAL ARABS
Cyrene
Ptolemais
Portus
EGYPT
NILE R.
Red Sea
palacios
D1213227

Theodora AND THE Emperor

by Harold Lamb

BIOGRAPHICAL NARRATIVES

Theodora and the Emperor
Suleiman the Magnificent
Genghis Khan
Tamerlane
Nur Mahal
Omar Khayyam: A Life
Alexander of Macedon: The Journey to World's End

NOVEL

A Garden to the Eastward

HISTORICAL NARRATIVES

The March of the Barbarians: The Mongol Dominion to the Death of Kubilai Khan
The Crusades: Iron Men and Saints
The Crusades: The Flame of Islam
The March of Muscovy: Ivan the Terrible and the Growth of the Russian Empire
The City and the Tsar: Peter the Great and the Move to the West (1648–1762)

FOR OLDER CHILDREN

Durandal
White Falcon
Kirdy: The Road Out of the World

Theodora AND THE Emperor

The Drama of Justinian

HAROLD LAMB

Doubleday & Company, Inc., Garden City, N.Y.
1952

Library of Congress Catalog Card Number: 52–8750

PRINTED IN THE UNITED STATES
FIRST EDITION

To

EDGAR J. GOODSPEED

"One who puts on the purple may never take it off."

THEODORA, *Empress of Byzantium*

Contents

The Ten Persons

JUSTINIAN, *the emperor*

THEODORA, *the empress*

PROCOPIUS FROM PALESTINE, *an historian*

BELISARIUS, *the soldier*

ANTONINA, *an actress, his wife*

JOHN OF CAPPADOCIA, *the economist*

NARSES, *the eunuch, also a general*

TRIBONIAN, *master of the laws*

ANTHEMIUS FROM TRALLES, *an architect*

ST. BENEDICT OF MONTE CASSINO

Theodora AND THE Emperor

I

The Palace by the Circus

THERE IS ONLY A GLIMPSE OF HIM AT FIRST, COMING DOWN from the mountains. Peter Sabbatius by name, he walked methodically down along the swift Vardar River, until he came to the edge of the sea.

Peter Sabbatius might have been eighteen years old, but he always appeared older than his age. A barbarian bred in a village of the higher mountains, he had amiable gray eyes, untrimmed tow hair, and an earnest way of trying to please other people. Vitality but no grace showed in his round ruddy face and long awkward body. A son of country peasants, he was on his way to the city in the hope of getting an education, with his clothes and some lawbooks and writings of the Christian Fathers carefully packed on a likable mule.

Somebody noticed that he believed everything he said himself, which was unusual in that uncertain time. Peter Sabbatius brought with him a letter from his elderly uncle Justin, who had made the journey long before to the city of Constantinople wearing a herder's cloak and carrying toasted bread—after Attila's Huns had looted through the upper Vardar Valley. Justin, it seemed, had made the journey for two reasons: because times were hard in their uplands after the raiding, and men from the farms were sought for the army, to take the place of hired Germans.

So much the bearer of the letter had explained to young Peter. The letter itself said very briefly in words printed carefully on a scrap of parchment: "Greeting to the son of my sister, Flavius Petrus Sabbatius in the village of Taurisium near to Scupi upon the upper Axius [Vardar] river." It was signed simply Justin. But the bearer, a merchant taking loads of eastern cloves, camphor, and sandalwood up to the Danube forts, had told Peter the message that the ill-schooled Justin had not been able to write out.

This almost forgotten uncle had reached the age of fifty years without a son to bear his name—at least without certain knowledge of such a son. Moreover Justin, after long service on the frontiers, had gained for himself a comfortable post as an officer of the excubitors, or household guards of the Emperor Favored by God. This post was profitable as well as honorable. So Justin desired to make use of his good fortune to educate Peter at the city college. Himself, he was too old a soldier to take to book learning, and he had heard from his sister that Peter manifested a zeal to study. If Peter, then, did well at college, he would be adopted by Justin and would also be in line for a government job. If not—well, no harm would be done. After delivering the message the camphor merchant had presented the dun mule to Peter as a free gift of Justin.

The mule had not influenced Peter. His mother assured him that Justin, who had gone from the river at his own age, possessed as much cunning as he lacked schooling. It seemed evident to Peter that his uncle desired a younger mind, able to interpret books, to aid him in his new moneyed dignity as officer and patrician at court. His mother said that Justin would not have sent the dun mule unless he expected to get back more than the price of the pack animal. And Peter craved, more than anything else, to sit at the feet of the masters of old-time learning, to be able to quote carelessly a line of Catullus about a charming girl, or to debate Aristotle's belief that a superior man is activated by ethics. Not that he dreamed of becoming a philosopher in the ancient sense of a lover of wisdom. He had lived too long on a farm. With the optimism of a self-taught boy he longed to draw into himself the magic of book learning in the city, in a sheltered room over a garden of fine plants, where, as a scholar and gentleman, he would be waited upon by body slaves as Master Peter . . .

The milestone stood on the paved road at the end of the river trail. Peter Sabbatius read the number upon the stone with a shiver of excitement because it told him the thousands of paces that would take him by way of this highroad to the New Rome, *Constantinopolis*, the city built by Constantine, where all the waters of the earth came together—or so his route book said. To enjoy his arrival on this coast road the more, he turned the mule with his serving boy into the wine-shop and stable by the milestone.

Across the road gleamed the long dark line of the sea. It stretched from horizon to horizon, with here and there a red sail moving. Standing under the arbor of the shop, Peter watched a sail coming out of the sunset toward Constantinople. Around him horses lifted their heads from water and voices argued over prices in strange dialects. A carriage drawn by white mules stopped at the arbor. It had silver rails and a shining gold initial V, and armed riders guarded it, although only a bearded barbarian captain stepped down from it to drink beer and talk with a loud voice. A German officer, it appeared, taking this carriage of the Illustrious Vitalian eastward.

Noticing Peter's pack mule, the yellow-maned captain stepped over to him, bowl in hand, and questioned him amiably about his name, rank, and destination. Learning that Peter fared alone from the northern mountains, the big captain laughed and said that only peasants made journeys on their legs, and there was plenty of room on the seat of the carriage for him. Peter laughed himself because the German spoke in dog Latin without proper verb endings.

"Youngling," quoth the good-natured man, "tie that pack beast behind. So, you sit, and we talk and go easy. You like that, my master?"

Peter said yes, he might, but the laden mule could not keep up with the patrician's carriage. It always pleased him to talk with whomever he met, even a Gothic warrior with a heavy sword who quite evidently meant to strip him of his belongings after dark on the road.

"So, we unburden the pack beast, and it goes well," decided the armed man, over his bowl. When Peter thanked him and started to refuse his offer, he drained his bowl of beer and shouted to his outriders. They finished their drinks and ran to the dun mule, throwing off the loads.

"Tell me no thanks," roared the Goth. "Only watch how well it goes."

So quickly did the trained men take to horseback and to the carriage that Peter could only watch. The jovial Goth climbed into his seat with a shout of farewell, and the equipage started off with Peter's dun mule tied behind. The escort did not even trouble to look back when they rounded a turn in the road.

Impulsively he started to run after them. Anger stirred him physically. Then, sensing the eyes of all those in the wineshop on him, he stopped and went back to his packs. Not knowing how to catch up with the armed riders, or how to claim his animal if he did so, he accepted the fact of the robbery and sold his bulkier belongings for a small price in silver. But he kept his books, and he took to the highroad with his boy, carrying packs.

It would be, he reflected coolly, many thousand hard paces now before he sighted the walls of Constantinople.

Peter Sabbatius journeyed in this fashion along the sea in that year 500 of our salvation. By the older Roman calendar it was the year 1254 from the founding of Rome on the palace hill above the marshes of the river Tiber. But in the last centuries that other, western Rome had relinquished the rule of the world and was in reality held by Theodoric and his Goths. During this same time New Rome had endured in the east, a citadel of culture besieged by incoming barbarian peoples, preserving within it the civilization of the buried Caesars.

His mother had pointed out that this very year was the midpoint between the birth of their Savior and the thousandth year when the rule of human beings would end, and the graves give up their dead, and the Devil return to claim his own.

Theodora was born about that same mid-millenium year 500. Her birth from an eastern circus woman attracted no attention at all. But at five years of age, more or less, she came before the eyes of the assembled men of Constantinople.

Just before the start of a day's races in the Hippodrome, when masculine crowds edged into seats to gossip and lay bets, an unscheduled event took place in the arena that had been swept and watered for the chariots. Three small girls paraded across the dirt. They had wreaths of flowers on their joined hands and on their heads, and they plumped down on their knees before the crowd at one side of the vast sunlit space. No one there gave them a second glance.

Then out stepped the official annnouncer. His sharp voice cut through the buzz of talk. These children, he proclaimed, knelt as suppliants to the Green faction. Their father, Keeper of the Bears, Acacius by name, employed by the Greens, had died. Their mother had married again to support these, her offspring. But the new husband had been refused the post of Keeper of the Bears. Now the children begged their Green faction to grant him the post.

No answer came from the throng on the Green benches. Those who listened were more intent upon the condition of favorite horses and the all-important selection of Green drivers. The races were the solace of their troubled lives. Besides, somebody else had bribed the Green dancing master to give him the job of grooming the bears.

"It is to keep these children from starving," rasped the announcer.

"No, no!" shouts answered. "What is all this about bears? Take them off!"

If the Green faction took no interest in its children, the dignified announcer had no mind to waste his breath in charity, and he strode off. The three girls, having been coached how to behave only up to this point, did not know what to do next.

Then they heard fainter shouts from across the arena. "What is this? . . . Does the Green deme cast out their own children? Ah, they would cast out their mothers, if they knew them. . . . Come over, little girls—come over here."

The invitation roared from the tiers under the portico, by the vacant imperial gallery. It came from the Blues, the antagonists of the Greens. The Blue faction of the city mixed no more with the Green than the blue sea mingled with the green land; at the race track or political rally as well as in street rioting the factions opposed each other, and as soon as the Green spectators refused the petition of the small girls the Blues took an interest in them.

Frightened, the children knelt helplessly among their wreaths.

"Your father can groom our bears. This way, girls."

Whereupon the three got up and hurried across the track to the shade of the portico. A troupe of acrobats came out then to form a moving human pyramid, and the incident was forgotten, except that the three girls, Comito, Theodora, and Anastasia, became the public charge of the Blue political faction.

Because she had come from the friendly Syrian coast where the sharing of bread is not an act of charity, the mother of the growing girls never seemed to be able to make ends meet in the greatest of cities. It is clear that she tried hard to do so. Whatever happened to her latest husband, the Syrian vanished after a while from the animal cages of the Hippodrome and appeared in its theater. There she earned money herself by going off with men.

Theodora at first carried her mother's stool around, in the audience. Then, when her elder sister Comito matured enough to catch the glance of men, Theodora followed Comito on and off stage clad in a slave's tunic with sleeves. Quickly enough she discovered that if she did something funny it amused the audience. This critical audience tired of flute music and dancing and choruses only too easily; a bit of unconscious fun cheered it up.

By falling over a stool, by tangling herself in the flowing scarfs of dancers, and by blowing out her cheeks when she was slapped, Theodora began to act as an underage clown. She did so perhaps because she could neither play the flute nor dance well herself, but she learned how to attract an audience by impishness.

There was a popular trick dog at that time on the Hippodrome theater stage. It was blind. It could count, and above all could run among the spectators to point to the one who might be the greatest glutton or woman fancier. For a human actor to perform such tricks would be boring; the blind dog, being an animal, achieved fame and profit for its trainer. Theodora in those early years may have taken her cue from the dog.

In the Syrian woman's family the mutual task was to earn food and sustenance by amusing gentlemen. No reputable women were allowed to attend the races, the plays, or the pantomimes. Nor had the Syrian's brood any such fame as the popular dog. Comito began to sleep with men when barely old enough to do so.

Theodora, slight in body, delicate in features, with a mane of black hair, did not manage to get along so easily. Acting as mimic and child attendant upon Comito, she attracted attention only when she could make the watchers laugh. "No one," rumor relates, "ever saw her embarrassed."

It would be no novelty for a ten-year-old girl to grow red and hang her head when male hands felt her body under her clothes. A smile, a quip, and a wriggle answered the situation better. Boldness paid off better than tears. To jump up on a festival table and walk around above the heads of the reclining diners with her dress pulled up to her armpits earned guffaws and *Aves* of approval, and kept an underage girl from having her dress stripped off by the servant louts waiting around the doors for their masters to emerge from the feast.

They say that the youthful Theodora lost no chance to take off her clothes, or as much of them as the theater allowed. She took them off herself. Like the fashionable dog, she had to depend on her tricks, and by them she gained some small reputation in the most sophisticated of all cities. It is certain, however, that while she lived with her mother she learned two things, never to forget—to watch out for good coined money and to laugh when she was hurt.

If she had had the skill of oriental girls in dancing with flying swords, incense, or veils, she might have been a success. If she had had the clear voice of a Greek islander, she might have hit upon a popular song and earned pay in gold by performing at the feasts of the aristocrats. Lacking such talents, she had only her imagination and naturally quick wit.

For she outgrew her role of child clown. A mature woman of fifteen, even though unusually slender, could not amuse an audience by getting slapped. Moreover Theodora had not the fleshy vitality of western women; she could not hold the eye of an aristocrat by a display of breasts or thighs. Nervous and pale, her brilliant dark eyes—heritage of her Syrian blood—under brows that met across her slim forehead gave her only an elusive, brittle beauty. At the same time her mother's looks were fading, while Anastasia had not become nubile. Theodora seemed to feel her responsibility for the family, while she had little hope for herself.

Circumstances had made her a pariah in the city. A woman of the theater was almost legally bound to serve as prostitute when sought by a spectator; the law barred her, definitely, from marriage with her betters—unless by dispensation of the Church, after leading a sexless life for a while. The same law kept her children from any life but that of the circus, unless the child were born after the grace period of redemption.

While the law bound Theodora to a performer's life, the huge Hippodrome was in reality her greatest antagonist—and by now she had learned to detect any influence hostile to her. In that edifice of brick arcades and marble sheathing lay a power against which no half-breed woman, lacking an influential male protector, could possibly strive. It was the power of the men, assembled from the streets of Constantinople, that had, by a whim, once bestowed on her family the pay of a keeper of the bears.

The Hippodrome was the heart of Constantinople. Stretching for a quarter mile along the height above the sea, it accommodated sixty thousand spectators on its marble benches, and when the chariots raced the trees and rooftops to the east held almost as many more. All those thousands were bound by delight in the speeding four-horse teams, by the lust of gambling and the relief of hours of oblivion. Along the Spine that divided the track shone monuments of Roman glory, the Colossus in bronze, the giant nymph holding a warrior in her outstretched hand, the ancient column of the twining serpents of Delphi, and the obelisk of forgotten pharaohs of Egypt. The portrait statue of the reigning emperor was also there. But the crowds gave more heed to the tablets bearing the names of famous horses, and the statue of the immortal driver who had won his races for twelve years.

No bodies were carried out now from the small Gate of the Dead. The games of pagan Rome, the bruising pugilists and deadly swordsmen—gladiators—had ceased to exist after the Christian Church became the supreme force in the empire. The refinement of two centuries since the founding of the city did away with the holocausts of human victims, burned or devoured by beasts, and the conflicts of massed animals. The bears and other beasts of the modern Hippodrome were merely pursued and fought by human hunters. For one thing, Asiatics like Theodora were not excited as the earlier Romans had been by war games and the mass shedding of blood.

The Hippodrome, then, had become the center of the world of men. Women had to place their bets outside and learn the results of the races or the rioting afterward. For the arena served also as a rendezvous of the factions; it provided a congress for the folk of the streets. It heralded triumphs and it springboarded revolts.

Curiously enough—although nothing in Constantinople was really curious except to visiting barbarians—the Hippodrome rose against the very walls of the Sacred Palace where the business of ruling went on methodically. There was even a way from the rambling palace through corridors, across a chapel, to the Kathisma, or imperial box, from which the emperor himself could watch the finish of the races or listen to the outcry of the crowd if it had a grievance. The old saying that the voice of the people was the voice of God lacked truth now that the patriarch of the Church had become the voice of God, but the outcry of the populace in the Hippodrome could send emperors hurrying into exile.

Several years before, Theodora had heard the terrifying roar of the populace—"*Give another emperor to the Romans!*"

The roar had gone on, menacing and insatiable, until after a moment's silence it had changed to a tumult of laughter.

Some wooden buildings close by burned, and a costume keeper said she had watched some men in the street catch a running monk and cut off his head to put it on a pole.

"Eh, it was the doing of Anastasius," a tightrope walker assured Theodora afterward. (Although only an Egyptian acrobat, he had been privileged to sit in the arena.) "He changed the orthodox words when he spoke the Trisagion, no longer saying 'Holy, Mighty, Immortal Lord' as he should. Well, some of us thought it sounded like heresy. Why should that old goat Anastasius change our greeting to God? Perhaps the Devil put it into his silly head. I don't know the truth of that. Then some of the Blues turned those houses into torches, and we all yelled 'Give us another emperor!' Anastasius ran back into the dressing room to wriggle out of his purple and gold in fright. He bobbed back into the box and made the announcer call out that he would never put on the purple again, so help him. It was really funny, and we had to laugh. We laughed so hard we told Anastasius to go and put on his clothes again."

Anastasius was the emperor, a very old and well-meaning person, who saved up the money in the public treasury. Theodora never forgot that outcry of the Hippodrome crowd.

Such things she could learn only by hearsay. From every entrance of the Sacred Palace she was barred as utterly as from the tiny palace in the garden by the sea where an empress in labor was carried, to bear her child in a chamber of purple marble. How few children nowadays seemed to be born in the purple!

A pariah, living in the side shows of the giant Hippodrome, she had left the stage where shapelier actresses bathed in tubs or wrestled in an odd fashion with men. The backstage of the theater is a place of hard reality. Theodora, having no role to play or patron to give her prestige, became inferior even to the drudges who mended the costumes or put make-up on the clowns.

In that reality she could only pretend that she was busy

and occupied. By trying to do so she had learned to read, and she had a bright way of chattering with the groups around the sporting aristocrats who sometimes wandered from the stables to look over the actresses in their dressing chamber. Where a quick word or an odd jest drew attention, she sparkled. It was easy for her to mimic well-known persons, and the older aristocrats found her a good companion.

But whether on a pleasure barge up the Golden Horn, or at a feast in the gardens of the uplands, over on the Asian shore, men would force her to submit to them until they were satisfied. After that, seemingly, few of them desired a witty companion. Like satiated animals, they would go to sleep or bathe or drink more wine.

Perhaps the girl hated them as brute masters. There was some talk—remembered and enlarged upon later—that such wooers found the child clown still extant in Theodora. Gossip had it that decent men lying with her in darkness had unnatural tricks played on them, as if a demon had entered her. It does seem as if her companions of the night would dodge aside if they met her by day, to avoid touching her garment—or to escape her eyes.

Out of this situation Theodora found a way, although not an easy one. She left the city. As a woman of one Hecebolus, a bearded and self-important merchant from Tyre—her own Syrian coast—she journeyed across the great sea to Pentapolis, in Africa, where Hecebolus was to serve as governor.

In that province she knew for a year the mild luxury of a governor's house, and dislike of its master. There she had a child, a daughter. Some time later she left the house of Hecebolus without taking jewelry or money or even the clothes that had been given her. After that for a while all trace of her is lost.

During these years Peter Sabbatius had remained unnoticed in the city—until the extraordinary happening of the summer of 518.

He studied. He hardly saw the Hippodrome or the palace area at the far point of the city. His orbit lay about the Auditorium that crowned the third hill with its halls where thirty-one orators and professors lectured students. At first, awed by the immense buildings and the dressed-up throngs hurrying over the paved streets, Peter had gone from lecture to lecture with the zeal of a neophyte. But after a while he ceased to be satisfied with the elderly lecturers wearing gray robes. They wasted so much time in argument, and they had a way of absenting themselves when the chariots raced. Since the students could follow their own inclinations—and Peter began to believe that all Constantinopolitans went where their inclinations led them—Peter started to study on his own account in the fine libraries, which had the additional advantage of remaining open at night. There he could investigate all the happenings of the past in the neatly copied manuscripts of Suetonius, Tacitus, and countless others. He enjoyed particularly delving into the private lives of the Caesars who had ordered those events.

Besides, Peter realized that he was older than most of the youths of the lecture halls; he had a poor background for the higher studies such as philosophy; he had to concentrate, and learn to read swiftly. Then, too, his practical mind probed for reasons and causes. *Scientia potestas est,* said the legend above the Auditorium portico. Knowledge was indeed power—if the knowledge were accurate, and not merely prating or preaching or the endless Greek theorizing.

For a long time the tall and clumsy Peter Sabbatius behaved like a starving man confronted by massed tables of unknown, delectable foods. He grudged each hour that took him away from his labor over the books. When daylight faded he would go out of the library, walking briskly to the main street, the midway, Mesé, toward the enticing smell of the bakeries where he bought a fresh loaf of bread; then on his way back he added olives and a flask of wine, to provide his supper, which he ate on a bench in the University

Forum, almost deserted at that hour. By then the oil lamps would be lit and he could go back to his study table until the closing hour, when he returned to his sleeping room and the books waiting for him there. It gave him a feeling of comfort to stretch out by his own lamp and draw the familiar volumes toward him. In the early hours of the morning the noisy street below him grew quiet as the fields of Taurisium and nothing disturbed him. Before sunrise he allowed himself to sleep. He had done well enough with as little sleep during harvest time in the mountains. Only here in the city there was an endless, strange harvest to be gathered.

Not that the barbarian-born Peter created for himself a dream world of the books. He did penetrate such a world of memory and imagination; at the same time he related it to the human beings and the city around him. His hard common sense gave heed to the gossip of the bakers and the light chatter of prostitutes waiting under the arcades. In the taverns sailors had much to say of cargoes brought from the land of Punt and the far Indian Sea. Whatever he heard went into Peter's memory to stay; he had never learned the trick of a cultured man, of taking notes of facts and then forgetting them. At the same time he made the mistake of believing almost everything he heard.

Count Vitalian reminded him of that. After finishing his supper on the bench Peter liked to climb up the column in the forum. Among the inscriptions about victories over the Goths on its base, he had found a narrow door that led to a precipitous spiral stair inside, up to the summit of the column and its statue of Theodosius the Great—who had built the mighty threefold walls of Constantinople across the land. Everyone said these walls were impregnable.

Leaning out by the statue, Peter watched specks of light appear in the dark streets below, as the hanging oil lamps were lit. At such a moment his city assumed the magical aspect of an illuminated island, surrounded by the darkness of the harbor and the seas and the far land. He thought of it as an island of knowledge and order, secure in the darkness of a world adrift, a Happy Island.

Then going down and out the door one evening, he almost stepped into a passer-by. The man turned sharply and two who followed him ran up, drawing short swords from under their cloaks. "Let him live," said the first quickly. "For he does not look to me like a spy, or an assassin either."

Peter recognized Vitalian, a noble although Bulgar-born—a handsome, assured soldier who seldom showed his face by day in the city. Hurriedly—for violence made him nervous—he explained how he used the column for a lookout.

This seemed to amuse Count Vitalian. "An island of security?" he murmured. "Do you believe there is any such thing?"

"Yes, Noble Vitalian. If its walls be impregnable."

"If! Theodosius had skillful engineers, and these walls will never be crossed by barbarians—until somebody is paid to open a gate or start a riot inside." As if exasperated, the soldier-patrician asked for Peter's name and identification. Then he said in parting, "Don't step out of monuments after dark, Noble Justinian. Or if you do, hire yourself a bodyguard. And for your own good, forget that you've seen me."

As if impatient at the delay, Vitalian strode off with the two swordsmen at his back. Peter wondered if he were not safer at his books than this distinguished soldier with his bodyguards.

By then his uncle Justin had made good his promise and adopted Peter Sabbatius as his son, with the name of Justinian. As Peter had suspected, his uncle thought well of his studies because he wanted his new son to serve as his secretary. Whenever letters came to the old man, he would have Peter read them and write down his answers. Justin kept insisting he could not read, but Peter caught him sometimes conning over the written answers carefully. Although more than sixty-five years of age, the mountaineer held his tall body erect; he never worried about what might happen, saying that you could not see Fate until the wench caught up to you. He married the peasant girl who had followed him faithfully. A simple soldier, he called himself, waiting to retire with his medals to his garden. Yet he dressed with the care of a young sportsman—criticizing Peter's habit of wearing shapeless tunics and drab cloaks—he had been promoted to lieutenant general after a successful campaign, and quite abruptly he was put in a cell by his friend John the Hunchback, Master of the Armed Forces, on the order of the emperor. Justin had been charged with conspiracy. This meant that Peter himself might be arrested as well, as a conspirator.

Startled by the news, Peter hurried by the courier road to the Asia shore where his uncle seemingly awaited execution. Inquiring his way to headquarters, he found Justin playing dominoes with John the Hunchback, who had decided to release the prisoner. "Officially," Justin explained to his nephew, "the commanding general has had a dream. In that dream a mighty being appeared to him—certainly no human being. It said to him that he should release me, because the prisoner and his family were fated to be of great aid to his country. That dream satisfied the emperor, our master. You are all my family except little Lupicina."

"It was a revelation," said John the Hunchback, over his dominoes.

"The most difficult situation," agreed Justin, "can usually be solved by a revelation."

Peter had heard Justin's name joined to that of Count Vitalian, who had caused trouble in the northern armed forces. When they were alone in Justin's quarters—no longer a cell—the veteran admitted that he respected Vitalian and had discussed politics with him. It seemed that Vitalian had angered Anastasius, the emperor, by starting rumors in the camps that Anastasius had relapsed into heresy. This affected the soldiers on the frontiers.

"The truth is that in Vitalian, my son, you will find the strongest will of all of us. But he is a nuisance because he cannot be controlled. Anastasius is weak as a water lily, and doting besides. Eh, he gets things done by making promises which he never carries out. Vitalian is so brilliant he gives us no peace of mind, while Anastasius keeps everything calm." Justin sighed. "Command brings worries with it. I had a better time with Lupicina, in the ranks of the excubitors."

Peter did not believe that. It seemed as if both Justin and John the Hunchback, while appeasing the irresolute emperor, did not want to make an enemy of the determined Vitalian. And he reflected that it was lucky for him that Vitalian had recognized his name at Theodosius' column.

When, thereafter, Vitalian made his appearance unexpectedly with a small fleet of galleys filled with seditious soldiery off the harbor of the *Chrysoceras,* the Golden Horn, Justin met him with an escort of government war galleys discharging flames. This fire from the ships was contrived by chemical experts borrowed from the university.

The result of the encounter was that the restless Vitalian turned back his prows and fled, while the simple soldier Justin was appointed Count of the Excubitors, or commander of the emperor's guard, and perforce took up his residence near the Sacred Palace. There he insisted that Peter-Justinian should join him.

And there, with his library moved to a great room over a garden, Peter realized that he would no longer be allowed to study at will. As Justin's adopted son he was expected to guard the mind of his tolerant uncle, to serve as an intelligent spy and adviser at need.

Henceforth he could only work at his books at night, while Justin enjoyed his sleep, but this he continued to do as before.

Justinian—as Peter was called thereafter—brought to the palace his consuming curiosity, his instinct for fact finding and remembering, and the quiet persistence of his peasant blood. His good nature made a pleasant impression and attracted no attention. Because he stopped to chat with the perfectly mannered custodians of the palace as he had done formerly with bakers and street girls, he got on their good side and passed for a harmless busybody. Silently—he had learned the value of silence—he discovered a great deal about the workings within the palace and the tensions within its folk. No one else took such pains to probe into situations.

The day came, unnoticed, when he began to lead his new father. Justin, who had acquired an education by the simple process of adopting an educated son, did not realize that Justinian was gaining notable importance through the celebrity of his adopted father. The veteran still felt a faint contempt for the studious man who, in the prime of life, had never heard the tramp of a disciplined regiment following him and could not parry a sword thrust at his ungainly body. Yet because Justinian served him faithfully, the old soldier trusted him. Justin kept the three hundred excubitors drilled and turned out like automatons of silver and steel; otherwise he devoted himself to enlarging his estates with the wealth that came by devious ways into the practiced hand of a Count of the Excubitors. Especially since the Master of Offices—the Secretary of State—was Celer, with whom he had shared command on the Persian front. Having taken hard knocks together, he and Magister Celer now watched out for each other. His wealth, of course, would go to Justinian, his sole heir.

"You should take a wife," he urged his son. "You should have children and a proper villa. You won't have 'em unless you marry."

There were patrician girls enough ready to mate with the adopted son of the majestic Count of the Excubitors. Perhaps for that reason, Justinian had not married as yet; perhaps he did not want to change his routine of constant work and occasional visits to attractive girls of the Mesé arcades. And as for the count's wife, even in the jeweled coronet and silk of court ceremonial she still resembled a dumpy camp cook.

Such little things disturbed Justinian's sense of order. It troubled him to discover that the Golden Milestone in the courtyard before the Senate chamber was actually not gold but gilded copper. This milestone marked, theoretically, the beginning of all the routes of the empire—or what remained of the empire. Over it stood the giant statue of Augustus, the founder, who had brought order and law and peace into the world for the first time. Or so Roman history said.

If the Golden Milestone had proved to be an illusion, Justinian realized that the living emperor was also something of an illusion. That is, the ailing Anastasius was far from being an Augustus Caesar. Along with the higher officials, Justinian prostrated himself when ceremony required before the dais of porphyry and gold on which rested the scarlet-hosed foot of the sitter on the throne, of the Autocrat, the surviving Emperor of the Romans. He felt the impact of the throne-room gleaming with gold mosaics under invisible lights and wreathing incense. He heard the chime of distant silver bells, more subtle than the call of trumpets. The figure of the motionless emperor might have been a statue encrusted with amethysts and rubies. But he prostrated himself, as did the others, to the majesty of Roman tradition, to the memory of Augustus the first emperor and Constantine the founder of his city. The real work of government, he understood now, was carried on by such personages as Magister Celer, the patriarch of the Church, the leaders of the senate, and the prefects of the provinces.

Anastasius himself had been a lesser official, chosen as consort by a widowed empress, Ariadne—a kindly man who had managed skillfully to avoid trouble ever since——

The extraordinary happening of July, in the year of Our Lord 518, was that at eighty-eight years of age Emperor Anastasius died unexpectedly in the night before anyone had been chosen to succeed him. It seemed to those in the Sacred

Palace at the time that Fate had intervened in their affairs.

Lacking children, Anastasius had spoken of his three nephews, without naming one of the three. The dominant Ariadne lay in her purple marble sarcophagus. In the midsummer heat most of the senators slept tranquilly in their distant suburban villas. So it happened that no one could be summoned immediately to became the new Autocrat.

Tradition required that one be named without delay, and tradition insisted that he be acceptable to the Church, the army, and the people.

"That night," Peter the Patrician wrote afterward, "some confusion occurred." This was a truly diplomatic understatement.

The man who took advantage of the confusion was Justinian. Roused by the silentiaries—the noble personal attendants of the dead emperor—the two veteran commanders, Justin and Celer, took charge of the armed men outside and inside the palace. Justin told his officers, "Our lord has ceased to exist, as a man. Now they must deliberate and elect an emperor, guided by God." The more sophisticated Celer watched the patriarch and high officials hurry into the portico of the great hall at sunrise. After listening to their arguments, he warned them briefly: "We should decide on a name quickly. If we do, all others will follow our lead without thought. But if we don't act quickly we'll have to follow them."

Still the arguing went on without result. As the sun rose the stately nobles in the hall began to hear the voice of the Hippodrome. Word of the emperor's death had passed through the city streets, and the populace was thronging to its meeting place. As Celer had anticipated, the people's factions gave tongue as soon as they beheld the curtains drawn across the imperial box. "Long live the senate! Roman senate, do something! Where is our emperor given by God, for the army, for the people?"

As the throng increased outside, it tired of shouting and

began to act for itself. Some soldiers sighted John the Hunchback, and hoisted him up on a shield, announcing that he was the choice of the army. A volley of stones from the Blue benches greeted him. Justin's excubitors rallied to the defense of his friend, and blood flowed. The riot surged along the passage to the Ivory Gate of the palace, where other soldiers raised the Master of the Armed Forces to a table and shouted that here was their emperor. "Bring out the purple, you in the palace! Bring out the crown!"

But the experienced guards at the Ivory Gate refused to open to a mob. In their turn the excubitors drove at the rival candidate. The fighting, between trained men, became deadly. It was more than unruly conflict of mobs: the faction fortunate enough to get its candidate accepted might gain great power.

Justinian, who had come out to watch developments, managed to hold back the excubitors and escort the man on the table away to a safe place. Whereupon the excited excubitors seized on the son of their officer and demanded that he offer himself as candidate. Justinian refused, and broke away. Then the factions joined together to shout at the gatekeepers to pass out the imperial regalia. This the guards would not do without knowing the name of the man to wear the crown. Name after name was called by the crowd, while the guards shook their heads.

While the tumult echoed in the hall, a late-comer took the lead there. Amantius the Chamberlain very quickly sensed the nervous frustration of prelates and senators. With the instinct of a politician he suggested a compromise, naming a certain Theocritus belonging to no faction—except Amantius' own. He had come armed with gems and gold, which he immediately turned over to the only spectator, Justin the Count, to distribute among the quieter senators while Amantius made the rounds after him to urge that Theocritus' name be cried. Unmistakably, there was no more time to waste.

Justinian noticed this, and saw a priceless opportunity in it. Going to his father's shoulder as Justin proceeded mechanically to carry out the Chamberlain's bidding, he whispered, "Do as he says quickly, but say nothing yourself at all."

There was such confusion in the hall that no one noticed him. He stepped over to Magister Celer, who was glowering at the frantic officials. Then he vanished from the hall. Justin continued obediently to hand out wealth to men in the corners. Clearing his throat, Magister Celer let out his voice as if in command.

"Long live Justin, our emperor given by God!"

Both Amantius and Justin were too amazed to protest. The senators who had been bribed added their voices for the munificent Justin; the patriarch, with a sigh of relief, bestowed his vote on a man who, at least, might preserve the peace; the senators quickly agreed. They hurried the bewildered veteran out the passage, where one of the mob cut his lip open with a blow.

Witnesses say that Justin acted like a man amazed. But he may well have suspected that his old comrade Celer would cry his name.

Silence fell on the Hippodrome as the curtains of the Kathisma were drawn back. There stood Justin, bleeding at the mouth, and voiceless.

At sight of their commander, the excubitors roared approval; soldiers cried the name of the friend of John the Hunchback; the Blues rose to acclaim a candidate of their own faction. Even the Greens had nothing at the moment against Justin. They all cried, "Justin, August, thou wilt conquer."

Hearing this consent of the patriarch and approval of the army and people, the guards of the wardrobe hurried to the box with the imperial purple mantle and scarlet hose. The guards of the box raised the military standards from the floor, and several held their shields as a screen over Justin while the purple was fitted on him. A lancer placed a gold chain on his head for a crown, the patriarch blessed the chain, Justin grasped the lance and a shield and stepped out to face the Roman people, his new subjects.

Unaccountably, Magister Celer, who should have presented him then, was absent, complaining of pains in his feet from long standing. Nor was Justinian to be seen in the box.

Justin promised five gold pieces to each soldier who had held a shield over him, then remembered that, as Autokrator, he should speak to the people. The patriarch prompted him.

"Emperor Caesar Justin, Victorious, ever August, says to you——" He sought for something to say. "May God aid us to accomplish what is good for you and the state."

"Reign as thou hast lived!" the crowd shouted excitedly. "Be abundant to the world! Live long, Imperator! Worthy of the city! Give us honest magistrates——"

"I will give each of you a pound of silver."

"May God protect the Christian emperor."

Justin had recovered his poise. Truly he made a fine figure, although his erect head was bloody. "Our care shall be to provide prosperity, with divine help, and keep you altogether at peace."

"Worthy of the empire, Justin, thou wilt conquer! God will surely help thee."

In this manner, according to the chronicle of Peter the Patrician, was the soldier Justin elected to the throne "beyond any expectation."

The election, engineered by Justinian and Celer on the spur of opportunity, had the great advantage of surprise. No effective opposition could be formed in a few hours. Vainly the startled Chamberlain, Amantius—who had no more money in hand—spread slander that the emperor-elect had been a swineherd and was an ignoramus, unable to sign his name. Being a eunuch and unpopular with army officers, Amantius rallied no following and accomplished nothing except to nettle Justin, who soon convinced himself that it was now his duty to serve his country as emperor.

There remained one final test: to manifest to the populace that the election had taken place by divine providence, as Celer had announced and Justin himself, prompted by the patriarch, had repeated. Fortunately, since he had assumed office early on a Monday, his new friends had a week to prepare for his recognition in church on the coming Sunday. Celer, still doubtful of the final result, continued to be invisible while he cared for the sudden pain in his feet, and Justinian kept out of the public eye. But tales went out into the streets and were repeated from mansion to tavern that John the Hunchback had dreamed that Justin and his family would be the salvation of the country, and that the dead Anastasius also had dreamed that he would be succeeded by the first officer to enter his chamber after his death. That officer, unquestionably, had been Justin.

Unquestionably, too, Justin was orthodox in his religion. Unlike Anastasius or Vitalian, he had never bothered his head about religious whys and wherefores. As a simple soldier, he had attended communion reverently; this attitude of mind was shared by the leaders of the Blue faction—wealthy magnates who wished to preserve the status quo here in life and hereafter beyond the grave.

So when Sunday came, the vast candlelit depths of the Sancta Sophia cathedral-church were packed with orthodox believers and their families, eager for the return of the old religion. This assemblage was keyed by the presence of women who had had no share in the Hippodrome election; they wore their finest dresses and egged on their husbands or lovers with growing excitement. For these women, satirical though they might be of their social life and even of themselves, held blindly to religious faith and, without understanding the nature of religion very well, insisted on the ritual of it. Their critical eyes approved the curled white hair and fine carriage of the new Autocrat and they felt instantly sympathetic to this "Old Justin" as they termed him in whispers to their men.

The congregation of St. Sophia was accustomed to debate as noisily as the crowd in the Hippodrome, and the appearance of the patriarch in robes drew its vociferation upon him. Standing without escort among the worshipers, Justinian heard the outcry with satisfaction. "Live long, Patriarch! Live long, Emperor! Live long, Augusta [the new empress, Lupicina, the peasant camp follower]. Why have we been without communion? Give us communion now, with your hands. Ah, go up in the pulpit. Comfort us! You are orthodox. What are you afraid of? The faith of the Trinity conquers! Why don't you proclaim it? An orthodox emperor reigns at last. Throw out the Manichaeans. Whoever does not say it is a Manichaean himself. Throw out the falsifiers. The faith of the emperor conquers—the faith of the Augusta prevails. Live long, the new Constantine: live long, the new Helen."

In two days it was all decided. The congregation held the floor of St. Sophia until its demands were satisfied with promises. The congregation did not raise the question of Justin's election, in its eagerness to have him accomplish all it wished. His sanctification as the ruler chosen by God went forward with only admonitions to hurry. With much truth Justin himself could dictate a letter to the distant orthodox Pope at Rome in the west, at Justinian's advice: "Against our will we have been elected . . . by favor of the Almighty, by choice of the highest ministers of the palace and of the venerable senate, after the nomination of the most powerful army."

This letter spoke of his wife, sensibly enough, as "most pious." In fact the former Lupicina, now empress under the well-sounding reign name of Euphemia, realized that the only thing she could do effectively in the public eye was to aid the Church. Euphemia declared that politics gave her a headache; she seldom showed herself at court ceremonies and began, as a religious recluse, to build a nunnery in the city. Justinian remained almost as inconspicuous, taking the title of Count of the Domestics (of the palace) which had been held by the unfortunate Theocritus who was put to death with Amantius on the charge of conspiracy.

So in the year 518 the surviving Roman Empire came under the rule of a handsome man sixty-eight years of age whose chief qualification was that he had been a popular soldier. To aid him he had Justinian, whose only demonstrated ability was that of a hard-working student.

II

Theodora's House

ONCE THEODORA HAD HAD FRIENDS IN THE CITY OF CONSTANTINOPLE; she had never gone hungry there for long because when the market men took down their stalls at the end of the day they would hand out stale sesame bread or leftovers to an alert girl who passed on to them the latest rumors of the Mesé. Uprooted from such familiar haunts, the city girl knew hunger in Africa.

She had the feel of dirt upon her each day, sleeping in it, soon neglecting to wash her food clean, for water no longer poured from city aqueducts. Skeletons of children around her would make a meal off a handful of decaying grapes from which the flies rose to their faces. Once Theodora had taken hours to cleanse herself in a public bath, in the scented vapor and cooling chambers. . . .

A young circus performer with a repertory of jests and a baby could not make a living in the desert. The desert had its herds of thin animals and wandering black folk fearful of being enslaved. The caravans that crossed it demanded silver from her; she could not walk carrying a burden like the black women. To reach the nearest great city she shared the tent of a caravan master, and slipped out of the tent on the night before the last for dread that she would be sold bodily in the market at the end of the journey. But she lost her way in the unmarked waste of clay that had never been plowed up or made into bricks by human hand.

When she started to walk toward a square outcropping of red rock that might have been a guardian fort, she found that the embrasures in the rocks were small caves. Evil-smelling rain water stood in a hollow hewn in the rock. One other woman lived in a cave, sleeping on a mat and eating only a few grapes and lentils at the end of the daylight. This woman amazed Theodora because she insisted she had been Caesaria, a patrician owning hundreds of slaves and ordering whatever she fancied for a meal. Now with shrunken arms and breasts she exposed herself to the burning sun; her skin had become like old parchment, her fingers claws.

Yet this Caesaria abode voluntarily in the cave, believing that by torturing her body she would gain eternal life; happily she numbered off the days when she would fast and eat nothing. Theodora listened to her with fear and took only a part of the green food the hermit offered her. It seemed that the desert had many such rock residences of people from the best society who starved themselves as a preparation for death. Theodora believed that suicide by walking into the sea, or buying granulated virus from a physician, would be swifter. Secretly she thought that to become an anchorite in the desert must be the newest craze of the Christians of Alexandria—although her hostess insisted that generations ago a certain Hypatia had walked the streets there unescorted, although shapely and young, to lecture to crowds that gathered around her. Having a fine education in mathematics and the science of the stars, Hypatia answered readily all questions put to her, and became the disciple of a bishop who saw in her an instrument for good. Moreover, Hypatia had gained a martyr's crown, when a crowd stoned her to death.

It seemed to Theodora that the hermit woman had a hidden purpose in telling her about the brilliant Hypatia.

Strangely, this woman eyed her with dread–Theodora could sense that–as if, strong and soft-skinned, she were an unhallowed pagan girl wandering the desert. Just as strangely the woman looked at the baby and made an awkward attempt to fix up a bed for it by laying fresh rushes on a pile of sand. This woman, shrinking like an ancient mummy within her baglike clothing, had never borne a child. . . .

In the great port of Alexandria, named after the legendary conqueror of the world, Theodora left her own child at a house of strangers. She fixed in her memory the name of the family and the number of the house. The sickness of the foul marshes had come on her, in her weakness. She could not even pretend to sing in the wineshops where slim brown girls rattled castanets against the legs of sailors for copper coins. Beggars wailed at the food stalls in the steaming alleys; Theodora was not yet scarred or emaciated enough to beg, and with a flash of her stubborn temper, she resolved that she would never hold out her hand for a coin.

To try to escape the stench of the alleys, she made her way to a canal. A houseboat lay tied in the shade of an archway, and she pulled herself over the side to lie down on sacks that smelled of spices from the east.

In her fever the merchant who tended her, bringing clean pomegranates and goat's milk, seemed to be a brisk fantastic being. Trying to talk to him, to thank him and to ease the ache of her body, she learned that he had set himself a task to travel the world. How could anyone do that without baggage or servants or money? she wondered. The merchant explained that he was making a book of the world. On the houseboat he had gone up the river Nile, to discover what made it flow.

Because of that they called him Cosmas the Merchant, but no one knew about his book because he had not written it down as yet. As for money, he did not need any because he went from hostel to monastery. At such refuges the folk aided him because he was performing a great task in writing down the manifold wonders of the world. He was eastbound, to locate the place of the sun's rising. According to the enthusiastic Cosmas, the sun did not rise daily out of Ocean—as Theodora had heard in Constantinople—and sink again into the same enveloping Ocean. No, it came out at dawn from behind a very high mountain and vanished at dusk in the same way.

Had the kind Cosmas ever seen this mountain?

Regretfully the sunburned wayfarer admitted that he had not, as yet. But he knew it was there. In proof, did not the sun take longer to pass around the base of the mountain during winter, when it hung low in the heaven? Certainly in summer, when the sun stood high, less time was needed to pass behind the summit of the mountain.

Theodora did not quite understand that. This Cosmas proved to be very awkward as a nurse; he stumbled over her and prayed when she talked wildly in delirium. It seemed ridiculous that he wanted to put the shape of the earth into a book, when he could not even pour milk from a bowl without spilling it down her throat. Of all things he fancied he knew where paradise could be found. Beyond the last great river, beyond the land of India and beyond the Land of Silk there stretched a gigantic canal, vaster than these canals of Alexandria that led to the outer seas. On the far side of this canal lay an island on which rose the mountain of paradise.

What would Cosmas do, Theodora asked with malice, when he found himself at paradise?

Cosmas knew what would happen then. He could not enter where Adam and Eve had been driven out by the angel with the flaming sword, because the sins of mankind had not yet been cleansed. That was why no human eyes could actually see paradise, high up where the angels sang across the stars.

There was something appealing in the clumsy Cosmas, as there had been in the hermit Caesaria; both of them believed in a strength that had nothing to do with their own bodies or minds. As if they expected to find a luxurious home and garden awaiting them around an invisible corner. Apparently they expected to die before reaching that home . . . like the lovely Hypatia. . . .

When the lilt of flutes and fanfare of trumpets came faintly from the shore, Theodora knew that a festival was going on, and roused herself to go out to it in the hope of something turning up. In Constantinople money had been thrown to crowds during festivals. She thanked Cosmas for the fruit and milk and said gently, "I am sure you will find the mountain of the sun."

Because the Admiralty harbor was lined with residences of white stone for the officials and *potentes* (magnates), who moored their yachts to their porticoes, Theodora had to find a fishing boat to take her there, where the northern breeze drove away the stench and the flies.

The yachts had bright awnings up, and Theodora could almost taste the comfort of the women upon the shaded decks, wearing bright silk shaped to their bodies, tinkling laughter against the mutter of men's voices. They were all merry, speeding an imperial war galley on its way, to music. Her bare foot tapped the gritty boards of her boat, and she asked impulsively what admiral was returning to the capital in such state.

After the manner of boatmen, the Syrian fishers, who did not know the answer, shouted her question over the water and the police of a customs skiff answered. The galley was taking Porphyrius, the sixty-year-old unvanquished charioteer, from his native city of Alexandria to appear at the games in the imperial Hippodrome.

Closing her eyes, Theodora could see the marble tiers of the Hippodrome, where on both the Blue and the Green side stood a gold statue of the matchless Porphyrius—

Who was giving the games?

The magnificent Vitalian, the police shouted, who had been named consul for this new year by the pious Justin, the emperor.

Then the police warned the fishermen back, the slim galley turned and moved seaward with a flashing of red-tipped oars and a fluttering of streamers. No one threw out any money.

Going back into the alleys to search for shelter, Theodora picked her way mechanically between the garbage piles. The memory of the Hippodrome with its wind-stirred awnings followed her, mocking her.

She did not try to beg. All fastidiousness had left her and she no longer cared where she went. . . . Cosmas had given her food, not like a woman in need but like a suffering animal.

When the great board in the courtyard of the basilica resounded at the hour of vespers, Theodora stretched out on the hot stones like an animal. Others waited there with petitions for the coming of the patriarch of Alexandria, but she lay motionless in his path to the church.

Being robed, the bearded patriarch did not pause on his way to the altar, but he noticed the outstretched woman and whispered to an attendant to inquire if she were sick. Weakly Theodora admitted that she was sick only from lack of food.

It was a part she could play without any effort, after watching Caesaria. And after listening so long to Cosmas she easily convinced the priests of the basilica that she sought to be cleansed of her sins at the altar. So readily did she recover strength in the kitchen, and so intelligently did she enter into the views of the priests, that very soon she was taken to the patriarch, Timothy, for his blessing.

Perhaps Theodora remembered the attention given Hypatia, because she contrived to be given white garments, and she scrubbed her thin body so untiringly in the tub of the nuns' dormitory and rinsed out her hair so often that her whole appearance took on sweetness and almost angelic fragility.

Under those circumstances she attracted the earnest attention of Timothy, who began to talk with her about salvation. The grateful Theodora, in touch at last with a powerful and educated man, began to call Timothy her spiritual father. She was careful not to try to dress or perfume her splendid dark hair.

Without holding out her hand for money, or begging for anything, she had been cleansed and clad and fed. More than that, she had won the approval of a group of men who had always been antagonistic to her.

When she went out of the cathedral courtyard with lowered head and hands clasped before her, even aristocrats in their gilded carriages turned to look after the lovely religious woman.

This approval stimulated Theodora more than the mild wine poured into small bowls on the refectory tables. Never before had she received so much attention. Never had she been given the run of such a commodious dwelling. In many ways the great church resembled the circus. It held performances for everyone who entered, at fixed hours of the day, starting very early. Noticing that it pleased her new sponsors, the sunburned, bearded priests, Theodora took her place with the women near the altar rail when the singing began. She liked the upbeat of the trained melodious voices that echoed back from the dome. Kneeling there, she could dream, after a nice supper, of a palace as large as this, with as many servants caring for her.

By degrees, especially when she waited to catch Timothy's attention, Theodora discovered that exciting things happened in the church. Strangers pleaded that they wanted to be married; whole families trailed in with a babe to be given a name—or with somebody dying. Or a rich patrician would come in to talk low-voiced to Timothy, asking what gift of how much gold value he could make, to insure his soul. Timothy faced every emergency without losing his courage or his temper. Before answering he seemed to listen, as if to an echo of music. He seemed to draw strength toward him from an invisible source. Although his enthusiastic servants did not manage to read aloud fluently from the massive, decorated Greek and Latin books, they were quick enough to lift up a sick woman. Like herself. Theodora wondered what they expected of her in payment. Men, in her experience, always expected something from a woman they fed.

After considering the many advantages and the few discomforts of the church in Alexandria, she decided to keep on with her new role.

Having discovered, or rather tested, Cosmas' method of travel, Theodora appeared very soon in her homeland of the Syrian coast. If she did not carry letters from Timothy, her spiritual father, she had hit upon the key that would unlock bishops' reception rooms. With her she brought the gossip of the churches.

For several years she must have been fairly content, although poor, because she left no record behind her. On the kindly, sunlit coast of her birth she must have drifted among remembered landmarks, along the waterfronts of tiny ports, up to the cool heights of the Lebanon. Here the folk would listen to a brisk Syrian-Roman—weavers at their benches, painters on the scaffoldings of ancient churches. More than the mild sun, the tranquil spirit of the east that takes no reckoning of time enveloped Theodora in her guise of church messenger at large.

It was a Greek spirit. In markets and docks they spoke the *koiné,* the patois of trade; around vine-grown temples young artists wandered, dreaming of the skill of a Praxiteles, intoning almost forgotten speeches of Homer. Idle, perhaps, and visionary, like Cosmas but much more intelligently—so Theodora believed—they sought for the great secrets hidden in nature. In the forsaken garden of an island she discovered an image of Pan, still wreathed with myrtle, and cleansed by careful hands.

It was the spirit of nearer Asia where the Greeks had wandered haphazard since Alexander's time; they had blended with the countryside, changing only the spouts of fountains or the flowering plants of a garden. Roman engineers had laid down the hard asphalt blocks of the paved roads and raised the massive rubble arches of aqueducts, striding from the hills across the deserts. Theodora had her superstitions. One of them was that you could not change the face of a land without suffering punishment. Yet wherever Romans dwelt rose fortified walls, and baths, and usually race tracks. Would the ancient gods, would Pan himself, take vengeance on these churchgoing engineers?

A change was taking place in Theodora, without volition on her part. Defensive and with no illusions, she distrusted the good will of these eastern priests. No one except a few women of the theater had befriended her before. Yet it seemed as if these guardians of the eastern dioceses meant to help her, after their fashion. They trusted her with messages. She felt, uncertainly, that the day would come when she would need to compensate them. But how? Theodora had learned how to injure those who harmed her. How would she make amends to a friend?

Only gradually she realized that the holy men of these shores were being persecuted. It had not occurred to her before that the vicar of a church might not be as comfortable as a landowner upon his estate. Timothy had been both defiant and anxious. Severus, in lovely Antioch, barely spoke to her of his great distress. It seemed that their churches, the earliest of all, opposed the orthodoxy of Constantinople. These Greeks, Kopts, Syrians, and Armenians, all had simple beliefs of their own which did not fit into the hierarchy of the New Rome. Anastasius, the emperor of beloved memory, had protected them, but the present emperor Justin challenged them and sent inspectors to annoy them. Often Theodora came upon processions of monks leaving their monasteries, carrying a few belongings toward the east where they would search for a new home beyond Justin's mandate.

It seemed strange and pitiful to her that these men upon whom she had imposed so easily should be driven out of the homes they had built. By gossiping around the race track at Antioch and passing among the prostitutes waiting for evening—while they made up their hair and put on scent—in the Daphne grove, Theodora tried to find out what was happening. The girls said the old-time festivals had been strictly forbidden in their vast, pleasure-loving city. Justin called them pagans! In Antioch, they declared, chariots had raced before Constantinople, the city built to order, had changed from killing gladiators to killing bears.

But what was happening in Constantinople?

Why, the girls said, at the games of the consul Vitalian, that veteran Porphyrius, sixty years old, had won his races against all competition. Porphyrius had put the crowd in a frenzy, until the streets were illuminated at night, and Blues and Greens paraded together in their colored mantles. Next to the incredible Porphyrius, the crowd had acclaimed Vitalian, a real Caesar, not like that figurehead of a Justin or his bookish nephew Justinian. Of that triumvirate the crowd wanted only Vitalian. So the precious pair Justinian and his old Justin had bidden Noble Vitalian to a feast in the Delphax dining room of the palace and had hidden assassins in the corridor to strike a half dozen weapons into him. Of course there had been a report circulated afterward that Vitalian had died in a brawl. But everyone there said he had brought no bodyguards, so that only two of his secretaries waited at the door. Since these had been killed, they could not testify. It was all a shame, and typical of the new hard times, according to the girls.

Egged on by the sympathetic Theodora, the girls of the Daphne park voiced their bitterness. They blamed the slippery Justinian more than Old Justin for the Blue laws. No soldier, in their opinion, would ever have thought of planting police in their Daphne grove, sacred to wine and love. Such rites of the grove might have been pagan long ago, but it was taking the cakes and wine from the mouths of the Daphne girls to forbid them by law. Only a brutal Roman would have passed such a law. Was it not Roman second nature to think up laws for other folk to obey? Hypocrisy, philosophers called it. Why, Old Justin had written to Severus, the patriarch of Antioch, that his blessed tongue would be cut out if he went on preaching his sermons—and him the Rock of Christ, the fertile garden of truth!

That, Theodora admitted, was unspeakable.

Wasn't it? And furthermore what did hypocritical Justinian do but contrive to have himself named consul, with Vitalian hardly cold in his honorary tomb. Well! At Justinian's games the next new year, he made all kind of show in the Hippodrome, sending in twenty lions and thirty panthers to be killed and scattering gold solidi as well as silver to the crowd—he who gave a woman of the Venus Square only a few obols for a night—but darling Porphyrius would not step into a chariot for Justinian—excusing himself by having rheumatic pains in his arms, the old dear. So, although Justinian spent a fortune on the games, they went cold, and the crowd gave him only one cheer, and it was a divine retribution on the unmannerly nincompoop for ending the festival at Daphne.

Theodora quite agreed. Whether these tidings from her old city spelled an opportunity for her, or whether some chance of making money drew her thither, she turned up next in Constantinople and as mistress in Justinian's house.

Their mutual reign of five or six years had strained the Justin-Justinian relationship without breaking it. The new Autocrat had followed a policy of ruling with a firm hand and otherwise letting well enough alone, and even the Quaestor of the empire could find no fault with that. Justin eased matters further by bringing about a reconciliation with the Pope, in old Rome (Justinian sending his personal invitation to the Pope to visit the patriarch of Constantinople). Being an experienced soldier, Justin prevented revolts by breaking up rioting (Justinian had eliminated the one dangerous army commander when the knife men of his comrades the Blues killed Vitalian).

In the stage setting of the great hall Old Justin could impress foreign ambassadors. Never had the palace guards resembled statues clad in white silk, holding to silvered axes, so perfectly as under his eye. Meanwhile the former Peter Sabbatius was becoming the mind if not the power behind this throne. He had years to study the work of administration without the strain of its responsibility. Voluntarily he labored without a rest—a surprising phenomenon in the Sacred Palace—and other officials were amazed to discover how much he had learned, quietly, about their duties. He had only the failing, common to a barbarian-born, of expecting them to accomplish whatever he suggested.

This tall, earnest Macedonian mountaineer seemed to cast his protruding gray eyes on every desk. By listening to them —while he judged them silently—he made friends of the older senators. By catching a certain John of Cappadocia falsifying accounts in the treasury he discovered remarkable ability in this same John and arranged for his promotion, thereby making a grateful friend. By spending his salary recklessly he delighted his faction, the Blue deme, which called him Justinian the Patrician. His vanity led him to make such generous gestures, and he liked to be called patrician.

Had he conspired in any way against Old Justin, keen Constantinopolitan minds would have detected it instantly, and his uncertain career would have ended. Had he ingratiated himself with field commanders of the army, he would have stirred up watchful suspicion. Old Justin, who had hoped to make a soldier as well as a scholar out of his adopted son, did not understand this. "Peter," he objected, "you could not drill a *numerus*. The men know what metal is in an officer. You can't expect 'em to respect you merely because they've been disciplined. No, they'll watch you to find out what you can do for 'em. Once I held Daras by telling my force of Huns that they could loot the Persians' camp if they waited long enough. Those Huns wouldn't have stayed put to defend a wall, but they waited for loot. Got it, too." His tangled brows twitched with satisfaction as he recalled the escapade. "What's that proverb? *Omne jus stat in armis*. Yes, all right depends upon might. If the army won't back you, Peter, you'll waste your breath spouting laws. Didn't any of the books teach you that?"

"They did, August," acknowledged Justinian, who always gave the old man his title. "Yet it occurred to me the armed forces have such respect for your leadership that it would be presumptuous for me to drill even a company."

Pleased, but unconvinced, Justin shook his head. "I'm feeling that hack in my foot, Peter. I can't sit a horse on parade. But I'm not blind. The army carries the old standards, but it isn't up to the legions of Theodosius. It can only stand behind fortifications. Mostly, it exists only on paper." Morosely he stared at his son's plump ruddy face. "The city can't survive without an army. That's the situation. I don't know what you can do about it. Remember, you can never delegate leadership to another man."

Justinian had ideas of his own about that. It seemed to him that Old Justin was grieving for the vanished legions of the great conquests. Modern warfare was fought with other weapons than swords and body armor. So he kept silent and waited for his opportunity.

It was a long time in coming. Old Justin had a way of pretending to be ignorant about questions he understood very well. His pose as a simple old soldier helped him a great deal. Because back-court gossip branded him as being too ignorant to sign his name, he had a fine gold stencil made with his name and title cut out on it, and in public he used the stencil to sign his name to documents. He wanted to be aided, not superseded, by his efficient nephew.

After thinking it over, Justin raised him to the final rank of Most Noble, and named him honorary commander of the excubitors. That would give the boy—as he thought of him—prestige without requiring him to go into the field with troops. In fact Justinian spent most of the daylight hours now within the palace.

The watchful eyes of the silentiaries observed every action of the favored man. They were the noble-born attendants of the emperor's person; they served him alone, although they might report to those who paid them enough. By their account, Justinian was a zealous busybody, content to wait for the emperor's death before trying to seize power.

Yet the balance between Justinian and Old Justin had shifted again. By now the man without a valid title had friends in important posts, while the emperor, secluded by tradition from his people, could do no more than make his rare appearances under veiled lights. At his rising one morning elder senators waited on him while he was robed and suggested that he name his son Caesar of the empire.

So quietly they insinuated the title, it took Justin a moment to reflect that the extraordinary rank of Caesar carried with it a true dictatorship over the military. Vitalian had been seeking it. "No!" he shouted, and clutched the purple mantle over his cloth-of-gold tunic. "Guard yourselves, gentlemen, against ever giving these to a younger man!"

Justin's anger came from his pride. He was angered the more because influential senators had spoken for Justinian. At that moment he might have degraded and dismissed his adopted son. Yet he had no other near kinsman; he felt the burning infection of the old wound in his foot; he knew that he could live for only a few years more, and he craved the last measure of the dignity that had come to him.

When the jeweled collar was clasped under his chin he said more calmly, "The people have no need of a Caesar now."

Assenting, the senators resolved to wait awhile before persuading the old man. For Justinian, uncertain of his authority at Justin's death, had convinced them it would be safer for his followers if he were acknowledged by the army and people as co-ruler now.

Then the wandering Theodora came to Justinian's house.

Many writers wondered thereafter how the woman from the circus could have met the man who was seeking a throne. Some said that she brought a letter from a mutual friend in Asia. But did they have any mutual friends? Others wrote that Theodora set up a spinning wheel in a poor house, and that Justinian, passing by, noticed her beauty. Theodora may have worked at a spinning wheel.

Justinian, however, was not hard to meet. Alone of the elite membership of the Sacred Palace, he walked the streets by himself and talked with the democracies—the butchers, the sailors, the corner orators, and all their like. Perhaps the girls of the Mesé arcades knew how the two met. Theodora had two sisters among them.

But the house drew Theodora and Justinian together. It was a small residence, half hidden by a garden wall, connected with the enclosure of the Sacred Palace only by a back stairway. It nestled under the high end of the vast Hippodrome on the slope leading down to one of the enclosed ports of the city. Since a refugee Persian prince had lived there once, it was called the House of Hormisdas, and it had miniature tiled rooms with a cool terrace overlooking the Marmora Sea, beyond the masts of the ships.

For the same reason that it had suited the exiled Persian, the house—listed on the tax rolls as a palace—appealed to the more energetic Justinian; it gave him seclusion from the watchers of the imperial palace; he could work there through the night in quiet; he could talk with friends without being overheard, and at need he could escape from it down a flight of steps to a ship.

To Theodora the door of this miniature palace must have seemed like the portal of earthly paradise to Cosmas the Merchant. The chambers within glowed not with silver fittings and gold wash but with carved jade and colored marbles set in mosaic patterns. The emerald green of Spartan marble was framed by the blood-red and white streaks of Phrygian. Here was an incredible thing, a home and security.

Stretched on the terrace at the hour of lamplighting, Theodora could close her eyes and dream that she was a favored Illustrious lying in her villa on an island of the Marmora with her yacht waiting beneath. But she did not permit herself to do anything of the kind. Instead, under lowered lashes she studied her antagonist, the man, the patrician who was also an Illustrious. She had no illusions about such as he, in Constantinople.

Watching him on the terrace, she realized that Justinian was somehow different from other grandees; his garments did not fit; he strode heavily back and forth between her and the long tables laden with papers; for supper, although he offered her some fruit, he took only lentils, bread, and milk. His massive shoulders sagged and his gray eyes were lined with fatigue that did not come from wine drinking. In spite of his bustle of activity, he seemed inwardly helpless.

She heard him tell a visitor in the hall to send a thousand pounds of gold to Colchis, and, coming back to her on the terrace in the twilight, he cried out as if shocked when he blundered against a glass bowl and shattered it.

There happened one night what neither of them had known for a long time. She slept with him, yielding him the satisfaction of her body, and he felt passionate desire for her.

Theodora discovered that Justinian was naïve, with a boy's belief in a benevolent Fortune. She had no such illusion. Her stay in the House of Hormisdas, she told herself, would end in a few days.

Yet it did not come to an end. For the slender, vital Theodora Justinian had the half-fatherly love of a middle-aged man for a girl still young. They had nothing in common. His blood was that of the insensible north, hers of the wayward south, and Asia. For a generation, while she had kept alive by her wit, he had been protected and enriched. Her schooling had been in the circus, his in a library of his own making.

Because they were so apposite and because their mating seemed so strange—as Peter the Patrician would have said, "beyond expectation"—the chroniclers who wrote down events invented a reason for it. Justinian, Illustrious, and Magister Militum in Praesentalis, made a bargain with the little daughter of the Keeper of the Bears—pledging her thousands of pounds of gold and large estates including the House of Hormisdas, while she stipulated she must follow a career of her own, more as a co-worker than a customary wife. So they said. And at least one historian, Procopius of Caesaria, wrote that the Devil had driven Justinian to make this bargain with the wanton Theodora.

But she was in no position to bargain with him. The roar of the Hippodrome crowd over her head on game days reminded her of that. All she could hope for at first was to stay longer in the house, as Justinian's favorite. Realizing that he idolized her, she devoted earnest care to her appearance. A thin woman all of twenty-five years of age, with only lustrous hair and good eyes as redeeming features, needed to select small necklaces and pastel coloring in garments. It suited her perfectly to do nothing but improve her appearance while Justinian was absent at his unending engagements. He proved to be as reliable as the water clock that dripped off the hours in the hall. She always knew where he was, and, having much the quicker mind, she soon learned to anticipate what he would do. And because he believed her to be a soul of wit, she tried to become so.

Undeniably she respected Justinian. No soothsayer of the street arcades had ever been able to conjure up the wealth of a province with a few words. Certainly he puzzled her, because he seemed to perform such miracles without thought of himself, as if merely attending to details of some great and unknown task. What purpose drove him to labor like a slave?

The memory of the pompous Hecebolus and the governor's mansion on the African shore was still strong. Only too well she remembered what had happened to her after Hecebolus. Justinian was quite affected because the woman he loved seldom ventured outside the gate of their narrow garden. It seemed as if she always waited for his coming. Naturally he did not realize that Theodora feared to show her face in a public square where, soon or late, she would be recognized.

When the Quaestor was announced one evening while Justinian studied reports under his lamps, fear stabbed at her heart. The dignified Quaestor served as general inspector and he was the one man everybody in the city admitted to be honest. When Justinian neither explained her presence nor named her to the visitor, the fear made her tense. After a moment she realized that the two men were merely discussing the fine points of some four-horse teams Justinian meant to offer as prizes in the Hippodrome. Cappadocian horses.

Theodora decided not to escape, as she wanted to. "Porphyrius told us," she observed, "that the Arab crossbred teams are faster in starting than the Cappadocian, and they can hold the barriers closer at the turns. Truly, he declared his secret is that he drives Arabians in the stake races."

They looked at her then, surprised, seeing a piquant profile, half veiled. "Theodora comes from his city of Alexandria," Justinian explained. "She has traveled more than you or I, Most Noble."

"Remarkable." The Quaestor's eyes changed, and he became thoughtful. "Remarkable. May I ask—was your portrait ever displayed at the Augusteon, Theodora?"

"No, Most Noble."

"I thought I had seen it." He nodded at Justinian. "She should be painted on ivory. Fortune favors you, in such a lovely woman."

Justinian was pleased. "The portrait shall be done at once. Will you accept it for your collection?"

"To increase my envy of your fortune? If you insist——"

From that moment fear kept Theodora from sleeping. Soon or late, the portrait would be recognized. In spite of all her care, she would have to leave the House of Hormisdas. It angered her that this should happen by the conceit of two men, who wanted her likeness made, like the memorial tablet of a favored horse. Her temper and her dread drove her to risk everything by speaking to Justinian.

With great attention she made up her face, grimacing at herself in the cold bronze mirror, and she chose a moment when he was chuckling, his tousled head bent over a new manuscript of the wars against barbarians.

"Do you know you are imagining something that does not exist?"

It took him awhile to detach his mind from the world of literary happenings. "There is no harm in trying, my Gift," he answered. He used trite sayings in his speech, and thought of her as her name implied, the gift of God. "The senate majority would probably agree with you. But the only way to test my plans is to try them out. Tribonian thinks the matter of the laws can be arranged."

His political plans. The Roman laws. Theodora nearly sobbed with rage and exasperation. The vital feeling in her poured out. Justinian had deceived himself in her—a child bred in the circus who had stripped off her clothes to exhibit herself on the stage. She cried that at him, but not the circumstances of Hecebolus or her daughter.

Putting his arm around her, he smiled at her, saying she should not have been afraid to tell him, who had been born on a Macedonian sheep farm. He was altogether infatuated with her. But his easy assurance did not drive the fear from her. She made him understand what she longed for—to share his life at night in the security of her house. In that lay her happiness. As for the rest—would the Chamberlain at the Chalké Gate of the palace allow an actress to enter?

His answer startled her. Theodora, he explained, would

need patrician rank to visit the palace, so she should have it. After that he would marry her.

Then Theodora had to struggle to keep from crying. It was the portrait all over again. Her likeness drawn and colored, held up to public view. For the laughter and mockery of her city, which craved nothing so much as a jest spiced with slander. From the Augusteon to the Golden Gate the jest would be whispered, how foolish Justinian had begged for noble rank for the daughter of a bear keeper, to marry her—the slut cast off in Africa, the beggar of the caravans. Not that her morals would disturb overmuch the women of society who often had bear keepers among their own ancestors. But to demand a marriage of state for a Theodora! To try to enter the Sancta Sophia with handmaidens holding her veil and mantle! Society would never admit her as an equal. It would destroy her by mockery, the most cruel of weapons.

Mastering herself, she tried to argue with the stubborn Justinian. Feeling that she was losing the only home she had known, she tried to explain the danger clearly, as a man would do. Suppose, by a bribe or by influence, he obtained noble rank for her? Still the Church would not bestow the sacrament of marriage upon an actress. The law forbade it. And if they tried——

"That law," Justinian broke in, "will have to be changed."

"But you can't!" She almost screamed at him.

"No, I can't. Justin can."

The dread did not leave Theodora until, formally named as patrician in the court register and clad in fresh garments of white silk, she passed behind Justinian through the statue-like guards of the gilded Chalké portal, through crowded reception halls to the sleeping chamber of an old man who still looked distinguished in a bedgown. No sooner had Justin, the emperor, apologized for his illness, caused, he said, by a wound in the Persian wars, than Theodora knew that he would help her.

Old Justin brushed back the curls of his white head and vowed that Hypatia had come before him in the flesh. Theodora, after one appraising glance, melted before his courteous admiration. The splendor of her eyes, the fine line of her throat, the swaying of her slim waist—she let the emperor note them all, to his satisfaction. She could do that, across the barrier of fifty years.

The matter-of-fact Justinian mentioned the ancient law that kept singers, dancers, and actresses from marrying.

"You never spoke of it before, Magister," murmured Justin, studying Theodora. "Ridiculous. Those very women keep up the morale of the troops. It's unchristian, to make 'em bear their brats in sin."

Then, after asking Theodora if she knew any new songs, he ordered a decree prepared for signature, invalidating the unjust law against the marriage of actresses. And he urged her to visit her ailing father-in-law by adoption at any time.

This Theodora did willingly. It still dazed her to listen to a few words that could set in motion vast sums, or move multitudes here and there. Very quickly she decided that an Autocrat was only powerless to change ceremony or the ideas of the people. Even Justin cautioned her to make a good impression on the patriarch before attempting to approach the altar.

Oddly enough it was Justinian who had misgivings about that, and Theodora who felt willing to risk it. To his surprise she knelt before the venerable head of the Church as if by right and responded fluently to his polite questions about her basilica in Alexandria. When she lifted her lovely eyes and begged for the patriarchal blessing, it was given her.

What Theodora anticipated happened as soon as she came into public notice. The talk started, of course, from unknown tongues, and the slaves of her house brought her snatches of it, picked up when she was driven through the streets with armed riders going before her. (These servants obeyed her with zeal after she had spoken to them once during Justinian's absence in the dialect of the Hippodrome; they soon decided that, while Justinian was oblivious, their mistress was implacable and could not be deceived.) The gossip ran that Theodora the bride-to-be of the Master of Militia was no other than Theodora the female clown of the circus, determined to make herself a great lady. No one, of course, repeated this to Justinian. And Theodora knew that such gossip could not ridicule the woman favored by both emperor and patriarch. The performers of the Hippodrome were grateful for the new law, and the spokesmen of the Blue deme recalled that as a child Theodora had been sponsored by their democracy. This gossip of the streets favored more than it hurt her.

Her wedding date was set when an unexpected voice forbade it. Euphemia, the empress who had been the peasant camp follower, refused her consent. This aged woman who had already ordered her tomb would not receive into her family a youthful and sparkling actress. Not even Justin could change Euphemia's mind on that point. The ladies of Augusteon society had petitioned the peasant empress not to allow Theodora's marriage, and Euphemia, flattered by their attention, remained adamant.

While Justinian raged helplessly, Theodora understood Euphemia perfectly. Her marriage would have to wait.

Inwardly she was glad of the delay. It kept her in the House of Hormisdas, and she began to feel that her home really belonged to her. Within the small garden wall every detail was familiar to her and important—even the oleanders growing up like trees around the pool among natural rocks that the servants had made for her. She had not wanted a pool of ugly Roman concrete or glaring tiles.

No other woman had occupied her chamber, since Justinian had taken the house. Justinian himself kept telling her that, of course, but any man would say the same. The servants bore him out, and Theodora believed them because she perceived no trace of another woman—no discarded comb or forgotten letter. Perhaps she loved Justinian devotedly because she felt so secure in her house. Protected and beloved, Theodora blossomed in new beauty, aided by her exacting care of her flesh and hair. The first time she heard a visitor say naturally "this house of Theodora's" she hugged herself joyfully.

When the games were on and the roar of the crowd drifted down through the curtains of the windows she no longer became tense and cold, hearing the "Nika—nika—nika! Win—win—win!" It was only the yelling of the men in the colosseum exhorting the drivers on whom they had placed their bets.

Theodora could assure herself that she had conquered the Hippodrome by escaping from it. It could no longer harm her in the house of Theodora. At the same time she tried to think of some way to avoid becoming an inmate of the Sacred Palace. She distrusted good fortune, knowing that retribution would follow it. More than that, instinct warned her that she must not antagonize the gods, who remained invisible and in consequence terrible. This fear was her heritage from forgotten ancestors in the east who had survived invisible forces of destruction, in famine, plague, and earthquake. Even the Romans, who had been victorious for a time over human armies, had never been able to defeat the unknown gods with their concrete walls and aqueduct water mains and lead plumbing. Although Theodora hoped that the prayers of a holy man like Timothy of Alexandria could prevail over the powers of darkness, she did not feel at all certain of that. Moreover, when she tried to imagine the intense and downright Timothy as a visitor to the Sacred Palace, she had to laugh.

So Theodora did not explain to the servants why she had them fetch stones from open fields for the pool, or why she tossed fragments of meat covertly into the burning brazier before eating.

"Promise me one thing," she urged Justinian, "that this house and its garden will be mine to come to and to dwell in, whatever happens."

When Justinian smiled and began to enumerate the property holdings of his father, and his own farm estates and merchandising ventures, she checked him and insisted that she wanted nothing in her name but the house itself. The next day he presented her playfully with a signed and stamped deed to the home; this she locked away carefully, trusting the parchment document less than the circumstance that, being deprived of the women's chambers in the Sacred Palace, this small property might belong to her in reality.

One hope she did not mention to Justinian. She could not send to find her six-year-old daughter in Alexandria. The child had become only a memory, bound up with the filth of the alleys. Deprived of the living child, she hoped she would bear another. A child, she knew, would hold the affection of peasant-born Justinian. And the patrician women of Augusteon society practiced abortion too frequently to ridicule a mother of children.

Unceasingly the girl of the Hippodrome was on her guard against gossip. It suited her to confine herself to the house, but Constantinopolitan tradition required it as well. Except when Justinian was at home, she never let a male visitor catch sight of her or hear her voice. When she rode forth to the silk shops or the Armenian bazaar or the Sancta Sophia, she veiled and took the kindly major-domo for escort as well as the impressive outriders—since Justinian relished having her appear "in state" as he called it. He enjoyed hearing the murmurs that followed her: "There goes Theodora."

Theodora, however, knew what filth might be cast on her name if she were seen to speak with another man outside her gate. Not that she dreaded any longer coming face to face with one who had abused her in the pleasure boats or screened-in feasts. There was always the chance that a man of her own age might stir her passion for him. Quite honestly

Theodora believed that the best way to prevent that was not to let it happen. It astonished her when Justinian, who had no such qualms about her, remarked that in ancient Rome married women had shown their faces in the streets and had answered anyone who spoke to them.

Weren't they disgraced, Theodora wondered, behaving like that?

No, Justinian assured her, the matrons of the Roman respublica had all the freedom of male citizens.

Then did the wives of that time sleep with other men?

No. They were proud of their chastity and would do no such thing.

Under those circumstances they must have been allowed to attend the games and theaters.

Justinian reflected, and explained that in those early days of austerity there were neither games nor plays. He thought that the matrons, although not the daughters, attended the mass meetings in the Forum, the temple ceremonies, and the legio—the drawing of the lots to fill the legions. But the early Roman matrons remained spectators, being confined otherwise to breeding children and preparing food.

This seemed to Theodora to be a strange, cold northern way of life. After that she questioned her lover frequently about what had changed Roman women. With some effort she could read, but she much preferred to get answers from Justinian, who had an amazing pattern of facts stored in his memory.

One evening the mistress of the House of Hormisdas felt an involuntary thrill of physical attraction toward a stranger, a Count Belisarius. At first sight of him in the fountain court, she thought that no woman could ever wear such a green tunic embroidered with eagles, a gold collar, and a bright red cloak. But this striking blond man from the Danube, no older than Theodora, wore them with a jeweled belt and sat there entirely at ease, saying farewell to Justinian before departing to take a command on the eastern front. He seemed to be rich as well.

His companion, a dark, undersized young Syrian, hardly dared to address the great men of whom he sat in awe. Quickly—for Theodora had learned to appraise the characters of visitors—she decided that her countryman, Procopius, felt insignificant beside the beautiful Belisarius. Her interest in the soldier grew when she heard that he intended to take advantage of the new law to marry an actress. Theodora felt a vicarious jealousy, imagining Belisarius married to a performer like herself. She barely listened to the farewell of polite Procopius, who bowed himself out.

Justinian told her when they had gone that this Procopius, named after the eastern saint, was an excitable man and therefore a poor lawyer, but he would do well enough as legal adviser to Count Belisarius in dealing with the tricky Persians.

"I imagined him lounging in the Augusteon."

"Procopius of Caesaria? Hardly, my Gift, considering his ignoble birth——"

"I'm a Syrian, too, beloved. I meant the young giant, Belisarius."

"He *has* been lounging in the Augusteon." Justinian answered her question literally. Then his gray eyes twinkled. "Half the noble ladies of court made excuse to go there to gaze at him."

It surprised and pleased her when he showed understanding of people's hidden natures. "But he's only a boy. Why do you think he is capable of commanding two regiments?" she asked obliquely.

"I don't know anything about it, Theodora. But they are his own comitatus—that is, his own enlistment of comrades for war." For a moment Justinian pondered and she waited, knowing that he was referring her inquiry to another compartment of his orderly mind. "Justin said men know the metal of an officer. Evidently those of his comitatus believe him efficient." He fished a note tablet out of a pile and read swiftly. "Belisarius, the Fair, a German-born. Graduate of military academy. Led defense of his estates beyond Danube against Gepid and Lombard raiders. Reported entirely loyal, and expert in tactics versus barbarians. A good record, Theodora, for so young a soldier."

It did not occur to her until long afterward that something must be lacking in an army that expected officers to supply their own troops. Musing upon Belisarius, she murmured, "I would like to see him with his com—comrades."

"You should, by all means, my Gift." Twice Justinian nodded his approval. "At the third hour tomorrow the new squadrons will parade out from the Mesé's end, past the Golden Milestone."

Among the spectators at that time and place Theodora sat in her carriage with silver rails drawn by two white mules. The horsemen of Belisarius disappointed her because they rode in leather rests called saddles, and they made a mass of dull gray in cuirass and helmets. The horses wore mail too. Carrying only small shields with short stiff bows and light lances, they lacked entirely the gleam and color of the excubitors. Their swords resembled curved German hacking knives, but they had a way of keeping their mounts in a close rank, as if one man were doing the riding of twenty. Although he was a wealthy nobleman, Belisarius carried a pack roll behind him like his regimental comrades.

Theodora heard old servicemen around her remark that this comitatus could strike with its weapons at any distance from fifty paces to handgrips. Before leaving she managed to hear that Belisarius' bride-to-be was older than he, and very wisely would follow him on the campaign where a woman would be most desirable.

To Justinian Theodora said nothing more about Belisarius, but she made occasion to visit Justin. Out of those visits to cheer the soldier-emperor with a description of such new weapons and tactics, two things transpired. Another law was altered by degree, permitting prostitutes to marry with the approval of their spiritual fathers of the Church. And Comito, her elder sister, who had been ravaged by disease, became the wife of a fellow officer of Belisarius.

At the same time, pressed by senators who anticipated an outbreak of war along the eastern front, the ailing Justin named his adopted son Caesar of the empire. Gangrene was eating its way up the veteran's leg. (Although Justinian, who had hardly left the city for seven years, understood no more of organizing armies than he had learned by reading Livy, and Vegetius' *Epitome of the Military Art.*)

Theodora did not confide in the new Caesar of the empire how she had contrived to get a husband for Comito because Justinian was buried in his work at the time. Then, too, Theodora decided wisely that her lover might not have the same regard for Comito, a listed prostitute, that he had for her. In the same way Justinian did not mention to his mistress that the Caesarian title had been planned for years by others more than himself. It was a necessary step, now that Justin was becoming senile as well as sick. But for the first time, in these new developments, they did not share their thoughts as before.

Yet at that time chroniclers of the court—seeking for ridiculous or sensational matters to amuse their clients—wrote down that Theodora the nude actress and Justinian the Macedonian sheepherder made an unholy bargain to gain supreme power and share it between them. That was not true. Nor did a demon settle upon the pair, to drive them to do what they did thereafter.

No, they were then much in love, as man and woman. Because the adoring Justinian believed his mistress to be gifted with almost divine wisdom, she tried with all her great determination to become educated and witty; because she was devoted to him, he made a dogged effort to achieve superhuman success. What happened to them thereafter came when they left the House of Hormisdas.

Having been raised in a poor home, Justinian, as Caesar, gave away money like a spendthrift. He was praised for his generosity, and he felt the need of displaying it in fetes and donations to the crowds. Such acclaim fed his vanity. It distressed Theodora to watch gold thrown away like confetti when the food on their table was no better than a bricklayer's victuals and Justinian himself wore mouse-colored, stained mantles. Not that he could have worn gleaming satin and gems like a Belisarius.

It startled her to discover on one of their last evenings together upon the terrace that the awkward and earnest Justinian was vain. As usual now he had spent the day in the palace, and he munched bread while he studied files he had brought back with him. Theodora, who had slept until noon, was wide awake and much interested in a peacock she had bought as an ornament, since they had so little drapery of cloth-of-gold or artificial flowers fashioned from gems. When Justinian, oblivious of her, began to end his labor by signing documents, she went to lean on his bulky shoulder and watch.

A wailing cry from beyond the wall caught her ear. . . . "Crawfish and sesame, O Most Noble! Taste and smell, and you will wonder."

The cry, in the patois of a street vender, made Theodora giggle. She understood the many tongues of the city streets, while Justinian really knew only the official and unmusical Latin. An imp of mischief stirred in her. "Nobilisssimusscaesaretmagisstermilituminpraesentaliss," she hissed.

He started as if struck. "What is that? You sound like a snake!"

She giggled in his ear. "Your titles, Caesar. All of them."

To her astonishment, he pushed away his documents, his dumpy cheeks flushing. Stammering over the words, he said such titles were honors, not to be mocked. The senate, not he, had wished to name Justinian Caesar.

Reflecting that he was tired, and wondering at the vanity

in him, Theodora murmured regretfully and caressed his throat. Then she slipped away, to find the peacock drowsing on the terrace rail. But he had fixed his attention upon her.

"What do you find of such interest in the street, Theodora?"

She did not want to disturb him again. "Just people," she said placatingly.

There was a pause. Then: "Did you ever think, Theodora, who the people are?"

The Greek word "*demos*" had slipped out of her; he used the hard word "*populi.*" A word to be carved in stone, on the pedestals of their gigantic statues. Populi Romani. The people were the Romans and the Romans were the people—when carved upon stone. Why did all the countless statues of dignitaries in the city tower like giants? The sensitive Greeks never made them more than human size. "I like to watch them," she ventured.

"Then tell me what *people* are passing under your gaze? Who are they, really?"

So challenged, she responded immediately. The fish and seed seller, carrying woven baskets on his bare arms, was a Greek islander, late in coming up from the harbor. The boys playing with the wilted jasmine blooms she had thrown out might be Jews, but no, they belonged to the Armenian from Nisibis who had the stall at the steps with enamel work displayed. He got his turquoise from the Euxine trading ships. The tall youth passing with torchbearers had his forehead shaved, his sleeves puffed out, and his mustaches grown long like a Hun, but he was probably merely a young gallant of the city, aping the fashion to make himself up like a barbarian.

Leaning on the rail beside her, Justinian nodded his approval. It always amazed him to discover what his mistress could notice in a street crowd. His mind had turned to a new train of thought. "You have said it yourself, my Gift. A Greek from the sea, two Armenian brats—and the only citizen dresses up like a barbarian Hun. Yet such as these are the surviving Roman *people*."

He leaned on the stone as if weary. He said senators talked of *the people* because they had always done so, in speeches. But the people no longer existed.

Curiously, Theodora gazed up at him. "Then who inhabit the city, Justinian? Ghosts? Demons? They look very much alive to me."

For once he did not answer like an elder teacher. His bloodshot gray eyes squinted into the darkness above the smoking lamps. Six hundreds of thousands of refugees inhabited this enclosure within the Theodosian triple walls, he declared—refugees seeking protection, wealth, kinsmen, pleasure, or simply bread and wine and fish. Not one man in a thousand thought about the government, except to try to escape taxation. Of the remaining few perhaps no more than a half dozen felt personal responsibility for preserving the empire. The other hundreds accumulated wealth, plotted for new dignity, or simply carried out tasks assigned them.

Silently Theodora conjectured that Justinian was one of the half dozen, with the Quaestor of course, and the three other Illustrious. Or did Justinian really mean those three? Until then she had thought of the government's bureaus as caring for all the people as immutably as the stars looking down upon the Hippodrome. Otherwise, how could a weak and gabbling old man like Justin rule? No, the bureaus ruled, by law. She said that.

"No, not by law." Justinian shook his head. "By custom. So many laws have been made that a specialist can always find one to suit his plea. Then he makes use of oratory and bribes the judges." His eyes crinkled with amusement. "How many of the six hundred thousands do you think, Theodora, do not lie awake nights to plan ways of avoiding those same laws?"

Because he seemed to have stopped worrying, she laughed. "That is very true, Justinian. My Armenian boasts that he escapes the import tax by pretending that he makes his own enamels. So he can sell them cheaper."

Justinian's mind had taken a turn in a new direction, and his voice was strained again. "In what do these *people* believe now?" He waited for her answer. "In what do they have faith?"

Thinking of the courtyard where she had lain in the dirt, Theodora answered that many had faith in a holy man like Timothy of Alexandria.

"Yes, they look for leaders everywhere. They trust in no strength of their own, and seek somebody to protect them. Have you heard the mob in the Sancta Sophia, yelling for a new patriarch? Do they believe, even in a church? Or do they, instead, look for somebody with rank, to pass out privileges and money? Is not money their chief standard?"

People did not put their belief into stilted words. They wanted to be merry and forget their troubles. That had always been human nature. So Theodora decided, silently.

But Justinian would not admit as much. His mind had gone back into his world of books, and he told her that in the time of Roman grandeur, before the empire, two elected consuls had ruled effectively because the people had obeyed the few laws and believed in the Roman state.

Fleetingly she remembered the old saying that those early Romans had conquered because they thought they could. They must have been very conceited. "But that is over with," she murmured. "Everything is different now——"

Suddenly, as if to relieve a torment of his brain, the man beside her cried out. There was no longer a Rome. The empire itself did not exist, except in written words. Their city, surrounded by walls, was no metropolis of all the peoples but a solitary island still standing above flooding darkness and ignorance and savagery. To this island crowds hurried to shelter themselves, snatching at wealth, listening to the loudest speeches, saying and pretending that they alone were safe within the walls of the empire. They imagined, because they were here on their island, that their way of life would endure. They feasted and played with ideas like toys, to avoid thinking of the flood around them.

It seemed to Theodora that he was tortured by some demon of doubt. Never before had she known Justinian to be confused in his thoughts. Holding to his arm, she smiled up at him and asked what he meant to do about the danger.

"What can be done?" he muttered. "Anastasius built the Long Wall inland—Justin sent soldiers against mobs. Otherwise they merely drifted." With his head sagging, he whispered, "I do not know what I can do."

It shocked Theodora, as if she had seen him crying. Justinian had seemed assured in his ceaseless labor; she had taken his assurance for granted. Her quick temper gave an edge to her voice. "Never let others hear you say that!"

Theodora did not know why she scolded him. But, for an instant, he had seemed to demean himself. Not Justin nor the impassive Belisarius would have spoken of their weakness. Was the man beside her a coward?

Justinian opened his hands. "It is the truth, Theodora. Why should I not tell the truth to you?"

For a while she did not answer. It was only clear to her that a leader could not show his weakness. If Justinian, who had done nothing for twenty-five years but study his task of ruling, could not trust his own ability, what did he have to depend on? Like a mocking echo, she remembered the saying, *The Romans conquered because they believed they could.* But Justinian had been born a Macedonian peasant.

Theodora no longer answered impulsively. "My lord has taken upon himself the tasks of many men." Carefully she avoided using his titles, or her pet names for him. "So he is weary. Can he not delegate to the others the tasks they should perform, and do himself only the work of Justinian?" Gently she pressed against his arm. "Surely you must always tell me the truth, and I must do likewise. Now I will say what I have kept in my heart with pride. You are more than the handsome Anastasius, more than Old Justin. Of all these people of the city only Justinian can devote himself to the empire."

With a heavy sigh, he blinked at the flicker of passing torches. After waiting a moment she went down to find the peacock wandering in the garden. The house was strange to her new pet and in that hour it had become strange to her. It had ceased to be a refuge.

At that point Fate intervened.

While Justinian's fears magnified the dangers that lay between him and the throne, they were great enough because intangible. Although he was the logical candidate of the all-powerful Blue faction and the Church itself, he remembered too vividly the sudden tumult at the death of Anastasius to be at all sure that the logical successor would be chosen at the ailing Justin's death.

Although he had every qualification of a ruler, he had not the personality to rally followers in the streets. He could not, therefore, hope to elect himself by the right of revolt. As for other rights, he was Justin's sole heir but only an adopted son. He had a marvelous education, fitting him to serve as Autocrat, but for a long time before Justin the emperors had been ruthless military leaders or harmless bureaucrats. Justin, the simple old soldier, had caught the popular fancy. But Justinian had nothing in him to catch the fancy of the unpredictable populace. He could not even make an election speech.

Moreover, Theodora stood in his way, being no more than his mistress from the circus. He could have won over the patrician women by casting her out of his house and marrying one of them. This Justinian would not even think of doing.

On their part the ladies of the Augusteon, who had nothing at all against Justinian personally, attacked Theodora with a phrase that the court commentators caught up.

"There have been empresses who became harlots, but who ever heard of a harlot becoming an empress?"

It was like Euphemia's feeling. These ladies had accepted an old peasant woman as Augusta, but they would not bend their coroneted heads to a young, lovely, and determined actress.

Thereupon, as if by response of Fate, Euphemia died in her bed of scarlet silk. Justinian married Theodora quietly, without public notice or the presence of the patriarch.

With Theodora established as his wife, and with popular enthusiasm roused by encouraging war news from Persia, Justinian gambled swiftly. He invoked an old Roman custom and pressed for his nomination as co-emperor.

The elderly and wealthy senatorial bloc approved of it, to preserve the status quo. The patriarch realized that it would aid the orthodox faith and prevent rioting in the city. Justin, helpless in his sickbed, with the gangrene spreading from his foot to his body, gave his consent without protest.

It was done on Easter Day, quickly, without stirring up the Hippodrome or indulging in public debate. An official summoned the Illustrious persons and the heads of the senate to an empty dining hall, the Delphax where Vitalian had been cut down. There Justinian was given the diadem, the purple robe, the scarlet half boots, and the scepter. The patriarch bestowed the regalia because Justin could no longer leave his bed, and it was not advisable for the people to behold the weakness of their Autocrat.

No sooner was Justinian crowned than tradition required him to crown his consort. Silent, Theodora knelt before him while the flaming woven jewels of empire were placed upon her head, throat, shoulders, and waist.

There was no speech to the public, no inauguration of the co-rulers before the worshipers in the vast Sancta Sophia.

Before that summer ended, the life of Justin flickered out. Word sped from the gates of the Sacred Palace: "Justinian reigns. Theodora reigns."

It was then the first day of August, 527.

The announcement of the fact drew echoes of approval. Priests from the east recalled the devout and lovely woman who had prayed at their altars, and hoped for much from her; priests of the west felt assured the new emperor would maintain their orthodox faith; experienced senators trusted that he would keep up prosperity. On the other hand, the democracies of the people hoped, as always, that a new ruler might change the old tyranny and tax-squeezing.

On the first Sunday, at the hour of candlelighting, Justinian took his seat, robed, in the carved ivory throne by the altar of the Sancta Sophia, and heard the prayers chanted for his name. Across from him, her slender body shimmering as the flames caught the facets of her jewels, Theodora heard the roar of the thousands who knelt below her in the splendor of court attire. In her hands she held the two candles of dedication.

"Justinian, thou wilt conquer! Ever August, God will surely aid thee! Live long, our Augustus! Live long, our pious Augusta!"

At the shouting a thrill of exultation went through her body. More than the taste of wine or the glimpse of splendor, it stirred anticipation in her. Never had the clown of the Hippodrome heard such an ovation.

III

Revolt

For Justinian the change from prime mover of the empire to ruler was a very satisfactory one. As emperor he merely had to speak his thoughts aloud to have them carried out. Under Justin he had served a long apprenticeship. He knew the ways and means of getting things done.

Only, during that apprenticeship, he had thought out certain things that he meant to have done, which had not occurred either to his court or to his people. They were changes which only as reigning emperor could he hope to have effected.

The first months in the palace slipped by joyously. At forty-five years of age, in the prime of his strength, the son of Sabbatius had a brilliant wife at his side and no discernible enemies. Supported by the powerful Blue political party, with a treasury temporarily filled, he needed only to play, with his consort Theodora, the role of a benevolent bureaucrat to make these first months stretch into years of magnificent anonymity. He might have done so if he had not possessed his peculiar imagination, with the persistence of a peasant-born and the vanity of a self-taught man.

For the daily life of the emperor was fitted by tradition into an old pattern. Accustomed to little sleep, Justinian woke before sunrise and usually read from a book by the lamp at his head, while he waited for the routine of the palace day to begin. (It was much easier to conform to the pattern, he discovered, than to change it.) The rising sun struck against lustrous white marble around him, and above him the blue mosaic ceiling set with the points of gold stars glowed as softly as the dawn sky it pictured. When the brass ball dropped in the water clock to mark the first hour of the day (seven, by modern clocks) the steps of the Grand Janitor sounded along the outer corridors. His keys jangled as he unlocked doors from the council hall to the Augusteon.

Finding the emperor awake at that hour, young serving-patricians brought him water in a silver basin; they set out fruit, dates, and barley cake; they waited to robe him in white-sleeved silk tunic with scarlet sash. After his food and drink they fitted over him the cloak of deep purple that only the Caesar Basileus of the empire might wear; under the right arm it had a diagonal panel embroided with gold thread, showing his emblems; on the right shoulder it bore the jeweled badge of the globe and cross. On his head they placed the diadem of priceless stones, with the four matchless pearls hanging down. And while doing so these silentiaries advised him of early morning happenings, of messages brought to him personally by hard-riding couriers who wore the feathers of imperial service—and used their eyes on the road for spying.

At the end of the hour the Grand Janitor knocked at the door. With the first step out of his sleeping chamber—they called it the Sacred Cubicle—the son of Sabbatius ceased to be a human personality and became the Autocrat of tradition. Pausing for prayer in front of the holy pictures, he led his entourage of silentiaries, guards, and eunuchs to the great audience hall, to the small fabulous throne behind the curtain. When Justinian signed for him to do so, the Grand Chamberlain drew aside the curtain that was like a veil. Outside in the anteroom waited the Illustrious, the ministers, the petitioners who sought a hearing, and whoever else Justinian had summoned into his presence. The business of the day began when the steward was admitted to report on the great household of the palace. All who followed kissed the purple hem of Justinian's cloak in salutation to the ruler chosen by God, before arguing their affairs with the man on the throne.

Justinian could not escape from this duality. Tradition made him the personification of power and sanctity. His decision was final *because* he represented the will of God on earth. If he chose, he could overrule the patriarch of the Church. But he had to depend on his skill as a human being to carry out such an act of divine finality. It was a two-edged sword to take up. How much safer to stay within this strange pattern, to sign with purple ink the documents put before him and to refer vexatious problems to the patriarch, who was supposed to be well instructed as to the will of God.

Even if he did that, Justinian would have remained unquestionably the busiest man in earthly governments. There was literally nothing that might not be brought before him to decide, to praise or condemn—from the prayer of a hermit of the Libyan desert to the claim of an adopted orphan against tax collectors, if both claimed a dead man's estate.

At any time between ten o'clock and noon the Grand Janitor might go out into the anteroom, rattling his keys to show the morning audience was ending. At the noon meal Justinian would meet with Theodora for the first time. By two he was expected to be back in the audience hall, or the council chamber where his chief ministers assembled—virtually his cabinet—the Praetorian Prefect, the Logothete of the economists, the Masters of Offices and Armed Forces, and often the patriarch himself.

The pattern itself provided for the bureaus to take routine administration from the mind of the solitary emperor. These surviving Roman bureaus were efficient; they ground out their paperwork like the mills of the ancient gods, slowly but surely. Emperors might come and go at the popular whim or military demand, but the civil service went on functioning unchanged. It pleased Justinian's sense of order to behold the documents neatly marked with colored filing emblems, with miniature purses or swords, or scrolls; reports from the provinces bore the tiny mountains, streams, forests, or highways that distinguished them; family data bore the crests of the family concerned.

This pattern which required reading, signing, listening, relegating tasks, and approving rather than objecting, really fitted both Justinian's special skill and his disposition. It tended to confine the emperor to his palace, where the son of Sabbatius much preferred to be.

As to meeting the people at large, tradition kept him remote from the crowds—in the guarded Kathisma at the Hippodrome or, on festival days, joining in the rejoicing only by riding a white horse with his entourage in procession through streets cleaned and strewed with flowers in bloom, or at night riding between the blocks of houses where lamps were set in all the windows. In times of crisis, on the other hand, the emperor still kept the semblance of an apparition, walking without his diadem in dark garments beside the patriarch mounted on a white ass, as if merely to exhibit his concern at the calamity and to relegate its remedy to the Church.

All this Justinian might have done, as Anastasius and Justin had done, if it had not been for his imagining. Understanding that he himself could be secure, he had grave misgivings as to the security of the empire. It seemed to him that the Roman Empire was weakening and dying. Its pattern of splendor had no reality for the peasant's son. He thought of it as an old man kept alive by expedients of physicians.

It never occurred to Justinian that the work of the old man might be carried on by somebody else. Other than the imperium of Rome, he could conceive of nothing to rule the world. For a long time he had brooded over some means to return to the vitality of the early empire. But how?

In his brooding over the problem he had been influenced

by the words of a seer and the inscription carved on a statue.

More than three generations before, when barbarian Vandals had been approaching his city of Royal Hippo, the learned Augustine, bishop of Hippo, had finished a book upon which he had been working against time. He called it *The City of God.* Before the Vandals stormed and sacked Hippo, Augustine had died.

Justinian read this book carefully. For the divinely wise Augustine had realized that the Roman Empire was breaking apart and might cease to be. And Justinian, who now wore the imperial purple, had much the same fear in his city of Constantinople. Of the great Romans in the earlier time of righteous Cato and ruthless Gaius Julius Caesar, Augustine had written, ". . . by love of liberty at first and afterward by the same desire for domination and glory they achieved great things. For when liberty was obtained, it was not enough unless domination also be sought."

That was it. One thing had led to another. The early city of Rome had become a military dictatorship to gain domination, and had changed perforce into an empire to rule its conquests. It seemed as if Rome, changing like a chameleon, had always tried to turn back toward its old form. Augustus claimed to rule only with the senate, but the turbulent Nero brushed aside the senate. Then for a while two emperors had been named. After that, Constantine the Great had acknowledged that he shared the rule with the Christian Church. True, Constantine had made the admission because many of his subjects had turned to the new faith of Christ the Savior. Thus from emperor-and-senate the supreme power had come to be emperor-and-Church. What form would it take next?

"He who gave power to Marius gave it also to Gaius Caesar; He who gave it to Augustus gave it also to Nero," so Augustine had written. "He who gave it to the Christian Constantine gave it also to the apostate Julian whose gifted mind was led astray by a detestable curiosity."

Thus Augustine's book revealed the passionate hope that when the ramparts of earthly Rome crumbled the survivors would escape into the invisible city of salvation. It was like saying that the citizens of Alexandria could preserve themselves in the deserts of the saints which Theodora had described to him.

Yet the population of the existing empire showed no desire to do that. Instead, throngs pressed into Constantinople, to greet their new emperor. They could not imagine a world without Roman rule. They fancied there would always be a Rome, prosperous and protected by God. . . .

When Justinian rode in his carriage of state drawn by white mules out along the Mesé, he passed through the forum of the great Constantine. Invariably he glanced at the honorary statue of the founder on its lofty column of porphyry. He knew by heart the inscription Constantine had had carved upon the base of the statue: *"O Christ, master and ruler of the earth, to Thee have I consecrated this obedient city, and this sceptre and the power of Rome. Guard Thou it, and deliver it from every harm."*

So Constantine had expected this city to become the new metropolis of Rome. In the day of the founder the city, apparently, had been more obedient, and the empire more powerful. Yet the first duty of Justinian, as of Constantine, was to preserve this city from harm. . . .

To join Theodora at the noon meal Justinian needed to go to the women's quarters in the Daphne palace. For tradition required the empress to have her own court and attendants. These attendants, from chamberlain to doorkeeper, he had selected for her with zealous pride. Theodora accepted them all, as if delighted by his care.

Habitually—and Justinian soon made a habit of everything he did—he took a turn through the garden slope on his way to the private gate of the Daphne. From habit also he glanced up at the stone beacon tower. This was the terminal of the sun telegraph, where signal officers watched for the flashes of messages sent by mirrors from station to station, from the far frontiers. Such messages announced invasions or disasters.

Soon from the ominous eastern frontier came word of an unexpected victory. The excited adviser there, Procopius, wrote, "In a day the Romans defeated the Persian army, a thing that has not happened for a long time."

The dying Justin had probably brought it about. He had given two young officers, Comito's husband and Count Belisarius, the task of holding Daras, the new frontier fortress. They had done so with youthful recklessness by going out to engage the Persian army of invasion. By tactics never written in textbooks Belisarius had held the Persians locked while a flying contingent of Huns emerged from hiding to rout them.

When he read the detailed report of the battle, Justinian shook his head. Obviously the victory had been gained by the hired Huns, a remnant of Attila's armies, not by the Romans. But on the strength of the victory he took a reckless chance himself. Over the heads of elder generals he named Belisarius sole commander of the armed forces in the east. It was just possible that if Belisarius could win such a battle he might avoid losing the war. And that is what he did.

The news from the east seemed to Justinian to be an omen of his own success. Armies might make gains elsewhere. In his imagination a new era of recovery took shape. It seemed to him that in some manner the decay of the state could be arrested; walls, even those of Theodosius the Great, could be rebuilt and made enduring; frontier armies could be mobilized on a new pattern; laws could be clarified to restore order; wealth that was now wasted in the amusements of the rich and displays for the populace could be devoted to new armaments. Above all a large fleet could be built, to utilize the open routes of the sea, now that the land routes were obstructed.

In this manner new power could be channeled from the capital city into the provinces, which would then be able to strengthen the city again, as in the lost days of grandeur.

It did not occur to Justinian, making his first plans in this fashion, that his people would oppose such expense and such activity, even while they expected Roman dominion to continue—at least for their generation.

Observers in the Sacred Palace reported that the new Autocrat appeared to be neither a bureaucrat nor a military dictator. He showed, however, two peculiarities. Keeping within the limits of the palace, he seldom ventured beyond the gilded bronze portals of the Chalké where the news bulletins hung, and he did not seem to rest.

His first move toward changing the city aroused no curiosity. He merely asked for a fresh code of law. Theodosius had done the same, with the result that legal experts were still at work over thousands of manuscripts of ancient civil laws, decrees, and decisions. It would take generations, the experts pointed out, to copy down such a multitude of texts in any kind of order. (The experts of course wanted their sinecure to last out their own lifetime, and they profited much because only experts could pass on the existing confusion between ancient laws and modern decrees.)

Justinian, however, was on his own ground when dealing with written records. Sending for one of the experts, Tribonian, an eccentric miser, he explained that he wanted preserved only the minimum best of the ancient laws, to meet modern needs. He wanted, in short, a single Corpus Juris, a Body of the Law, to apply in every hamlet of the empire. Since Tribonian had hewn out a fortune for himself, he should be able to bring a cosmos out of the chaos of the Roman laws. Besides, Tribonian himself had suggested doing something of the kind.

Immediately Tribonian pointed out the danger. Nowadays prefects and judges were accustomed to make their own decisions; if a single Body of Law were set up, like a colossal inanimate judge, what authority would be left to the officials to decide such all-important matters as property rights? The Body of Law itself would decide inflexibly. Before such a Body of Law a Samaritan olive grower would have the same rights as the Noble Tribonian.

That was exactly what Justinian wanted. He asked how quickly it could be done, and in how many volumes. Tribonian, piqued, said five years and twenty volumes—if Justinian believed in miracles.

Justinian said three years and twelve volumes, and the Noble Tribonian could choose his own assistants. If he accomplished the task he would be an Illustrious.

So challenged, Tribonian went to work with all his eccentric energy.

Evidently Justinian hoped to bring about his new imagined state by giving certain men the task of doing it. The gossip gatherers of the court picked up a phrase of Tribonian's and repeated, "He merely hopes to bring a Cosmos out of Chaos." Constantinopolitan society smiled with appreciation, remembering that it was a human failing of new emperors to order such reform.

Officials in the War Department, however, demanded the recall of Count Belisarius. The youthful commander of the eastern front had lost his second battle with the Persians and only saved his army by wading out to islands in the river Euphrates. Justinian pointed out on a map that the islands and the Euphrates were deep in Persian territory, so that even if Belisarius had failed in a battle, he had protected the frontier. Belisarius stayed in command despite the elder generals.

Justinian had an instinct for picking men. He made John of Cappadocia chief Logothete, or Economist. This manipulator of finances, who had the morals of a Bulgarian bull, could extract from the tax collectors—who had been accustomed to hold out a goodly portion of the money that passed through their offices—almost all the tax money due the treasury. On the night of his promotion the burly Cappadocian raced his chariot up the crowded Mesé to the Venus Square and threw open the taverns to the girls and boys.

A rogue at heart, this stalwart John of Cappadocia took care to win the affection of the street crowds. And he said such people enjoyed their vices more than any virtues. He had a way of speaking his mind, even to the new emperor. Like Justinian, John was peasant-born and self-taught. They understood each other, and a strong tie bound them together. Whatever Justinian imagined, John was capable of contriving—so long as it could be done with money, and most things could. There the similarity between them ended. Abstemious in his habits, Justinian was devoted to the wealthy Blue faction; gargantuan in his appetites, the Cappadocian peasant envied the rich from whom he had been unable to steal as a boy; he belonged to the radical Green faction. Moreover, he hated interference, and so he had little good to say of Tribonian's herculean labor with laws that interfered with John's highhanded methods of finance. Tribonian, in his opinion, was not only rich but a miser and a weasel.

"Blasphemy, dicing, and grabbing girls for theater brothels are all natural vices, Thrice August," he argued. "Should we attempt to deprive the people of their amusements?"

"They have consequences, Logothete."

"To the persons, Ever Victorious? Isn't that their concern, not ours?"

"The consequences come upon the communities they live in. A town, Noble Logothete, can be destroyed by the sexual perversions of a few people."

"Sodom and Gomorrah?"

John of Cappadocia realized that he could not understand the mind of his new master. The doctrine of divine punishment was archaic—that fire, plague, or earthquake would visit a city where human sin existed. If that were true Constantinople itself would have been destroyed instead of thriving for more than two centuries. He recalled that, officially,

Justinian was an orthodox churchman, and changed his tone. "As the Augustus declares, a law should condemn every vice. Yet how will the sublime Autokrator enforce such a law?"

When Justinian stared at him, John, who was never abashed, described how the evening before a band of pleasure-bent Blue swordsmen in a boat on the harbor had sighted a desirable woman, a young wife out rowing with her husband. They had dragged her into their boat. Whereupon, unfortunately, she had jumped into the water and drowned. What would the new law do in such a case of suicide-by-compulsion?

"Hang the Blue youths." Justinian was curt.

"By all means, Ever Glorious! But, precisely, how?" When the new Economist reflected on the remarks of the Demarch of the favored Blue faction upon such a legalized murder of that party's young assassins, he repressed a smile; but when he reflected upon some of his own escapades he did not feel so amused. "The boys really didn't kill the girl. Who would hang them?"

"The Prefect of the city."

John of Cappadocia told his drinking companions, between their dice throws, that the new emperor had Platonic ideas. He must have been reading, while burning his midnight oil, Plato's *Republic* that described an ideal commonwealth in which no human being could live comfortably.

Already John sensed some public exasperation because taxes had not been diminished. He decided that popular resentment would be stirred by an attempt to enact the new laws—so they would soon become dead letters.

No one realized then—although the news commentators began to suspect it—that Justinian was being influenced by Theodora in what he planned.

The daughter of Acacius the bear keeper gained her influence over those around her very quietly. In no case was it yielded to her until she had won it.

Tradition bound her new life as Augusta of the Roman Empire. From the minute when the Grand Janitor passed noisily through the outer corridors and softly moving patrician girls bowed before her bed, each wearing a peplon of white embroidered with purple and gold, to the last minute when her silentiaries made the rounds of the halls, locking doors for the night, Theodora's actions were governed by palace routine. She shared Justinian's light midday meal, and often did not see his face again until lamplighting.

When the eunuchs of her private chambers approached her before noon, she paraded to the bath building, with the noble girls carrying the salts, ointments, and perfumes behind her; when her Grand Chamberlain bowed before her, Theodora knew that her councilors had matters to discuss in her audience hall. With apparent pleasure Theodora yielded to the routine, while she studied all these human beings who served her—aided by her ability to understand every dialect they spoke.

Very soon she realized that, although she was dressed and paraded about like some fragile imperial effigy, much was expected of her. The empress had her duties no less than the Most Sublime Autocrat.

Long before, women had been cast to the surface of affairs only by convulsion, as it were. Livia had been so uplifted during the suicidal family struggles of the first Augustan age, after Cleopatra—the Egyptian, sixth of the name—had risen on the bloody tide of civil war. Here in the east Christianity had bestowed a certain dignity on women; and in ancient Byzantium women had shared the work of men of the palace. Those Byzantine ladies had been too astute to remain yoked, like the early Roman matrons and virgins, to house service or breeding.

Theodora, who seldom read a book, learned about this from the gracious and highborn Mistress of the Women's Chambers, who wore purple almost as dark as her own. She learned more from the delicate eunuch Narses of the Sacred

Cubicle, who fed his own self-esteem by admonishing women. Narses' dignity was almost intolerable, being so easily offended. In imagination he believed himself superior to the generals of the army, and Theodora decided that he would be a useful confidant but never a friend.

From him and the old bath women Theodora heard about the ghosts. These had left vestiges of their beauty and their unhappiness in the shadows of the Sacred Palace. The ghosts had all been illustrious—courageous Pulcheria, who had tried to rule for the headstrong Theodosius; Ariadne, who had gone into the Hippodrome to appeal to the people; but most of all the Athenian, the lovely pagan who had been chosen for her eyes and matchless figure, and who had ended her days alone, an exile in Jerusalem. The bath slaves agreed that the Athenian had had lovers undetected but had ruined herself by giving away an apple.

Whenever Theodora felt deft hands fit over her forehead the diadem with sprays of jewels and the pearls that fell in strings against her ears, she felt the presence of the vanished ghosts.

Warily she attempted to appear as gracious as the Athenian. Because she had so little physical strength, she lay late in bed; because she distrusted her pallor and tense mouth, she let the handmaidens anoint her and tint her flesh, softening the tint with powder; because she could not endure the long work hours of a dogmatic Pulcheria, she seldom showed herself to her councilors. She liked better to lie under canopies on the roof of the Daphne, as if waiting for Justinian. There, overlooking the Hippodrome, she could greet petitioners graciously—as if allowing them to disturb her rest.

Unlike Justinian, she felt no sense of security in these early years. The patrician ladies who had opposed her marriage did not willingly salute her as empress. At her first mistake these women might join together to attack her.

At first she trusted nobody, and then only those women who confessed their private troubles to her. After she had aided them with money or authority, she believed they might be loyal to her. Yet she understood too well that the rise of a new leader, especially in war, or a turn of popular fancy, would send her from this palace, back to the House of Theodora. Among courtiers who habitually played a part, she proved herself to be an actress more skilled than they.

Insensibly she began to crave the luxury of her new chambers. Since Justinian seldom left the palace grounds, she was confined there. She craved the snow-chilled pomegranates and Syrian dates the stewards placed, in gold vessels, on her table. When she heard the familiar murmur, "Glory of the purple—the joy of the world," her body tensed as if at the kiss of a lover.

Theodora had visited the empty purple chamber in the southern garden of the cypress trees. But she was not with child by Justinian.

When Justinian wrote out the wording of his new decrees On Marriage—for Tribonian to deal with in law—she sat with him and did not smile when he wrote that women needed to be protected from "the weakness of their sex." Such a preamble did not matter, compared to the mandate that women of any blameful past should, after marriage, become "free women differing in no way from those who have not erred as they." Or that their children and inheritance should be different in no way.

Theodora persuaded him to put that in, and he seemed pleased to do it. Although she watched him carefully as they discussed it, he did not appear to wonder how much her early life had taught her. Surely he had not forgotten that she had amused men on a stage. Had he learned more about her than that? Justinian never would speak of it.

Very quickly she discovered that his mind dwelt on points of law. A particular thing, to him, was lawful or not lawful. He did not wonder, as Theodora was apt to do, whether it might be desirable or not. Moreover, he gave his judgment with a deep inward contentment. Caesar had spoken.

Almost at once—when she perceived that—the daughter of the bear keeper resolved that she would never beg of her new Caesar, or worry him into doing something she wanted. If her husband now regarded himself as clothed in the authority of Caesar, she would appeal only to Caesar, invoking the laws and if necessary the will of God to do so. She did not relish that.

It seemed silly at times, all this breath-taking ceremonial that surrounded them. The sleeping room she shared with Justinian was not called the Sacred Cubicle; it remained anonymous, put apart, as it were, for their bodies to mingle in love. Once she stepped out of it, she was within his court, or her own. Even in communion at the church the Augusta was seated apart up in the balcony with her court around her. Theodora actually saw more of her Mistress of the Women's Chambers now than of Justinian—and she felt afraid at times of the poised elderly woman who arranged the furniture of her chambers, to the very flowers in the crystal bowls, by tradition and not by the inclination of the new empress. Under the eyes of this Mistress, the lithe young Augusta could not hurry across a room; she had to take slow steps as if dragging a train. At such times she had a mad impulse to stand on her head, just once, to observe the effect.

A day came, however, when she no longer felt frustrated before the eyes of the Mistress. It happened because of forbidden wine. Since Justinian never touched it, no wine appeared on the table of her private dining hall. After going without it for a long time, Theodora began to ask the steward for figs soaked in sweet Cyprus brandy, for honey-brew, and grapes flavored with wine. After that, to her surprise the water poured for her to drink changed mysteriously to a pale wine of Cyprus. Tasting it, Theodora glanced curiously at the table servitors. They appeared impassive as always. Then she became aware of the Mistress standing behind her, as if to make certain that the meal was in order. Impulsively she sprang up and threw her arms around the patrician lady. "It's such a nice gift!" she whispered.

The Mistress flushed, and smiled. "It's from our vineyard on the island," she whispered in response.

"I'll have nothing else. Anyway, not so much fruit now."

The appearance of the wine made Theodora quite happy. But she had learned that Justinian did nothing on impulse. While he was writing and crossing out the *novellae,* as he called them, of the new laws, she exclaimed that all brothel keepers should be exiled from the city.

When Justinian considered that, he objected that they were within their rights; they paid a tax for their establishments and did not seek to injure anyone. Checking her exasperation, Theodora invoked what she could remember about the laws.

"Will Caesar tell me this? Is a man a criminal who takes for himself the pay of another person? Is it lawful to make an underage girl sign a bond that profits somebody else?"

Thus she persuaded her husband to outlaw brothel keepers. He did not mention John of Cappadocia's objections, but wrote, ". . . for we have found out that some people travel about the districts offering poor young girls shoes and clothes, and in this way carry them off to dens in this fortunate city where they are shut up and given little food and clothes, while putting their bodies at the service of the public. These brothel keepers have the girls sign bonds binding themselves to this, and the keepers pocket the fees they get. Some of these men are unholy enough to pollute girls less than ten years of age . . . we were secretly informed of this, and it is our determination to free the city from such pollution."

The decree appropriated money to buy the release of the girls and condemned their keepers, upon conviction, to exile.

Justinian was quite earnest in wishing to cleanse his city. He warned John of Cappadocia, "Keep your hands clean," and John obediently swore that he would.

But Theodora had a different way of looking at it. It seemed to her that "the weakness of her sex" was neither a curse nor a physical disability but a weakness caused by the brutal whims of males. Her body had been the test of that.

Very quickly all those who wore the *propoloma*—the tower-like hairdress with floating veil of the court ladies—realized that in the new Augusta they had a protectress. More, they could bring their friends to her, to complain of a husband, to appeal for a divorce, or demand acknowledgment of a child. In these women who served her Theodora found her first following, and a most loyal one. The girls of the new Augusta spied for her, warned her of hidden enmity, confided in her, and never, in all that followed, betrayed her.

Before long the outer city heard about "Theodora and her women." A fantastic story went the rounds. It made some of the hearers laugh, but most of them grew red with indignation. It was about the patrician Timothaeus, who appealed to the new Augusta to aid him in collecting debts from some of her people.

Timothaeus, at that time, did not know the risk he was running. In his own opinion he had a just claim, and he fancied himself a much put-upon, well-meaning man. But he had the reputation of squeezing even obols out of those who dealt with him, and Theodora's following had taken pains to acquaint their mistress with their view of the case.

So Timothaeus, entering confidently to the private audience hall, prepared to play his part of a defrauded benefactor. He did not know that he entered upon a stage prepared for him—with eunuchs and the girls of the propoloma ranged in attentive lines, and ladies of honor gathered about the throne. It surprised him when the Chamberlain made him advance on his knees to the step before the throne and kiss the slender foot of the empress instead of merely inclining before her. But Theodora made a lovely picture, smiling as if enjoying his salutation. And Timothaeus fancied he could beg effectively on his knees, although the position was painful.

"Most Clement Augusta," he began, "hear the plea of a devoted servant, who is, as Your Omniscience knows, also a patrician." He paused, but Theodora said neither yea or nay. "It is hard, in these trying times, to be a patrician, and poor——"

Close to him the girls sighed in concert, murmuring, "Poor Patrician Timothaeus!"

This chorused assent surprised the nobleman but rather encouraged him. "May it please the Most Magnificent to remember that a patrician must spend money to maintain his station in life. Moreover, I have had certain dealings——"

"What a big hernia you have," intoned the eunuchs, as if making response in church.

This time Timothaeus did not think he had heard aright. He started to get up and remembered he had to stay on his knees. With difficulty he resumed his carefully prepared argument—that moneylenders, being common men, plagued a patrician to pay his debts to them, while he, being a patrician, could not say a word about money that was owed to him.

"Poor Patrician Timothaeus!"

It was the girls again. And surely like a chorus. Exasperated, he threw out his arms. "Let me appeal. It is outrageous! I am burdened beyond endurance——"

"What a big hernia you have!"

Choking, Timothaeus groaned, and heard a ripple of laughter. Frantically he backed out, to the refuge of the entrance. Theodora said nothing.

But most of the powerful magnates with summer resorts up the Bosphorus and over in Chrysopolis began to feel that Theodora's whims and Justinian's naïve ideas of reform were dangerous. In this opinion the radicals of the city, particularly the Green party, quite agreed.

The revolt came without warning. It came from the streets of the city and it attacked the Sacred Palace.

This palace enclosure formed a separate city, as it were.

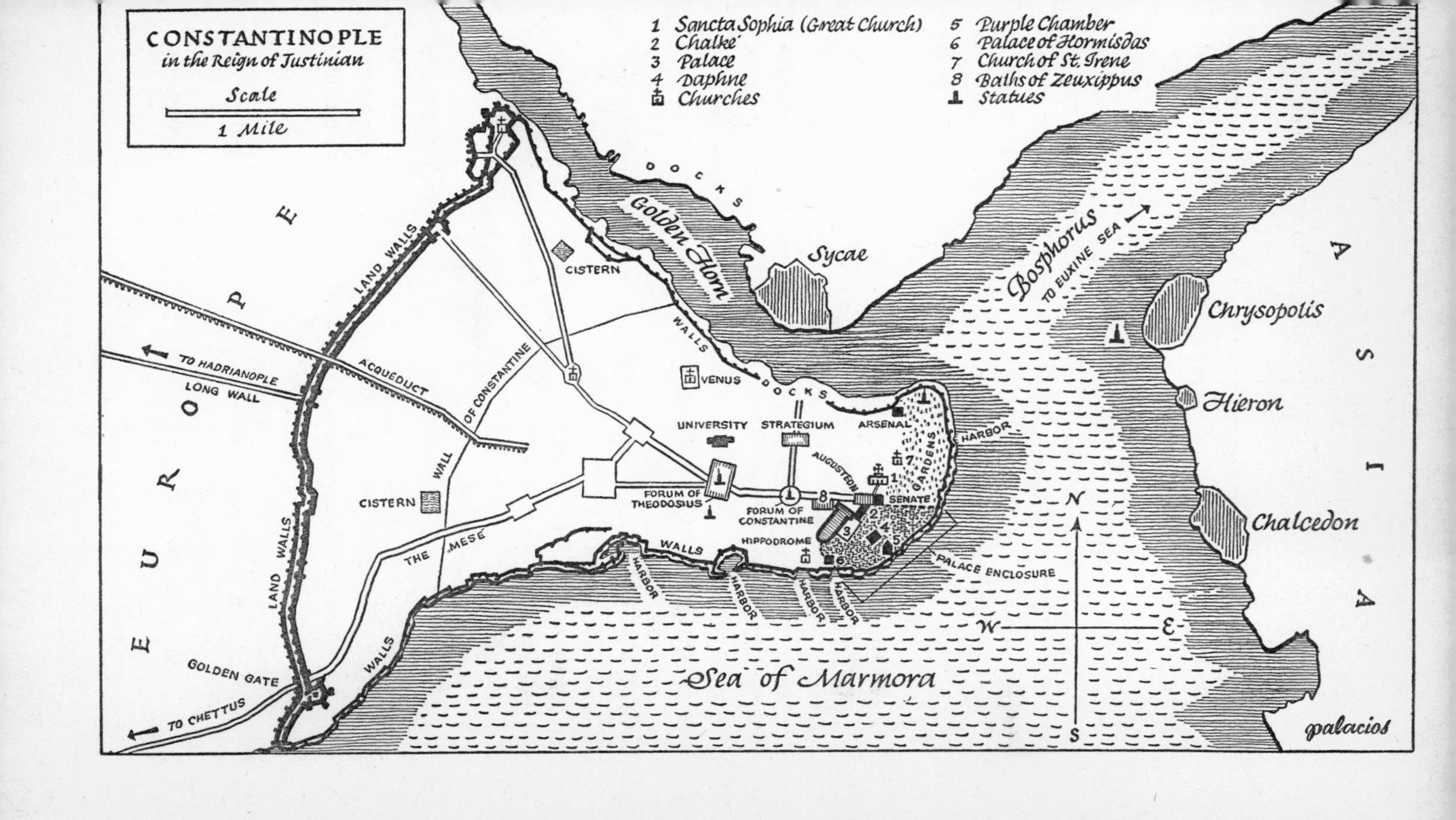

CONSTANTINOPLE
in the Reign of Justinian
Scale
1 Mile
1 Sancta Sophia (Great Church)
2 Chalke
3 Palace
4 Daphne
Churches
5 Purple Chamber
6 Palace of Hormisdas
7 Church of St. Irene
8 Baths of Zeuxippus
Statues
DOCKS
Golden Horn
Sycae
Bosphorus
TO EUXINE SEA
Chrysopolis
Hieron
Chalcedon
A S I A
E U R O P E
LAND WALLS
CISTERN
WALLS
VENUS
DOCKS
TO HADRIANOPLE
LONG WALL
ACQUEDUCT
OF CONSTANTINE
WALL
UNIVERSITY
STRATEGIUM
ARSENAL
HARBOR
GARDENS
AUGUSTEON
SENATE
FORUM OF THEODOSIUS
FORUM OF CONSTANTINE
HIPPODROME
CISTERN
THE MESE
WALLS
PALACE ENCLOSURE
HARBOR
HARBOR
HARBOR
HARBOR
N
W
E
S
LAND WALLS
GOLDEN GATE
WALLS
TO CHETTUS
Sea of Marmora
palacios

When the great founder, Constantine, had marked out the limits of his metropolis-to-be in the year 326 of salvation he had tried to make it appear as much as possible like the old Rome—although the beautiful point of land jutting out into the blue waterways was actually as different as possible from ancient Rome, built upon a malarial plain athwart a muddy river. Constantine had pointed out seven heights, like the ancestral seven hills, and he had built his residence on the first and best height facing the sea, where the palace of Byzantium had been.

The city not only outgrew Constantine's original wall but spread over the greater Theodosian ramparts, seventeen miles around. Procopius, the Syrian who had abandoned his legal duties to write a history of his age, took note of this great influx of people. "A throng of every sort of men comes to the city from the whole world. Each of them is led by an errand of business or some hope or chance . . . to petition the Emperor. All of these become residents, impelled by ambition or fear. It also happens that these persons are in want of living quarters."

As the city expanded, the palace grew over its favored height. Other residences like the Daphne, and office structures like the senate and treasury, sprang up around the old house of the master, so that by Justinian's time the Sacred Palace, as it was called (from the Sacred Cubicle), formed a labyrinth of government quarters and churches stretching from the little House of Theodora (actually outside the enclosure) to the equally small church of St. Irene above the boat landing on the Golden Horn.

This kremlinlike height had its own fortified ports, beacon tower, and protecting wall. Such massive walls had not been known in ancient Rome; they had appeared after the first barbarian invasions.

Not that the Sacred Palace sheltered all the great edifices. The university, for instance, lay within the city along the Mesé main street. And the Hippodrome itself, which the democratic factions still claimed as their assembly place, not only adjoined the Sacred Palace but was connected with it by corridors. So it was not so much that the court walled itself off from the common people—as would be the case before long in feudal Europe—but that the rulers sheltered themselves from the ruled. That state of affairs could be changed overnight by revolt. All segments of the people outside the palace walls, including the university students, held stubbornly to their legal right of revolution if they discovered they were misgoverned.

Until the winter of that year, 532, the outer population had been annoyed rather than angered by Justinian. Against Theodora no one spoke then. But the Economist, John of Cappadocia, enforced the collection of taxes, and Tribonian's new laws caused anxiety. Moreover, Count Belisarius and another commander, Mundus, a Hun or very much like a Hun, had been recalled from the frontiers, not to preserve peace but to start a new war.

It was Justinian's idea. The emperor wanted to prepare an expeditionary force to be transported over the sea to recapture for the empire the lost province of Africa in the west, which had been a Vandal kingdom for three generations.

It was a fantastic idea, to try to regain the lost western empire—Africa, Sicily, Italy, Spain, Gaul, and even ancient Rome itself. Belisarius was known to have expressed no joy at the prospect of mobilizing an army to put to sea. The last imperial fleet sent out to recover Africa had burned mysteriously; the last remembered expedition had been led out by the apostate Julian and had been annihilated in the deserts of the Tigris and Euphrates. Whatever happened, the cost would be tremendous. The Economist spoke against it openly. "If we win, what do we win? A province. If we lose, what do we lose? The field army, and that means everything. It's a bad gamble."

Besides, John pointed out, there was already civil war in Palestine, where the government was trying to suppress the heretical Samaritans. It took soldiers and it cost money to kill the evil-minded Samaritans.

Most of the people wanted no war at all. Street speakers, tavern drinkers, and dockyard workers went so far as to demand of their hearers that if the August Emperor would not change his mind he must be cast out. But the emperor did not change his mind. Preparations for war went on in the dockyards and the Strategium barracks.

At this point one faction complained bitterly of its grievances. The Green party suffered, in reality, from the domineering of the favored Blues.

Now the circus factions, as they were called, had their roots deep within the populace and far out within the provinces; they were more active in turbulent Antioch and nervous Caesaria than in the well-policed Constantinople. Originally they had been the defense forces of the cities, where Blue, Green, Red, and White had been responsible for manning certain sections of the walls. They still had arms of sorts, but in the prevailing security they devoted themselves more to sports than to drill. They sported their colors, however, and fighters carried forbidden knife-swords under their mantles. The Green color prevailed among the poorer sort, or jobless, and in the heretical churches—and so were called Manichaeans and Jews and Samaritans by the Blue spokesmen. (As if political parties in the present day were formed out of the militia, Masons, athletic clubs, workers' unions, betting mobs, and gangsters.)

The most dangerous element in the factions was the lawbreaking youth. The lads who prowled the city at night went armed and aping the garb of Huns. "They got themselves such clothing," Procopius testified, "from stolen money. They hid small, two-edged swords along the thigh under their mantles and they gathered in groups as soon as dark set in, to rob their victims of clothing, gold brooches and whatever else they had."

By then well-to-do people habitually put on old clothes

and cheap jewelry when they ventured out after dark. The Blue gangs counted on their immunity from arrest, and violated women by daylight, heedless of observers. After the Blue murder gangs had driven the Green fighters from the streets, other citizens began to call on the knife men to kill off their own enemies.

"There even began a sort of competition among them," Procopius relates, "to show off their strength and manliness by killing with one blow any unarmed man who fell in their way. . . . If any judge ignored the advice of these men, the penalty of death hung over him. Money-lenders were compelled to give up their contracts of debt without any money being paid them. Sons of men of high station mingled with the lawless youths, and tried to compel their fathers to hand over money to them."

Girls joined the successful gangs; disheartened Greens began to change their colors or flee the city. At the same time families and delegations trooped in from the villages and provinces, to protest the tax levied on shopkeepers, farmers, and all who owned a boat. These simple folk came to appeal to the Emperor Chosen by God; they held to their old rights of free speech and public assembly.

That assembly began, by their reckoning, at the opening of the games in the Hippodrome before the Ides of January, 532. Owing to the disorders, Justinian had named no consul to provide the sports. He gave the games himself and trusted to the Prefect of the city to keep order. "The government," Procopius noted with relish, "behaved like a tyranny, but not like an effective tyranny."

It was Sunday. During the quiet between two races, the Demarch of the Greens stood up and called until he got Justinian's attention in the imperial box. Scribes noted down the argument that followed. Since Justinian's voice could not carry across the arena, the announcer answered for him.

Demarch of the Greens: "Live long, Justinian Augustus.

Be victorious! Kind lord, I am aggrieved. God knows I am oppressed, yet I fear to name the oppressor."

Announcer: "Who is he? We know him not."

"Oh, he is to be found in the Street of the Shoemakers."

"No one has wronged you."

"You know the truth, Thrice August, about the one who oppresses me!"

"We know no one who oppresses you."

Driven to give a name, the spokesman of the Greens identified an officer of the guard. "He will perish like Judas."

"You haven't come here to watch the games; you've come to insult your magistrates."

"My oppressor will die like Judas!"

Evidently the Greens were complaining of more than one guardsman. Sensing the threat, Justinian retorted, through the bull-throated announcer: "Silence, Jews, Manichaeans, Samaritans!"

"Oh! Do you call us Jews and Samaritans? Now, the Mother of God is with us."

There was a stirring and a muttering along the benches where the crowd hung upon the shouted words.

Announcer: "Be silent, you—or your head will be cut from you."

At this the orator changed his tone. He begged the Most Magnificent not to be angered by his pleading. For he had good reason to make his complaint *at this moment*. Here he spoke for all those who could not find a way into the palace or get a hearing in any public office. He himself had had to enter by a back way, for mules, and truly he wished now he had not come at all! He, who asked for a hearing, was being threatened with execution!

Announcer: "Everyone is free to come where he wishes, without danger."

The Demarch, skilled in oratory, faced the audience behind him. "I am told that I am free, yet I must not make use of my freedom. If a man is free but is known to be a Green, he will be punished. Justice goes blind at sight of the Green color. Stop all this murdering, and let us be punished lawfully! Human beings can't endure being oppressed, as if it were punishment by law. Would that Sabbatius had never been born! For his son is a murderer——"

With the uproar drowning Justinian's protest, the orator flung his voice over it. "Yes, a seller of wood, a spectator here in the morning, was cut down in the junction this afternoon. O lord of our lives, who killed the woodman at the junction?"

Up to this point the leader of the Blues had been listening critically. Now he gave tongue. "Your party is the only one to enter the Hippodrome with murderers."

Demarch: "Yes, with your party. You can do murder and run away under protection. Lord Justinian, who killed the woodman at the junction?"

Announcer: "You yourselves."

"Justinian, who slew the son of Epigathus?"

"You are trying to fix guilt on the Blues——"

"Now may the Lord God have pity on us. The Lord God does not wrong us. I will argue willingly with anyone who says God brings all such things to happen. Who is it that wrongs us? Explain that!"

"You are blaspheming! Be silent!"

"If that is the pleasure of the Most Majestic! Now I know the truth—but I shall be silent. I should not have called for justice here. Our bones will be in the earth if we stay here. Pick up your bones, spectators!"

At that signal the Green faction rushed out of the amphitheater with their orator, to be followed after a moment by the aroused Blues. Street fighting began.

Watching from the roof of the Daphne palace, Theodora knew that Justinian had not come off well in the angry debate. He had heard himself threatened, and had been unable to quiet the mob. Old Justin had chastened the parties by using his authority on both, in equal measure.

Justinian ordered the Prefect of the city to arrest and execute the leaders of the riot immediately. Seven men were hurried across the harbor under guard to be hung. By odd chance the ropes broke with the weight of two of the victims, who survived. This stirred the superstition of spectators, and some friars from the Hospital of St. Lawrence carried off the survivors to safety—since the hospital was a religious sanctuary. The harassed Prefect threw a cordon of guards around the place. By chance one of the survivors of the hanging was a Green, the other a Blue.

All day Monday excitement rose in the city. Tuesday, Justinian decided to go on with the races as if there had been no disturbance. Crowds thronged into the Hippodrome and he was beset at once with calls to release the two who lived, although hanged. Having been worsted in the earlier debate, Justinian elected to be silent now. As a result, after every race he had to listen to the shouting. "Set free the two who were hanged by your servants and spared by the Lord!"

Whether his inaction gave the crowds courage, or whether invisible leaders planned the revolt, Tuesday ended in general demolition. Massed armed men paraded down the Mesé and broke into the Praetorium, firing the buildings. Encouraged by such easy success, the mobs entered arsenals, seeking more weapons, and smashed the portals of the Augusteon at the end of the Mesé. They demanded that senators appear to consult with them, and when no senators came forward, furniture was piled in the senate house and fired. The flames spread to the Great Church of Sancta Sophia.

After dark the conflagration became awe-inspiring as it reached the adjoining Octagon Forum. The mobs were now clearly under leadership. Criminals escaping from a burning prison joined them, and the guards of noblemen antagonistic to Justinian were seen directing them. Blues joined with Greens—always a danger sign—and they found a slogan: "Long live the humane Blue-Greens!" They also had a watchword, the cry of the circus: "Nika."

By the end of the night the Sacred Palace was cut off, by fire and armed bands, from the rest of the city. Besieged in his palace, where he had secluded himself for so long, Justinian knew that his life was at stake.

Separated from the surviving city guards, protected only by those shut up with him in the labyrinth of the palace, he had to listen to grim news on Wednesday. Mundus, the impassive commander of the Herule barbarians, had gone out with two other officials to hear the demands of the rebels. They reported that the populace demanded the dismissal of his executives, John of Cappodocia and Tribonian among them. They believed that the revolt now was a major effort to remove the son of Sabbatius from the throne and elect one of the nephews of Anastasius who had been passed over by the crowning of Justin.

Hearing that, Justinian realized that the revolt had a religious impulse and was in addition the protest of his people against the African war venture. His servants reported that food was giving out within the palace, packed with dignitaries who had come in for the Ides of January festival. Pent up with such a throng, he sensed that he could depend on very few of his courtiers. Leading senators, well aware of the crisis, would give no official response to the rebels; the excubitors and other palace guards, of whom he was the honorary commander, remained idle at their posts, except to fight the fire outside the Chalké gate. He remembered Justin's warning that such men knew the metal of a commander. And the last thing he could do would be to lead a few hundred irresolute guardsmen, gleaming with silver and gold, into his anger-torn city.

Instead he asked Count Belisarius and Mundus to drive back the rebels. Luckily the field officers had with them part of Belisarius' comitatus and a Herule regiment from the battle front. These three thousand trained men would obey their own commanders, if they took no heed of Justinian.

Thursday morning the two sections of the army moved out, around the smoldering ruins of the Great Church. But they did not penetrate far.

A city defending itself is like no other battlefield. The young Belisarius and the half-pagan Herule and Goth soldiers were confronted by blocked-up streets and massive buildings from which missiles poured down. When they cleared a house they might find the roof burning over their heads; if they broke through a barricade, loaded carts might be rolled against them. A great marble bath building and the skyscraping Octagon became fortresses for the poorly armed but wildly excited populace.

Mistakenly, devout priests paraded out with candles and holy pictures, to stop the conflict. The ignorant Herules, believing themselves taken in the rear, scattered the procession, thereby arousing the throngs that watched this seeming sacrilege. And the conflagration broke out again, driven by the wind, from the harbor to the Mesé, enveloping a hospital with all its patients.

For two days Justinian watched from the palace roof, hoping for some miracle of achievement. When food ran short he ordered all persons not of the army or his own following to leave the gates. Some went unwillingly, but most of them seemed glad to escape while they could. The rebels, having no quarrel with mere senators and servants, greeted them with cheers. But their departure nearly emptied the palace grounds, and when Justinian hurried through the vacant corridors he felt watchful eyes studying him as if calculating his chances of life.

Theodora kept apart with her women in the Daphne, where wounded men were brought in. After the first futile day of street fighting she seemed to have lost hope of victory, and she no longer watched, unobserved, to be certain that her old home was safe.

By Saturday night the surviving soldiers were back within

the gates, most of them blackened with smoke and bleeding. Belisarius wore ordinary mail and steel half helmet. Sweat stained his blond hair and beard, and he sagged with weariness. Curtly he said that his forces could hold only the ruins of the church and Augusteon. They could not open a way through the city.

Waiting for Justinian's response, she sensed the indecision of her husband. The soldiers had explained the situation; no one but he could direct them what to do next. Narses kept whispering to her about the mistakes that had been made, in not sending for more troops, and in letting the races go on. It exasperated Theodora to hear this muttering. What had been done was over with. What would they do now?

"I will go out to the people myself," announced Justinian after he had talked with John. It surprised Theodora, this decision to act himself. But he murmured then that he would make a last appeal, taking the Scriptures with him. She did not believe that talk would gain anything for them, after their defeat.

Escorted by priests and excubitors, Justinian went out through the corridor from the Daphne across the chapel to the Kathisma box. The guards, eying him curiously, gave him their rigid salute.

When the curtains were drawn back from the box, crowds surged into the half-filled arena. Expectantly they waited below for their emperor to speak, and Justinian began to speak too soon and too quickly.

His hoarse voice did not carry over the stirring of the restless crowd. Impassively the announcer stepped forward, past the silvered figures holding the standards of the Roman eagles and the cross of Constantine. The announcer's trained voice, projecting one word at a time, quieted the mob.

"I . . . the Caesar, your emperor . . . give pardon . . . to everyone. . . . I condone . . . all that has been done."

Tense with expectancy, the populace listened with satisfaction. Mobs of youths and bodyguards pushed into the tiers, to hear the defeated emperor. Justinian declared that he had dismissed his obnoxious ministers; Probus—a man known to be honest—would be the new prefect of the city. Not a soul in the favored city would be arrested. The hanged men would be safe. Justinian pledged his faith as a Christian and his word as emperor.

Many in the crowd were satisfied. (If Justinian had faced them in this way on Tuesday, the revolt might never have gained momentum.) But all the leaders were skeptical; they had agreed to depose Justinian, to liquidate his following and elect one of the nephews of Anastasius. They had gone too far to draw back.

A single voice cut through the cadence of the announcer.

"Ass! That's all a lie!"

When thousands of human beings are tensed by conflict and edged by uncertainty, such a voice can start them into action, forward or back. Laughter and jeers echoed the shout. Justinian was doomed.

He made the mistake of lifting the heavy illuminated Gospels in both arms. His hands shook. His weak voice rose in a cry. "Be at peace! I swear it upon these holy words. My sins have caused the burning and killing. I alone am guilty. I swear it. No one of you is guilty. I am guilty. I swear——"

"So you swore to preserve Vitalian. Where is he now—after you shared the bread and wine of the Eucharist with him?"

The crowd, prompted by its varied leaders, roared approval. The spectacle of Justinian baited in his Hippodrome stirred a gale of laughter and the monotonous shout: "Who murdered Vitalian? Son of Sabbatius, who murdered Vitalian? Perjurer, who murdered Vitalian?"

Justinian could make no answer, and ran from the box. He had been condemned by the democratic convention of his people. (Immediately the senators and officials released from the palace learned the result of the emperor's last appeal, and—since the senate house had burned, and was still held by the Gothic soldiers—assembled in the nearest forum and agreed upon the next steps, the crowning of the new emperor, the attack upon the palace of Justinian. Since that was the plan of the leaders of the revolt, the senators merely had to put their consent on record. Only one voted against the attack—one who believed that no attack would be needed because Justinian would flee the palace.)

The weary Justinian faced his remaining officers and followers in the gold-sheathed Delphax chamber, where Theodora waited. This small group remained because all of them except Belisarius and Mundus would lose their lives when Justinian fell. John of Cappadocia shouted out what must be done. There was not a moment to lose—a galley was manned in the palace port, and the bullion and jewels from his vaults were being loaded on it.

Justinian agreed that they must escape, to his Macedonian coast. Hurried arguments rose—who should be taken, and whose goods? The troops would cover the evacuation.

Around the gleaming walls the robed domestics listened avidly to the arguments of the grandees who had become fugitives. Slaves slipped away to loot and report the flight to the rebel forces.

A woman's voice was heard. Theodora stood by her chair.

"Caesar, you can leave. The sea is there. The ship is ready, and you have money enough. I shall stay. I believe that those who put on the imperial purple must never put it off. May I not live upon the day when they cease to call me Augusta."

Her slight figure turned to face the officers. "I like the old saying that purple makes the finest shroud."

After that there was silence. They knew she meant it. No one tried to make Theodora change her mind. Justinian's face darkened with a rush of blood, and his mouth hung open. No officer was willing to be the first to speak again of the evacuation. Instead they asked what else could be done. John of Cappadocia threw his big body into a chair and made a motion with his hands as if washing them.

The shout of the Hippodrome penetrated the uneasy silence. "Nika . . . nika . . . nika."

By mutual impulse the military commanders, Belisarius and the bandy-legged, hideous Mundus, left the conference to go up to the roof to learn what was happening outside. Mechanically other officers followed.

What they sighted in the Hippodrome brought Belisarius and Mundus to frozen attention.

The populace had found its new emperor. At some time in the night the rebel leaders had discovered that two nephews of Anastasius had forsaken the palace and were in their homes. Thereupon the leaders had hurried to the house of one, Hypatius by name, a well-meaning, middle-aged veteran of the Persian war, fond of his gardens. In carrying him off triumphantly they were hindered by his wife, Mary, who held on to him, weeping and crying out that they were taking him to his death. With some difficulty they had thrown off this woman.

Early in the morning Hypatius had been lifted on a shield in the forum of Constantine, which had not been gutted by the fire. Having no crown, or patriarch to bestow it, they had put a gold chain on his head. After Justinian's hurried exit from the imperial box they had thought the moment right to present the new emperor to the throng now pressed into the Hippodrome, and they had hurried Hypatius to the box where the impassive guards still stood. The time, indeed, was right. The crowd had roared salutation, and that shout had penetrated the palace walls to the Delphax chamber.

Hypatius was agitated. Half hysterical after his wife's hysteria, he caught hold of an imperial guard named Ephraim and gave him a message of some kind to take in to the besieged Justinian. Whether the nephew of Anastasius tried to warn Justinian about the coming attack, or whether he tried to clear himself of guilt, there is no knowing. It was a spoken message, and this Ephraim, hurrying back through the corridors, ran into a certain Thomas, a physician of the palace, who was hurrying to the box to be the first to announce Justinian's flight by warship. Quite naturally, learning of this, the guard Ephraim turned and ran back with the physician to have a share in spreading the all-important news. When the crowd in the Hippodrome heard that Justinian had fled, a new tumult of rejoicing began. . . .

This, then, was what Belisarius and Mundus observed from the roof of the palace in the full glare of noon. For long moments the two of them remained motionless, fascinated by the vista below. To civilian eyes it was merely uncounted thousands of exulting townspeople swarming about the great arena. To the trained eyes of the soldiers it showed perhaps three tens of thousands of their enemies of the street fighting penned within a walled amphitheater from which only narrow doors offered a way out. Most of the thousands had weapons, but poor ones. As leaders they seemed to have only rabble rousers.

Belisarius and Mundus had somewhat more than two thousand disciplined men. Together they estimated distances and time, and chances, and agreed that a surprise attack could be made. When they ran down to the Delphax chamber, Justinian gave his consent.

Waiting only for his first numerus to catch up its belts and weapons, Belisarius, guided by Narses the eunuch, led the way through the private corridors to the Kathisma doors.

These he found to be bolted against him. The guards on the far side had no least desire to take part in the conflict, especially when the Hypatius forces appeared to be victorious. They remained deaf to Belisarius' hurried commands. The bronze doors stayed shut.

Wasting no more time, Belisarius swung his numerus back through the corridors. Picking up the rest of his comitatus, he hurried out the ruined Chalké gate, meeting the Herules in the blackened Augusteon. The two commanders led their small columns around through the deserted fire zone, through debris and smoke, while Narses, tense with excitement, hurried ahead to scatter rumors and prophecies to confuse the populace.

But these were scarcely needed. Bystanders along the gutted Mesé kept out of the way of armored troops bound for an unknown destination. Confusion held all the streets that Sunday morning. Leading his column across the black ruin of the bath building, Belisarius headed at a trot for the nearest gate of the Hippodrome, which happened to be the one leading to the stair to the Portico of the Blues. Mundus raced his barbarians on to another entrance, the Gate of Death.

Belisarius jumped out into the colonnaded portico. He had to lead. The days of the old Roman legions were gone by, when a commander could expect his men to execute an attack without going first himself. But his mailed comitatus followed, into the tumult of the crowded benches, opening the way with their swords.

By the time the mob realized it was attacked, Belisarius had cleared the upper tiers and his armored line was wheeling down into the throngs. Groups flung themselves at the soldiers spasmodically, leaders yelled incoherently, before the arrows and javelins of the comitatus killed them.

It was a strange spectacle in the Hippodrome, a line of armed men moving slowly down into thirty times their number. If there had been any organized mass or clear-minded commander to oppose the line it could not have done so. But the mob tried to do a dozen things at the same time, and the hardest thing was to climb up over the marble benches to reach the armored line that killed every person in front of it.

Then the Herules burst into the throng at the far end. The barbarians had no steel on them; they had only leather and small round shields and curved hacking swords. But they rushed down savagely, howling their eagerness to take blood vengeance for their comrades slain in the streets.

The turn in the fighting came when the crowd, collectively, became insensate with fear. Belisarius knew what that turn in a battle meant. Wiping his sword clean, he sheathed it. Beneath him, beyond the soldiers, the throngs made thick human clusters at the passageways, men tearing at each other to inch themselves into a way of escape. Most of them died, because Belisarius and Mundus held the exits toward the city, and there was little way out toward the palace. The weary soldiers went on killing, like surgeons operating on a multitude of patients. Procopius says that thirty thousand died in the Nika revolt, and that may well be the truth. Few of the soldiers were hurt.

Hypatius and his brother Pompey sat helplessly in the imperial box. At first they had been too stunned to move. Then the guards of the box, perceiving the turn in the battle, decided to hold them there. Still wearing the gold chain, forgotten on his head, Hypatius waited until officers of Belisarius came and took him by the arms, to lead him through the corridors and the bronze doors now swung open by the guards, into the palace. The unlucky man kept swearing that he had sent a message to urge Justinian to attack his followers, and that he had never wished to be crowned. The gold chain gave evidence against him and his messenger, Ephraim the guard, said he could not remember what Hypatius had said to him.

That evening these two nephews of the former emperor Anastasius were put to death by the soldiers on Justinian's order.

For days silence held the burned area, except where women came to search for bodies in the Hippodrome. Their wailing went on without ceasing. Many families had fled from the city to escape the fighting. There was no one left to carry on the revolt. For a long time there was no semblance of a Blue or Green faction, and Justinian reigned unchallenged by spokesmen.

As soon as she could Theodora went to her house. She found it deserted with the doors locked. The servants had sought safety in the adjoining church that Justinian had built to add to the garden. It was a very small church, that of Sts. Sergius and Bacchus, but beautifully designed in all its details by the young architect, Anthemius of Tralles.

So it happened that Theodora went alone with her women of the propoloma, through the locked-up house, finding the terrace littered with leaves and the tiled rooms smelling still of smoke.

When you return to rooms where you have lived with the hope of other days, the rooms may be the same, the windows opening upon the same treetops, but they have become different because the feelings you shared with them have changed. Theodora went from her sleeping chamber to the terrace and looked instinctively at the wall where the peacock had roosted in the sun. When she turned around as if searching for something, a handmaiden stepped forward, asking softly, "The Augusta desires?"

Theodora said that the monks of the Samson hospital no longer had a roof over their heads; they could be sheltered here. There were many holy men from the east wandering the streets like beggars after the fire. They could sleep in her house, with the new church at hand for their needs; they could walk in the garden, where the pool needed to be cleared of ashes.

The women who wore the propoloma murmured agreement. When they had been pent up in the Daphne, listening to the conflict, they had realized that they owed their lives to her, but they had not thought she was a pious Augusta.

Nor did Theodora explain why she gave up her old home. It was an instinctive act, to end her life of those years, after the catastrophe, and the sight of the Hippodrome, and the certainty that Justinian was a coward unable to play the part of emperor alone. It was, perhaps, some gesture of restitution to the monks of the east that made her give the house to them, as if by doing so she could pay what she owed.

Her women noticed a new decision in her. Once she spoke, she would not change her mind. At the same time she began quietly to form a system of spies who would report to her daily the talk and happenings in the city. The closest cells of the spying agency were of course her women and eunuchs; from them the cells connected outward with the markets and harbors, and beyond the city. What happened henceforth, Theodora wished to know each day.

Then, too, without explanation, she made a journey. Departing alone from the city for the first time, she crossed the water to the Asia shore. With her own guardsmen, counselors, and ladies of honor, she went from village to village along this far shore, turning into nearby Bithynia, passing under the snow peak of Mount Olympus there, even riding up to the monasteries on the heights.

Ostensibly she made the journey to give donations to refugees as well as to enjoy the hot mineral baths herself. She also contributed to the monasteries and started temporary hospitals, needed during the crisis.

Actually she met in this manner with new groups of country folk, the most dependable in the empire; she made the gesture of giving away her money, and let the Bithynians know that she had authority upon which they could call in an emergency. After her tour of this Asia province, she let it be known that she wished foreign embassies to call upon her as well as Justinian.

Such envoys she met with a new, hard brilliance. When strangers sought her presence she obliged them to wait, often for days, until she had learned much from her agents of their affairs and natures. She had a way, too, of forcing dignified men to prostrate themselves to kiss her foot, which no Augusta had done before.

For Theodora was no longer playing a part. She had staked everything, including her life, for empire, and had won—to the extent she was still alive. She was attempting to learn, and to help Justinian carry out, the task of ruling an empire without appearing to do so.

For a while after the week of terror Justinian seemed to be in a stupor.

In fact a sense of terror lay upon Constantinople itself. The palace and the city alike had been scarred by blood and fire. The best part of the metropolis had become a black waste of burned brick. Theodora and her people went about caring for the maimed, the military commanders brought in supplies from the suburbs, and the priests proceeded with their business of praying for the sufferers. But the surviving populace waited, keeping within doors, to learn what vengeance its emperor would take.

Justinian could not rid himself of the memory of those sleepless nights when servitors had watched him like some trapped animal. He found himself facing again the crowd in the Hippodrome, trying to speak and make clear that he meant to punish no one . . . he had never meant the multitude to be slain. He had been patient with them, and had made every effort not to anger them. And his city had burned, and most of those human beings who listened to him that morning had been made into cadavers by the weapons of a few Herules and hired Goths.

In Justinian's orderly world of imagination there had been no concept of disaster so close to himself. Not understanding what had happened, he could not think what action to take now. Briefly he thanked the unperturbed Count Belisarius for the brilliant operation that had saved the palace. Whereas John of Cappadocia threw his arms around the young soldier, kissed him, and swore that Michael Archangel could not have done more.

A sagacious emperor like Diocletian, Justinian knew, would have carried out a blood purge of all who had shown themselves in the ranks of the rebels. Justinian ordered the Hippodrome closed indefinitely.

Then, unexpectedly to all observers, he made an effort to carry out some of the promises he had given in the Hippodrome. "He restored to the children of Hypatius and Pompey the titles they had held before, and much of their [confiscated] property. He did that also with members of the senate who had turned against him. . . . Tribonian and John were deprived of office, but were given back their posts later on. Tribonian, a plausible fellow, made use of his great learning to cover up his avarice, while John inflicted blows on everybody, plundering wealth without respect for any owner."

Justinian, then, gave general pardon to the survivors of the Nika insurrection. Something odd came into his mind at this point. The bodies of Hypatius and Pompey lay where they had been thrown into the sea. He, Justinian, had murdered Vitalian as the crowd had charged, after swearing that Vitalian would not be harmed. Justinian did not mention such things again in a public speech. But so long as he lived he put no other political offender to death.

Probably neither Justinian nor the populace perceived it, but a change had taken place in their relations. The blood and fire of the uprising had weakened age-old institutions. The senate, which had played a wavering if not a treacherous role, did not regain its former prestige. On their part, the popular democracies were left crippled, deprived of the Hippodrome that had been their areopagus. So two ancient institutions, one Roman and one Greek, became moribund. There remained a single ruler, an autocrat, facing a single people. The great question was, how would this solitary ruler conduct himself in the future toward his people?

Tribonian and his companions were set to a new task, to arrive at an explanation of the laws—the Roman law of the civilized world—to make clear in what way and under what circumstances they could be enforced.

A dynamic head of state like the great Constantine would

have rebuilt the burned portion of the palace enclosure as a fortress more secure against attack. Justinian spent weeks in wandering afoot over the devastated zone, talking with priests and populace. To them he made clear—for the memory of the jeering rabble rankled—that his city when rebuilt would shelter no drifters and idlers; his streets would be closed to the mobs of gamblers, beggars, and extortioners. No longer would semi-military factions march to music in colors of their own. Every person who came henceforth to the gates of the new city would need to have a family, work, or business to care for.

All the listeners agreed to that, and most of them decided that it was a Platonic idea which could not be carried out.

For Justinian had determined in reality to rebuild the devastated heart of the city in new splendor—to erect the monuments of an empire for public use.

In particular he set his mind on the ruined Sancta Sophia. Through long hours of the night he sat in discussion over drawings with young Anthemius of Tralles, who called in a master builder of masonry, a certain Isidore, and others. Justinian asked the architect what he had disliked about the burned basilica, and Anthemius explained that it had been dark, like an ugly parallelogram in shape, and so low in the ceiling that you felt confined rather than uplifted within it, and besides, a structure built largely of wood endured no weight and burned down frequently. The Romans, he said, designed magnificent baths and hippodromes but had never been able to erect a church of God.

After this study and discussion, Justinian asked Anthemius to design a structure radiant with the light of the sun, vast enough to hold all who came to worship, and lofty enough to give the feeling of the sky within it, and of such strength that it would endure for the ages.

Seldom had a young architect been called on to build such a new wonder of the world. (For the existing wonders had been rather solid masses, to serve as personal tombs, like the pyramids of ancient Egypt, or to gratify the whim of a tyrant, like the hanging gardens in Babylon, now defunct.) Anthemius sobbed for joy and declared the new wonder could be built, to contain five thousand people and exalt them.

He would raise the structure on four piers, massive as mountain pinnacles, with galleries behind them. He would lift it higher upon half domes, which would be the foundation of a single mighty *sphaira,* or central dome, lofty as a portion of the sky. Isidore and the builders demanded stone faced with marble—not a single beam of wood—for the main structure. The incredible suspended dome, they announced, would rest with Anthemius and the Lord God.

Other architects, who had not been given a share in the contracts, declared that such a dome could not be built. It was an eastern idea, not Roman at all. If built by any chance, it would fall on the heads of those thousands of worshipers. Businessmen grumbled that such a monstrosity, as huge as a mountain, yet finished like a jeweled cameo brooch, could never be paid for.

Both the experts and financiers proved to be more right than wrong. But Justinian had the persistence of a mountain peasant and the carelessness about money of a boy who had never possessed it. At the end of five years the new edifice stood completed, and it was a wonder.

Before then observers—quick to sense any change from routine within the palace—noticed that Theodora had drawn insensibly apart from Justinian. Envoys from abroad were careful to make gifts to the court of the Augusta as well as to the officials of the Augustus. Theodora's spies might be anywhere; she certainly had her people to serve her, while Justinian was immersed in building projects, and trying to clean the streets of human refuse. Women especially sought Theodora, who showed herself to them in lovely new dress creations. She afforded them a sense of infinite power, while the emperor tramped his corridors as before, or shut himself in with papers and secretaries.

The shrewdest minds gave out the opinion that this was a clever trick of the pair. Theodora, they said, took up one side of a question if Justinian favored the other. By doing that openly, they could compare notes on the quiet and solve the secrets of all petitioners. This opinion gained belief, because the minds of the Constantinopolitans turned to what was hidden more than to what was apparent. A few observers decided that this difference was caused only by the determination of the sovereigns—the empress merely doing what a woman wished, the emperor following a man's pursuits.

Baffled by this duality of the throne, most persons studied Justinian to discover the answer to the riddle. They knew it would be useless—even if possible—to watch Theodora. But they were careful to offer their choicest gifts to the inscrutable Theodora.

Justinian, however, did what nobody anticipated. With his city still maimed, and his government disturbed, he insisted on sending the expedition to Africa.

Having every reason for not doing so, he returned to his old project, that had started the Nika revolt, of attempting to reconquer the lost half of the old Roman Empire. He said the past could be restored. That could not be, of course.

Yet a year after the slaughter in the Hippodrome, he organized the expedition and entrusted it to Count Belisarius, to accomplish the impossible.

IV

Recovery of an Empire

FLAVIUS VEGETIUS, A STUDENT AND CIVILIAN, WROTE IN HIS *Epitome of the Art of War* that "Victory can be gained by wise skill and discipline over greater numbers and untaught courage . . . a small trained armed force guarantees success; an undisciplined throng is doomed to destruction . . . in time of apparent peace, prepare for war."

True, Vegetius gave examples that dated back rather far, to Julius Caesar and the handful of legions that conquered the then savage Gauls, and the slight Roman legionaries who had once withstood the physically powerful Germans. But were not his axioms still true? Justinian, who had read Vegetius, must have believed them to be true after witnessing the massacre in the Hippodrome. Furthermore, Vegetius counseled doing what he himself had done—choosing officers from trained, brilliant young citizens rather than relying on foreigners.

Even though most of his officers, including Belisarius, were born of foreign barbarians, they were Roman by inclination and training. They had, as it were, become Romanized. While very few ancestral Romans wanted to serve a lifetime in the army or, if they did so, made more than routine generals who depended on orders and sought honors for themselves.

By now Justinian had studied a good deal of history. He must have understood what caused the downfall of the old Roman armies. The old-style legions might have given way before the terrifying attack of Goths on horseback with long swords at Hadrian's City not far from Constantinople itself, some century and a half before. Yet Roman strategists had learned the lesson of that disaster—Vegetius himself wrote after it—and had by slow degrees evolved a new army relying on cavalry (like the Goths), protected by iron body armor and using the weapons of the barbarians, the light spear and longer slashing sword. These were the lancers, the cataphracts—the "iron-covered"—and they soon added to their equipment the stiff handy bow of the formidable barbarians from the eastern steppes like the Huns. Such mailed and mounted fighters made up the comitatus, or private army, of the energetic Belisarius.

But the collapse of the old armies in the west had been caused not so much by lack of equipment or training as by the failure of manpower to use the equipment and by the rotting of Rome itself, the central government that directed the armed forces. Slave labor had enriched the estates of wealthy citizens until they naturally forsook the dirty business of war, while the privileged lower-class citizen—and it had been still a privilege to be registered as a Roman citizen—forsook armed service to share in the dole of grain from Africa and the games of the Colosseum. The reigning city, consuming instead of producing, had become a gigantic parasite, draining sustenance from the outer provinces.

It collapsed not because the barbarians from the northern forests or the eastern steppes invaded it, but because it began to hire barbarians to fill the ranks deserted by its own citizens. World peace, the pax Romana, seemed at that time—at least during the splendid Augustan age—to be a permanent state of affairs, and the empire an everlasting world order. It seemed natural enough under those circumstances to hire garrisons for the *limes,* the frontier lines.

For a long time barbaric fighters had been hired as auxiliaries to the armies. Then entire tribes were employed as *foederati* or federates. Yet disintegration only set in when the empire was torn apart and all standards lowered in the civil wars of the third century after Christ. The vestige of the empire that endured after that in the west enlisted slaves, debased its currency, and settled accounts with barbarian federates by ceding them territory within the frontiers. Actually Gothic and Visigothic leaders usually tried to hold together the semblance of Roman rule, while emperors-in-name retreated to Ravenna, protected by encircling swamps. Migrants under such leaders as Alaric and Gaiseric merely marched into Rome to collect their share of the vanishing wealth of empire.

They had settled down in various parts of the empire, to farm their own lands, being careful to stamp the imperial effigy upon their coins and to acknowledge the existence of the surviving emperors, who were now in the east, in Constantinople. (Under the sagacious House of Attila, the Huns, last comers from the steppes, had attempted to establish a rival dominion throughout Middle Europe, based on the Hungarian plain, but the Hunnic confederation had broken down at Attila's death.)

Now the Vandals held Africa, the Ostrogoths ruled Italy, the Visigoths Spain, while the more barbarous Franks overran Gaul, and the distant Anglo-Saxons swept over southern Britain.

In the east, the emperors of Constantinople had had the advantage of observing the different stages of collapse in the west. At times they had tried to send military aid, but they had little to send and could not arrest the internal decay of the west. They had shunted the Goths and Huns, the most dangerous migrants, westward by massive gifts of gold and by building strong fortifications along the lines of the Danube. They had checked the tendency to hire German fighters, en masse, not long before Justinian. Guard units like the new excubitors were recruited from wellborn Isaurians in the highlands of Asia Minor, or Armenians in the mountains of the Caucasus.

The empire in the east, however, had not escaped without damage. Migrating barbarians in quest of loot and land had overrun and sacked the Greek peninsula; Justinian's home province of Macedonia had been raided but not vitally hurt; the fertile Asiatic provinces—the Asia Minor peninsula, Syria, Egypt, and Cyrene (where Theodora had traveled)—had been guarded so far from invasion, and their wealth served to buy off the more dangerous barbarian peoples pressing down upon the Euxine Sea and the line of the Danube. Moreover, the strategists of Constantinople learned to play off one chieftain of a horde against another—a dangerous game. Both Anastasius and Justin had tried to build more walls, but as Vitalian had pointed out, walls meant little without men to defend them. So the task of the occupants of the Sacred Palace had been to find brains to balance the weight of manpower that could be thrown against them.

They had a new weapon, the secret of which was carefully guarded within the War Department. Chemists had discovered that sulphur and saltpeter, mixed in a mortar with powdered pyrites and then treated with quicklime and other ingredients, would burst into devastating flame when projected upon an enemy ship or troops. Flaming oil had been employed to defend walls before then, but this chemical flame ignited itself and could not be extinguished, even on water. (It came to be known as Greek fire or sea fire.) Being still experimental—the compound had to be handled carefully and kept out of the sun—it was used only in an emergency, as Justin had used it, close to Constantinople.

It was Justinian's idea to make Constantinople secure by attacking in turn the barbarian kingdoms of the west. After three peaceful generations they would not expect such an attack. It could not progress far by land, but it might be thrust unexpectedly across the Middle Sea (Mediterranean).

He had prepared for it with care by arranging a perpetual truce, after a suitable gift of gold, with the Persian King of kings, by sending agents to Africa to stir up sedition, and by befriending the daughter of the great Theodoric, king of the Goths in Italy, recently laid in his splendid tomb at Ravenna.

With the expedition launched in the spring of 533 under command of Belisarius, after the patriarch prayed for its success on the landing of the Golden Horn, it remained to be seen whether Justinian could support his general and keep the army supplied in the tremendous gamble it was taking.

For the army entrusted to Belisarius was too small to be thrown against the warlike masses of Vandals and Goths.

Justinian himself was taking the chance that Belisarius might elect to stay in Africa as a monarch in his own right, if successful. The great Theodoric had started his career as an officer of the empire. The African coast was fertile and rich. If it managed to arrive there, the army might follow Belisarius, not Justinian. The 10,000 regular infantry resented going because for the most part they wanted leave at home after the Persian campaign; the 400 Huns disliked putting to sea; so the staying force lay in the several thousand cataphracts of Belisarius' comitatus. Moreover, the brilliant young commander in chief had taken along his family, his actress wife Antonina, and his grown-up godson Theodosius. That caused trouble, but not the kind Justinian expected.

Belisarius' first task was to exert the authority he was supposed to have. The 500 small vessels of the flotilla, needed to transport the army's supplies and 5000 horses, were owned mostly by Syrian and Egyptian traders and had never taken part in a great naval cruise. Belisarius had the upper sails of the three flagships painted red, and lanterns hoisted to poles above the masts at night so the ill-found mass of vessels could follow in convoy. Whereupon his fleet-to-be nearly piled up on itself by following blindly into a small harbor after dark. Procopius says the seamen displayed great skill in warding off other craft with their poles. Water fouled in defective casks. (Antonina, wife of the commander, kept her own supply of drinking water clean and cool by hiding it in glass jars in the sand ballast of her ship. "She was a woman," commented Procopius, "with a genius for accomplishing the most impractical things.") Biscuits furnished by the imperial Economist (John of Cappadocia was back again in office because only he seemed to be capable of raising enough money for a war and the rebuilding of Constantinople at the same time) turned out to be moldy, and caused many deaths from dysentery. Belisarius landed long enough to buy reserves of grain with his own money; he also executed by impaling on stakes two Huns who had got drunk and killed a comrade. This was a serious step to take. The Huns, invaluable in a battle, did not acknowledge that they were bound by Roman laws or discipline. After the execution Belisarius could not be sure if they would go into action for or against him.

So his ill-found fleet hugged the shores, from island to island. The army officers—many of them jealous of the young commander, and some ready to conspire against him—reported that their men would not accept a battle at sea against Vandals on such vessels.

Ahead of them stretched unknown waters where barbarians had roved for three generations. The soldiers did not know what they would find there, except the charred wrecks of the last imperial fleet to venture against the Vandal conquerors of Africa.

They landed on Sicily beneath Mount Aetna. This happened to be Gothic soil. With his ships becalmed and his men weakened by the long voyage, Belisarius began to show signs of nerves. "He was restless as soon as he went ashore," Procopius relates. "Wondering how he could go further, his mind was tormented because he had no idea what sort of combatants the Vandals were or how he ought to wage war against them, while his soldiers remained in fear, saying they would not meet two enemies at once—the Vandals and the sea."

The Syrian Procopius had begun to admire Belisarius, and to his joy he was able to relieve the mind of his hero. Going into Syracuse for information, he discovered a servant who had left Carthage only three days before. Carthage was the reigning city and seaport of the Vandals where the king, the army, and the fleet would ordinarily be. Justinian, however, had opened the way for his expedition remarkably well. His provocateurs had stirred up anticipations of a move by the imperial forces against the desert coast of Tripoli and the far-off island of Sardinia. In consequence the Vandal fleet with 5000 of the army had gone to Sardinia, while the king, Gelimer, and his court were four days inland from Carthage with no suspicion that Belisarius was at sea.

Moreover, owing to Justinian's correspondence with the Gothic court, his fleet was given supplies at Sicily. As soon as he could do so, Belisarius put to sea, crossing to Malta where a favoring east wind drove his vessels over to the African coast.

Their landfall came at a point known as Shoal's Head to the Romans, but far from the coveted Carthage. The bare red coast looked inhospitable but uninhabited. Belisarius, anxious to advance quickly, called his commanders to his ship and asked what they would do. This council of war voted for remaining on shipboard and rounding the promontory to Carthage. It would be a nine days' march without water overland to the city, and what would happen to the army if a storm destroyed the fleet on this shelterless coast?

The officers, apparently, wished to keep a way of escape open. Belisarius could be both courteous and caustic. "I don't blame you," he answered them. "We can look for no shelter, for a base in this desert. But I for one agree that I don't want to meet with the Vandals and the sea at the same time. It's true what you all say, that if a storm comes up one of two things will happen to the ships; either they will escape far from the coast or be sunk. And if we're still on the ships, what else will happen to us?"

Belisarius advised marching overland with all speed, to reach Carthage before the enemy could defend it. Then the fleet, following along the coast, could shelter in the harbor, and Carthage, with its wealth and supplies, would serve as a base for future action. (In this way he would force the army to find security in walled Carthage.)

The others, perforce, agreed. Procopius announced with glee that it was a good omen when they found water by digging at the first camp. But Belisarius, with his comitatus and the Huns mounted, was in no mood to humor the expedition more. He hurried the march, and severely punished men who took fruit and livestock from a village. "These countrymen were Romans as of old—they will aid us unless you drive them to join the Vandals. Why do you persist in making two enemies to face?"

He forced the expedition to pay with good silver for its food, and to keep going. (He was then following roughly the route of the Eighth Army closing in on Rommel's Afrika Korps, more than fourteen centuries later, when Carthage had become Tunis.)

He did not win the race to Carthage. When the Romans came in sight of the natural barriers of the great port—the chain of hills ending in a dry salt lake and the great lake of Carthage—they heard from their well-wishers, the farmers who had been paid with silver, that the Vandal horsemen were coming in from all sides. Belisarius halted his column and built one of the old-style entrenched camps. Here he left his baggage with the weaker units of infantry and his wife. Then he started cautiously forward along the highroad which ran through a long defile in the hills and between the wet and dry lakes to Carthage. His comitatus he held in the rear because it was the only force he could rely on not to retreat to the fortified camp on the appearance of the Vandals.

What happened then was a matter of luck, with the difference that Belisarius was prepared for bad luck while the inexperienced masters of Africa were not. The four hundred Huns, sent ahead to probe the hills to the left, discovered one body of Vandals coming out across the dry salt lake. When they observed the glittering gold body ornaments, the fine cloaks, and large fat horses of the noble Vandals, the Huns lost their ill humor, or decided that these horsemen were a more desirable enemy than the inflexible Belisarius. Their devastating arrows swept the massed human loot in front of them, and their swift mustangs outran the heavier horses of the Vandals, who scattered in flight over the salt depression.

The Roman federate cavalry, advancing through the defile, collided with the Vandal commander of Carthage, who happened to be Gelimer's brother. They rode over him and his small escort at the Ten Mile road marker, and finding similar detachments coming up along the road, they kept on attacking, gathering up loot and looking for more Vandals. They had almost reached Carthage itself when they sighted Gelimer's main array trotting through the hills at the side. Whereupon this Roman cavalry turned to fly back to protection. In so doing they encountered Belisarius with a small following, who stopped them.

Almost anything might have happened then in the hills. What did happen was that Gelimer, the king, reaching the road at the Ten Mile post, found the body of his brother. No enemies were visible. Gelimer was still a barbarian by instinct, which meant that he had affection for his own family and felt the need of burying the dead with religious ritual. This he did on the spot, grieving, while his army waited out the funeral. Belisarius, feeling his way along the defile, came upon this unexpected panorama and allowed his dubious cavalry no time to become afraid again. He led it in a headlong charge into the startled and dismounted Vandal array. This, believing itself to be attacked in force, mounted in haste to ride off with Gelimer.

So at the end of the day the main Roman column found

the defile occupied only by dead bodies of the enemy. At dark the Huns reappeared with their gleanings of brooches, silver-plate belts, and gold-inlaid weapons. The remaining ten miles of highway were open to Carthage, and the city itself illuminated with lamps and flares to welcome the invaders. Vandals in the walled city moved into sanctuary in the churches. The townsfolk had been prepared by Justinian's espionage agents for this coming of the liberators who would restore the African coast to the benevolent rule of the empire.

Belisarius would not allow any detachment of his Romans to enter Carthage that night. He had taken the measure of the Vandals in combat and had no more anxiety about the campaign, but he dreaded the looting that would follow if his underpaid Romans entered a friendly barbarian city at night. Even Procopius admitted that "some confusion" ensued whenever a Roman army entered a city.

The next morning Belisarius paraded his men in and did not allow them out of ranks until guards had been posted around the luxurious villas and palaces of the prosperous city. So his entry was something of a triumph. The common folk, egged on by Justinian's spies, threw myrtle before the marching Romans. When the gilded eagles of the standards passed, the Africaners wept and shouted their joy at liberation after three generations. Belisarius policed the streets, gave immunity to the Vandal nobles in the churches—but kept them there—and went off to dine in Gelimer's palace, to be waited on in royal style by the house servants. After the reserves and baggage came in from the road camp, he let his men rest.

Even with the port illuminated and well-wishers sailing out to guide it in, his fleet had difficulty in entering the safe haven of the lake of Carthage.

Luck seemed to follow his every move. The old inhabitants of the coast felt religious exultation in his advent because under Justinian the old religion would be restored to their churches. The Vandals were Arians, not orthodox believers. A Vandal vessel loaded with treasure tried to escape and was forced back, later, by a storm, to fall intact into his hands. And in Carthage he held the only fortified base of the Vandal coast. At the time of their conquest of Africa the barbarians had demolished the walls of other towns in the logical but mistaken belief that they would be more secure in Carthage if no other fortifications existed.

This resulted in Belisarius being secure within Carthage while Gelimer had no such fortification available. It being the end of summer by then, the Romans (actually the trained Balkans, Armenians, former Goths and Huns) aided the liberated inhabitants to get in the fruit and grain crops. When the Vandal fleet returned at last after having a very easy time in Sardinia, it was astonished to find its home port occupied by a Roman fleet.

The Vandal sea commander embraced his king, and they both wept, in true German fashion, because they had lost their city, their wives, and their crops. Whereupon they made a vow to reconquer all, or to die.

When Gelimer mustered up all available Vandal manpower to advance on his city, Belisarius refused to leave it. Incapable of siege tactics, and unwilling to engage the now dreaded Romans behind walls, Gelimer's host broke down the aqueducts, gathered up the remains of the harvests, and retired along the coast for a day's march, to build a camp and wait on events.

This situation pleased Belisarius, who could get supplies enough from Sicily by his ships. Probably those very ships had convinced Justinian in the beginning that the impossible could be accomplished, and the empire of the west reconquered.

In the time of its supremacy the empire had never maintained a strong navy on the Middle Sea. It had devoted its efforts instead to developing an invincible army. With frontiers far inland from the sea, this army had seldom availed itself of sea transport, although it might have done so to advantage. With peace enforced, the Mare Nostrum had no need of warships. Egyptian and eastern merchants took care of the carrying trade.

Very much the same state of affairs prevailed under the early emperors at Constantinople—until the Vandals began to construct a fleet, in defiance of the law that no war vessel might be launched without imperial permission. Leo had tried to destroy this nascent barbarian sea power and had lost his own fleet instead; Anastasius had built some new dromons, "speeders," in the Golden Horn and these had escorted Belisarius on his test voyage.

For it seemed possible to Justinian and his advisers that, if the land routes were to be forever closed by hostile barbaric manpower, still the small expeditionary forces mustered in Constantinople might be shunted westward by sea, where the hostile land armies could not reach them, or at least arrive on the coast in time to prevent their landing. Islands might be recaptured, and bases established to the west. By regaining, as it were, the Middle Sea through naval power, the surviving empire might recapture the surrounding coasts, ports, and outthrust peninsulas. Having no land routes to the west, it could open up the sea lanes.

Naturally the first step in the undertaking was the most difficult, and Justinian had taken the sound risk of striking at the farthest nation, the most seemingly secure, with the one dangerous fleet. The risk had been in attempting to cross the sea to get at the Vandals by land, while avoiding the Vandal fleet. Although his nerves had suffered on the way, Belisarius had accomplished this.

In doing so, he had fanned Justinian's hopes that the future of the empire lay across the sea. . . .

Oddly enough, the appearance of the invaders from the sea shook the spirit of the Vandals who might still have driven off the expedition by weight of numbers. There was a prophecy that not until soldiers came out of the sea would the Vandalic kingdom end.

Early in their migration across the face of Europe, these particular Asding Vandals had mixed with a nomadic group from the steppes; they had gone their own way, harried along by the more warlike Germanic migrants. Driven down to the coast of Spain, they had faced extermination, or slavery, when Gaiseric, their one dynamic leader, had accomplished the miracle of transporting his people entire in crudely made vessels to the African coast. There Gaiseric had rounded out a miniature empire by treachery and keen foresight, deceiving the Roman commanders more than vanquishing them in battle. In so doing, he had discovered the usefulness of a fleet in threatening the weakened western empire; by ending the shipment of grain from the fertile African coast and by raiding Italy, he had made himself more dangerous in those last decades than Attila, who chose to bleed the empire with tribute. Gaiseric had even raided Rome itself, searching out concealed valuables with a care that made his people's name proverbial. They found the treasure of gold, the candlesticks and vessels that Titus had looted from the Temple in Jerusalem, and Gaiseric bore off the women of the imperial family as hostages and future wives for his sons.

Had there been a second Gaiseric to succeed him, the remnant of Rome in the west might have been starved and blockaded into subjection to the new Vandalic dominion of the sea. But the next generation relaxed from the hardships of the long migration and conflict. As overlords of a rich coast, with a fabulous treasure in their coffers, and only the Berber tribes of the interior to contend with, they made life as easy as possible, convinced that the fleet would protect them on the sea where no rival fleet existed.

"These Vandals used to take to the baths every day, and they enjoyed having the best sea and land food on their tables," Procopius observes. "They wore gold ornaments all over their bodies, and clothed themselves in Medic [Persian] garb which they called seric [silk]. After dressing up like this they went to theatres and hippodromes, and most of all to hunts. They had their dancers and mimics, with music. They lived in private parks, and gave themselves banquets, and all kinds of sexual pleasures."

This picture of barbarians softened by the arts of civilization had been known, also, to the strategists of Constantinople. But it remained for Belisarius to prove that they were only shadows of their ancestors.

After all the Vandalic people had gathered in the coastal camp of Tricamaron, Belisarius moved out his small army. The massed Vandals came out to meet him with much show but only shields and swords for weapons.

Immediately Belisarius began to disturb the Vandal array.

Squadrons of cataphracts rode against different points in the rough Vandal line, drawing it into a confusion of advances and retreats. Then Belisarius' comitatus charged the center of the Vandal mass and drove it back into the camp. The Huns, knowing the battle decided, joined in to plunder; Belisarius led the regular infantry hastily through his cavalry, which was scattered in the pleasant occupation of looting—and Gelimer fled on horseback without warning his people. At sight of the king riding off, panic emptied the camp of all Vandals who could get to a horse or run.

After that, Belisarius lost control of his army entire. All the women, the valuable property and hoarded gold of the small African empire were left within the wooden palisades of the camp, and the Romans ransacked it through the night. Their commander tried to prevent the taking of women against their will. He had no sleep himself, because any enemy force could have cut its way through the wine-soaked encampment. But no Vandals appeared. At sunrise his trumpets rounded up a few of the comitatus. Taking them to a hill, he sobered them down and led them into the camp to beat a semblance of order into the others and escort the Vandalic treasure to safety in Carthage.

By the end of the day Belisarius had his army together again and had started cavalry in pursuit of the fleeing Gelimer. The war, as such, was over. Belisarius had won it by brilliant leadership and by using in battle only his dependable cavalry, with the four hundred Huns. Those same Huns immediately begged to be sent back to their homeland in the steppes with the great wealth they had won, and the young conqueror of a continent had to swear that he would do so, although he hated to lose four hundred supremely able fighters. The Huns, it seemed, were weary of civilization and homesick for their prairies.

Without a courageous leader, with their women and towns lost, the scattered Vandals roved around as partisans, migrated to the interior, or offered to serve under Belisarius. They had paid a heavy price for their devotion to the baths and theaters of Roman civilization. Gelimer, cornered on a mountain where the Berber tribes protected him, could not endure life among savages and sent to the Roman officers to beg for a loaf of real bread, a sponge to bathe with, and a lyre to sing his miseries. The officers, rightly interpreting this request as a bid for terms of surrender, sent back with the desired articles a suggestion that the Vandal lord consent to travel to Constantinople, to occupy a luxurious estate with good servants, and a pension and esteem from Justinian, the emperor. Gelimer agreed, if Belisarius would swear that the estate and other stipends would be forthcoming. Belisarius did so.

Now throughout this unusual campaign the co-operation between Justinian in the capital and Belisarius in the field had been almost perfect. Justinian had given his commanding general full authority. (No other official, of whatever rank, was allowed to question that authority.) "Your orders shall be as orders given by myself."

Justinian's first message after the news of Tricamaron was

typical; he congratulated his soldier on the victory and asked that the islands of the sea be gathered in also. Being now possessed of the Vandalic shipping as well as his own misfit fleet, Belisarius was able to seize for the empire its former areas along the Tripolitan coast (thereby joining the new province of Africa to Egypt), the craggy islands of Corsica and Sardinia, and even the far trading ports at the Gates of Hercules (heights of Gibraltar and Ceuta). He conciliated the interested Berber chieftains with medals, regalia, and money, while he planned new frontier posts to keep them out. His rule now stretched across the west of the Middle Sea, so long lost to Rome.

Then, abruptly, he was recalled. Procopius explains indignantly that some officers, jealous of his success, slandered him by writing secretly to Constantinople that Belisarius was preparing to set himself up as king in the new conquest. Procopius adds that Belisarius heard of the accusation from his informants in the city, and that Justinian himself ignored the letters. What Justinian did, however, was to send out a legate, Solomon the eunuch, with an invitation to Belisarius to make the voyage back to the city with Gelimer and the Vandalic treasure. As to that, Belisarius must please himself; he might stay or return as he thought best.

This put the general of the western army in a dilemma. He knew that he was needed in Africa. Yet to stay there would make it appear that he had refused his emperor's summons. On this point his wife Antonina expressed herself sharply: her husband had only one safe alternative, to go back, face Justinian, receive his honors as victor, and finish the palace he was building by the Golden Gate. (Like many another ambitious woman—and Antonina was some years older than the handsome Belisarius—she had more fear of plotting at home than of foreign enemies on the horizon, even if her husband believed the opposite to be true.)

He went. Leaving Africa to the rule of Solomon the eunuch, he sailed in the new fleet with the captive Vandals, the gold bullion, and most of his comitatus, his biscuit eaters (*buccelarii* "hard-bread eaters"—the hardtack-feeding professional soldiers), to back him up if the need arose. As he had promised, he also took along the homesick Huns.

But he knew he should never have left Africa to play politics.

Justinian was jealous of the careless man who could face danger and turn difficulty to his own advantage. Laboring as he did with his mind eighteen hours a day, Justinian had the illusion that he slaved against hostile forces. He had not taken a rest because he did not know how to rest. Whereas the unthinking Belisarius greeted him as cheerily as if the soldier had landed from a year's outing. "Our thanks go to you," Justinian said stiffly, "as our devoted benefactor."

When Belisarius reported that the treasure of Solomon the king had turned up in Africa, Justinian remarked that it had brought ill fortune to Titus, who took it from Jerusalem, and to the Vandals, who carried it off from Rome. Theodora was pleased with Belisarius and eager to see this celebrated treasure of the Jews. Instinctively she disliked the war in the west, and she felt relieved that Belisarius was back again with such incredible gains. She said gaily that the ominous treasure could always be sent back to its place in Jerusalem, but Justinian did not approve of that.

He was more than fair to Belisarius in public recognition. He named the victor consul for the coming year, and ordered a triumph to be staged for him in the old Roman way. No such triumph had been held since the time of Constantine, and perhaps Justinian wanted to revive memories of ancient conquests.

Whatever he desired, the city turned out to cheer Belisarius. The Constantinopolitans cleaned the whole of the Mesé, strewing this main street with myrtle and hiding vacant lots in the old burned area behind emblems of victory and floral wreaths. They crowded every tier of the Hippodrome, under the bright silk awnings, where soothsayers and stargazers rose to proclaim the advent of a new Golden Age, and to pick up the silver tossed them. Even favored charioteers took seats in the audience, without display, and acrobats did not show off on the vast empty track.

Watching from the imperial box with her noblewomen, Theodora could tell where Belisarius was marching in; she recognized the roar of delight rising from the new Baths of Zeuxippus, and the musical shouts of applause from the Augusteon gateway.

Then, with the chanting of a hymn, monks and priests marched into the arena with incense swinging, and the grandees of the empire riding after. But Belisarius rode no horse, nor did he wear the laurel crown of a triumph of the old days.

In a soldier's mantle and half helmet he walked on foot, at the head of his biscuit eaters who had triumphed at the Ten Mile and at Tricamaron.

The masses in the Hippodrome raised no chant of greeting, they threw down no flowers or rings. For once, they wept and shouted and beat their hands together.

Behind Belisarius and the comitatus rode the Huns and behind them walked Gelimer, the vanquished king, in his robes with his nobility escorting him, and all bearing chains for the occasion on their wrists. Behind them paced the horses and carts bearing the Vandal treasure, with the seven-branched candlestick, the shewbread table overlaid with gold, and the golden Seat of Mercy, from the Temple at Jerusalem.

Eying the moody, flabby face of her husband, Theodora wondered if it had been generosity or weakness that had induced him to give this triumph to a better man. For Justinian would never draw from his people the adulation that had been given Belisarius. . . .

Alone, and unperceived by Theodora, however, Justinian recorded his claim to victory. He wrote it upon a manuscript that was the second edition of the new Code of Law. Carefully he traced the words: "In nomine Domini nostri Iesu Christi—In the name of Jesus Christ our Lord, the Emperor, Caesar, Flavius Justinian, victor over the Goths, Franks, Germans, Slavs, Alans, Vandals and Africa itself—the pious, happy, renowned conqueror in triumph, always August."

So he signed himself, at that time. Peter Sabbatius had become in his own estimation victor not only over the Vandals but Africa itself—without mention of Belisarius—and not only that, but over all the surrounding barbarian kingdoms and peoples, some of whom barely knew his name. Then he had added every triumphal epithet of the real Caesars of ancient Rome. Scipio Africanus, who conquered ancient Carthage and Hannibal, had been content with less.

Was Justinian maudlin with vanity or insane with hope after his first successful campaign? Hardly. Certainly he was vain—in the solitude of his study—and hopeful, and he must have known that what was inscribed in the Code would be read by other eyes for ages. Apparently he put on record all that he intended the empire to achieve. Yet the sum of it, the subjection of all barbaric powers that had invaded Roman frontiers, was impossible to achieve.

Elsewhere Justinian added to his personal record of would-be triumphs. "Divine providence enabled us to end the Persian wars with an Everlasting Peace, to overthrow the Vandal nation and to join again to the Empire, Carthage, and even all Libya—to bring by our watchful care the ancient laws out of the heavy burden of age into new beauty—and this is an achievement which no one before us hoped for, or believed to be possible."

Again he wrote that he had accomplished this "by unwearied toil and hardship through the watches of the night."

So Justinian compared himself to a conquering soldier. And what he recorded indelibly for future generations he meant to accomplish. He meant to persist until he did it. Secretively, witnessed only by his candle flame, he was laying plans beyond the comprehension of others for Justinian to become in the eyes of the world Justinian the Great.

On Palm Sunday Theodora sat beside Justinian in the throne seats behind the decorated table of the Triclinium, when the grandees came in to salute their sovereigns, to offer gifts and verses in their honor. Paul the Silentiary read a poem in praise of the beauty of Theodora; Gelimer, who had been a king, bowed his head—he had been forced to do so at first—and some said he muttered words from Scripture: "Vanity of vanities—all is vanity." A monk of the east held up his pilgrim staff and recited a greeting to Theodora the Augusta: "The empress sustained by God," he cried, "to aid the oppressed." This greeting came from Severus, patriarch of Antioch. For those who sought an audience with the sovereigns had learned that Theodora could do more for them, if she so desired, than Justinian.

Belisarius came, followed by admirers, tossing out gold to the throng at the Augusteon gate. (He had kept a great share of the spoils of the Vandalic war, and Justinian had not objected.) His wife Antonina wore a collar of pearls and a shoulder vest sewn with rubies; she bent her bejeweled head before the other actress, Theodora, murmuring salutation to the glory of the purple, while she ached with envy. She was older than Theodora, and she looked like a dressed-up matron—she, the wife of the foremost man in the empire—before the dark, piquant beauty of the circus brat. And Theodora cried out clear salutation to the most noble lady Antonina, while she reflected how her spies repeated that Antonina smuggled the handsome Theodosius, godson of her husband, into her chamber at night. . . .

The little Syrian, Procopius, watched the illumination of the Sacred Palace to which, as a staff secretary, he was summoned only for duty. Robed eunuchs like Narses and Solomon held responsibility and gained honor there, but not Procopius. Restlessly he wandered through the lighted garden paths at the edge of the sea, where the nobles exercised their favorite horses by day, and young excubitors off duty embraced their girls after sunset. By the boat landing he noticed a dark statue, more slender than Roman work. It was made of imperial porphyry, designed by Anthemius of Tralles as a portrait of Theodora. It was a beautiful statue, he said, "but not as beautiful as Theodora herself, and it reveals clearly, even far off, that it bears the likeness of an Empress."

At such times Procopius felt a strange love akin to hatred for the Syrian woman. He sat alone by the statue, with a sense of possessing it, and a longing to destroy the likeness of an empress, so that Theodora herself might become a wanton woman again.

The sensitive Procopius imagined at times that the city itself impelled its people to do strange things. Justinian would talk to him kindly, but his mind would be off elsewhere as if drawn from his body by some malignant power; Antonina, who schemed to advance the career of his beloved Belisarius, could not keep her eyes off the stupid, golden-haired Theodosius. Surely the Christian God—for the moody Procopius believed in miracles, even pagan ones, more than in the remote, idealized divinity of the Christians—had never intended such weaklings to have such power.

In the closed chambers of the strategists during that spring of 535 Belisarius the Most Noble Consul of the Roman Empire learned that Italy was to be restored next to the empire, and that he would be sent to accomplish it. He objected. Africa was not secure yet, he said, and they did not have men enough to face the Goths.

The strategists showed him on wall maps of the Middle Sea how they meant to do it. Of course they understood that not even Belisarius could be sent to land on the ancestral peninsula and retake Rome itself, as he had—so brilliantly—liberated Carthage. No, his new expedition would sail to

Sicily, as if on its way back to Carthage. He would explain that he was merely stopping over there; then he could easily overpower the Gothic garrisons in Sicily. The natives would not oppose him. The way had been prepared for him by secret agents, as in Africa. Meanwhile his old acquaintance, the courageous Mundus, would lead another expedition, the western frontier force, through the Dalmatian ranges down to the strait across from the heel of the boot of the Italian peninsula. Simultaneously, Belisarius would cross the other strait, from Sicily to Messina, on the toe of the Italian boot. Striking inland rapidly, these two expeditions could meet, cutting off the extreme south of Italy below, say, Neapolis (Naples). That military operation could be accomplished, could it not?

Considering it, Belisarius admitted that it could easily be done, except for one thing. The Goths.

The strategists complimented him on his acumen. How right he was, to mention the Gothic nation as the decisive factor in the new war! Were not these German Ostrogoths a real nation in arms, victors over the old legions at Hadrian's City? Indeed yes. And they had not taken to Roman vices like the Vandals. They did not even limit their children by abortion; they bred like animals. But they had one weakness that could destroy them.

Whereupon the strategists revealed to Belisarius how they were exploiting this weakness of the Goths, to prepare the way for him to attack. . . .

The weakness of the Goths lay in their kings. For they had the Germanic notion that one man of one family must rule. They believed in mythical heroes, descendants of their one-eyed Woden. Their present heroic—hence kingly—family was the Amalung. The late Theodoric, greatest of the Amals, had seized Italy from the other Germans and had ruled wisely, although handicapped by his sense of personal honor. He had actually kept intact the Roman bureaus under his German army, also intact. But his solitary grandson had died not long after him, and his handsome, educated daughter Amalasuntha had tried desperately to follow Theodoric's example in keeping peace and order. Germans, however, would not be ruled by a solitary woman—even after the resourceful Amalasuntha had contrived the deaths of the three Gothic nobles most outspoken against her. Those deaths, although necessary, had started a blood feud. And Germans would leave everything else to carry on a blood feud.

Amalasuntha had appealed to Justinian, who immediately offered her sanctuary in Constantinople and sent a fast dromon to transport her thither with her personal treasure. But the anxious Amalasuntha had changed her mind, like a woman. She had not availed herself of the ship; she had kept on good terms with the empire, instead, by offering supplies to Belisarius in Sicily when he voyaged against the Vandals; then she had offered herself in marriage to her cousin, the other Amal, a scheming man who tried to write poetry and called himself a philosopher. A woman's mistake. What happened? The Philosopher, having been duly crowned king by the Gothic warriors, then had the lovely Amalasuntha drowned, while swimming, by henchmen of the three purged nobles.

No sooner had he murdered his wife than the Philosopher began to fear for his life—having raised up a blood feud against himself—and agents from Constantinople persuaded him to appeal to Justinian. The Philosopher made the mistake of fancying himself to be as clever as the Roman agents. He had tried to carry water on both shoulders by making secretive offers to Justinian to yield up territory in Italy in return for a pledge of security for himself.

The Philosopher began to be more afraid, for the still barbaric German nobles were sniffing suspiciously around the pond where the Amal woman had deceased, and they disliked any man, Amal or not, who called himself a philosopher. At this point a special agent, a very gifted and persuasive agent, Peter the Ambassador, played upon the growing fears of the Philosopher. The two of them had met secretly along the Appian Highway, and the Philosopher asked anxiously if Justinian were not pleased by his offer. Peter said he supposed so.

Then the Philosopher—that was the code name for the Gothic king in the secret files of Constantinople—worried because Peter appeared dubious about Justinian being pleased. "But if," he asked, "he is not pleased at all, what will happen?"

"Why then," said Peter the Ambassador, "you will have to wage a war, Most Noble Lord."

"What! Would that be fair, my dear ambassador?"

"And why would it not be fair and fitting? You, Most Noble Sir, are a philosopher; Justinian is a worthy emperor of the Romans; is it not fair that you should reap the results of your thinking and planning; is it not fitting that Justinian should seek to regain the land that was Roman of old?"

The more he pondered the words of Peter, the more this last surviving Amal became worried. He realized that Justinian had a quarrel with him for eliminating the talented Amalasuntha, who had been, officially, under imperial protection. Only too well he realized that the chivalrous Gothic nobles would kill him as a traitor with their shields and swords if they had evidence of his dealing with Justinian.

At this point the strategists—who had ordered Peter to stay close to the Philosopher-king—planned to loose Belisarius' expedition upon Sicily and Mundus' force upon the opposite Dalmatian coast. As soon as that was done, Peter would have a new hold on the scheming Philosopher, who might be persuaded to yield up half Italy without further conflict. He was like that man Damocles who feasted with a sword suspended over him by a single hair; Peter could always betray him to the noble Goths; if, on the other hand, the noble Goths killed the Philosopher, they would have another blood feud to work out among themselves, and no leader at all. There were no more Amalung heirs.

Therefore, whatever happened, the formidable Goths would be without a leader, and might be thrown into civil war. Belisarius could count on that. And more.

The old Roman populace, being orthodox Catholics, would join the invaders against the Arian Goths. More, Justinian, in his careful planning, had set up another enemy for the Goths to deal with. He had sent a written offer to the still more barbarous king of the Franks, who had only the last year engulfed the Burgundians beyond the Alps. The proposal ran as follows: "The Goths who seized by violence Italy, which is ours, have refused to give back the land, where they commit other acts of violence. Such injustice is not to be endured. We have been compelled to take the field against them. This war will be yours as well as ours, because you are joined to us by the orthodox faith which rejects the Arian heresy, and by the enmity we both share toward the Goths."

This suggestion had been accompanied by massive gifts, with the promise of more to come if the valiant Franks moved across the Alps to raid north Italy. Nothing was more certain than that a true barbarian would snatch at gifts offered him for looting a neighbor's lands. In fact, the Frankish king had done so.

If events, inconceivably, should go contrary to plan within Italy, Belisarius could count on the Franks coming in, thus catching the Goths between hammer and anvil.

When the strategists had revealed all this staging for his attack, they asked: did the Illustrious Belisarius find any flaw in their planning?

The attentive Belisarius could not point out a flaw. It humbled and amazed him to learn the care and labor that had made his task easier. For the victor at Carthage could not think clearly in terms of such high strategy. He never learned to do so. He could visualize a conflict only by thinking of the numbers of enemy in front of him. And no one in the conferences had spoken about that.

When Belisarius hesitated, Justinian spoke.

"The world is growing old."

Usually the dumpy body of the emperor sat impassive at a conference. Now some instinct forced him to explain his brooding. He said it seemed to him as if they sat talking in a lighted city, while all around them lamps were dimming and going out. From remote Britain, where Angles and Saxons held their kingships in huts, to the forests beyond the Danube where voiceless Slavs stole tools to dig the earth, barbarians had become masters of civilized men. These barbarians had taken on the vices of the Romans. The former Romans, on their part, became brutalized while they struggled for food with the tribal farmers. The tools in their hands were old tools. No people outside of Constantinople knew how to make new ones, nowadays. Water flowed, out there, in ancient aqueducts, until they broke down. No one rebuilt them. The civilized world was dying slowly of old age.

Constantinople, Justinian said, could survive from year to year by bribing chieftains of hordes to fight each other, and by ceaselessly repairing the old fortifications. It was like a tired old man, buying the food he could not produce for himself. The city could buy more years for itself.

Or it could go out of its walls. To re-enter the darkening hinterland, bringing its arts of manufacture and living back, land by land, into the lost empire. It could enlighten the barbarian hordes by conquering them, one by one. By enforcing again civilized Law.

To accomplish this he, Justinian, was building a new fleet and a new army to take the place of the vanished legions of Constantine. He was asking Belisarius to take the second step outward by recovering the dying Rome. Belisarius would conquer. He would march in another triumph through the forum of the great Trajan, under the arch of Titus. But in so doing he would be the harbinger of a new world of intelligence. He would lead the way for a new empire, with one church and one law.

So Justinian said, not eloquently but earnestly. He looked

so old himself, with his eyes dull in folds of white flesh.

Belisarius felt grateful to be serving a man who exhausted himself in labor for other people. Justinian's vision, as he thought of it, inspired him, so that he longed to lead his comitatus under the arch of triumph in the old Rome. And Antonina egged him on, urging that this was his opportunity, while she planned to add to the new palace of Belisarius an enclosed garden court in the style of Pompeii so unfortunately buried by a volcano.

Preparations went on swiftly. The Mesé hummed with whispered secrets of Belisarius' expedition. Yet when the strategists informed Belisarius of the strength of the expedition, he shook his head mutely. To his own comitatus they would add two mounted regiments, and four thousand Isaurian infantry, with some federated Huns and Moors from Africa. Isaurians, Huns, and Moors to discipline. Eleven thousand men in all, to land in Italy where sixty or seventy thousand Gothic horsemen might assemble.

"The name of Belisarius," cried Narses eagerly, "is worth ten thousand men."

"Twenty thousand!" echoed the Constable (*Comes stabuli* —the Count of the Stables).

Belisarius did not know how to argue with the dukes and counts of the strategic council who planned to usher in a new era by force. Better than they, he knew that a time would come inevitably when his army would need to stand against the massed Goths, who would not suspend a battle to hold burial services. "Grant me twenty thousand," he begged, "and I will ask for no more."

Then Justinian pointed out that Belisarius was forgetting the advantage of the ships. Going in on their fleets, both Belisarius and Mundus could land where they chose, avoiding the Goths. They could withdraw to safety at any time. So the new armies would escape danger. He promised that Belisarius would command twenty thousand by the second stage of the war.

Belisarius sailed that autumn. He could not have refused, in any case, because the quick little war the strategists planned had already begun. It was to last, however, for eighteen years, and to become a world war.

The landing at Catania in Sicily went as the strategists had planned; the island was deceived, surprised, and overrun swiftly. The Gothic garrisons made a stand only behind the walls of Panormus (Palermo), whence Belisarius forced them out by the fire of archers he placed in the mastheads of his ships, laying the vessels against the waterfront wall. It seemed to Procopius that it was a fine omen that his hero should end his year as consul in the captured stronghold of Sicily.

Then in came Solomon the eunuch, exhausted after being rowed over from Africa, telling his story in one brief word, "Rebellion."

Half the varied Romans left on duty in Africa under Solomon had gone off with the Vandal and Moorish partisans, declaring that they were a Soldiers' Republic. Wine and ease had turned their minds to politics; tax collectors from Constantinople had angered them by claiming all conquered farming land for the state; orthodox priests, raging against Arian heretics, had made the former Vandal women—now the soldiers' women—hysterical by barring them from church doors and calling their newborn children pagans. Solomon himself had barely escaped assassination in a church, and had fled to sea in a small rowing vessel.

Belisarius decided that he could leave Sicily for a few days, no more. Solomon was temporarily discredited as a commander. For a few days the Goths, lacking ships, could make no move against his island of Sicily.

Selecting each man himself, he ordered a hundred of his cataphracts into a fast galley.

"What more are you taking?" demanded Antonina.

"No more can leave here."

"Are you mad, Belisarius, or do you crave a noble Roman suicide in the ancient fashion? May I ask—what do you intend to do with me?"

"You will stay with the comitatus and keep up appearances —that I am cruising the island ports."

Belisarius could not delay for a woman's mood. But Theodora's spies reported that when he left his wife in that fashion she summoned Theodosius the godson to carry her orders and attend her at night.

While Antonina solaced herself with the hesitating Theodosius, Belisarius was too preoccupied to take thought of anything in Sicily. His fast galley landed him and his hundred picked men in Carthage by night. Through the streets he rode with his standards and veterans, and word that Belisarius was back brought out the regulars who had not gone off to be a Soldiers' Republic, with some Moors who admired him, and even ex-Vandals who decided they would be safest with him. Belisarius' name, in Carthage, mustered two thousand fighting men, whom he led out at once toward the rebel army.

This dwindled in numbers at the news that Belisarius was back in command. It grew still smaller when the rebels sighted his familiar restless figure beneath the old standards of the cross and the eagles. When it had to form ranks to face him, there was confusion in carrying out the orders of the new officers of the Soldiers' Republic. And as at Tricamaron, Belisarius led a charge directly at the confusion, avoiding the steadier front of the rebellious regulars. Before the charge Vandal partisans, Moorish looters, and escaped slaves gave way and ran. The regulars laid down their arms and appealed to Belisarius.

It troubled him greatly that these soldiers did not speak of the empire; they spoke of Justinian's men, and the republic, as if all armed men served not the empire itself but fought either for or against Justinian. They explained that they had not deserted Belisarius; they had merely killed the tax-gatherers—the Squeezers—who had tried to take away the land they had won; they had only beaten the police who had driven their women away from holy communion.[1]

Belisarius showed them a coin of gold, a solidus with Justinian's head on it. They were soldiers, he told them, paid by the solidi of the empire, and they had deserted their service to loot. A soldier, he said, must be guided by nothing but the orders of the emperor who paid him.

They said many of their officers had held back their pay, or else Justinian had not sent the money, and they wanted Belisarius to remain in command over them.

That he could not do. Restoring what order he could among the African garrisons, he hurried back to Syracuse with his escort. There Antonina complained that the other army commanders had refused to carry out her requests. Angered, Belisarius summoned them to explain why they had not heeded his wife, left in his place. The Roman officers informed him that they did not care to carry out the orders of a woman, and particularly such a woman. Then Belisarius learned of the gossip that his wife had been intimate with his godson. He did not believe it. Consequently a certain bitterness came between him and his lieutenants in Sicily. But at the moment Belisarius had a greater anxiety, in the form of a new order from Justinian.

The timetable of the strategists in Constantinople had broken down at another place. Over on the Dalmatian coast the small expedition under Mundus, the former Herule, had encountered Goths in surprising strength. Being still a barbarian by nature, Mundus had given battle and had been killed. The Goths had suffered but they had remained on the coast, while the surviving Romans withdrew into the moun-

[1]The soldiers had a just grievance. New recruits were paid only one gold piece a year; veterans received one coin for each year of their service; they all depended on land allotments near the frontiers for a living. Apparently they had claimed such landholdings in Africa, and these had been taken from them by the assessors. But the Vandal women may have caused them to revolt.

tains, losing touch with the expectant fleet. Justinian had sent the Most Noble Constantian, Constable of the Empire, to restore the Dalmatian prong of the pincers that had been intended to nip off southern Italy.

Justinian now ordered Belisarius to proceed with the invasion of Italy as planned. Although Mundus had been defeated before reaching the heel of the Italian boot, Belisarius was to cross to the toe, at the Strait of Messina.

To Belisarius this request came as an order. Not knowing, as Justinian knew, what was happening elsewhere, the soldier accepted the order to go forward. After calculating how few detachments he could leave as garrisons in Sicily, he took to his ships and crossed the tide-ripped narrow strait—between legendary, perilous Scylla and Charybdis—from the heights of Messina. There he had a bit of his famous luck, because the Gothic coastal commander, not knowing his strength, surrendered.

Yet Belisarius, forming his march column on the tip of the toe of Italy, faced the one situation he had dreaded. With no more than eighty-five hundred men he was marching toward the aroused Gothic nation in arms.

Aware that his command would have little chance in the open against the mass of mounted Goths, he took the road to Naples. Probably he hoped to do as he had done in Africa, slip into a great city and use it for a base. Because he was desperately anxious, he rode the length of the Roman column with all his officers, calling out that luck was with them and victory in sight. He called for the battle hymn, and the deep chant of the Trisagion sounded after him, from regiment to regiment. "Holy, Mighty, Immortal Lord——"

To Theodora, in Constantinople, it seemed as if the war council had really gambled on Belisarius alone. Until then the single-minded soldier had accomplished every task given him. The strategists, no fools by any means, wanted to make the test whether Belisarius without aid could master all the

Goths. As to that, Theodora had no opinion. Having spoken her mind once in a war council during the Nika revolt, she did not do so again.

Meanwhile the news from Italy upset all the well-laid plans of Justinian's strategists. They had counted on the co-operation of the Gothic king, the Philosopher, who was being kept in play by their agent, Peter.

The distraught Philosopher failed to be of further service, because the Gothic chieftains and warriors realized that this was a war in which their king seemed to be hindering more than aiding them. Aroused, they had called an old-fashioned German council of warriors and had elected one of themselves, a noble named Vitigis, to be their king to carry on the war. The unfortunate Philosopher, fleeing to Ravenna, had been followed by a Gothic knight, who had slain the last of the Amals with proper ceremony.

(Vitigis, who had the German virtue of personal courage, was given a daughter of the murdered Amalasuntha for wife, to keep the semblance of Amal blood in the kingship; but his election changed the situation in Italy decisively. It ended the orderly nation of Theodoric and turned the Goths again into a barbaric army in conflict with the imperial armies.)

A third point of the timetable of the civilized strategists in their attack on the barbarians miscarried about this time. The Franks, or some of them, duly appeared on this side of the Alps. Expecting to plunder a countryside, however, they found a great Gothic army gathering in the north. Shrewdly, Vitigis greeted them as if they had come on a friendly visit, and they decided to wait where they were, to discover what military force the emperor could produce, and what further gifts he was prepared to make to them. With the Frankish visitors halted, Vitigis sent to Justinian to ask why he would not restore the peace between Goths and Romans.

What Justinian answered is not known. But he did not agree to a peace.

Theodora had no faith in the western war. She simply felt

convinced that the heart of the empire lay in the east, where beat the pulse of peaceful trade, where grew an abundance of all that was needed, where stirred the spirit of religious faith as she knew it. It had been her home, and it might be a refuge when retribution came after the war effort in the west.

She hated the Roman fasces carried before her pompously—the ancient axes tied up in bundles of sticks—and she was cold to ardent writers like Procopius who invoked the phrases of Caesar and long-dead Suetonius. Envoys from the west, prostrating themselves to her scarlet slippers, were often startled at hearing something like the hissing of snakes among the girls behind the throne seat. The girls were only whispering "Illustrissimi" as Theodora pronounced it.

Outwardly—and astute politicians like John of Cappadocia watched her movements closely—she devoted herself to a garden estate in the Asia suburbs which she had made into a home for prostitutes, and to her old home, now known as the House of the Monks. There the monks and pilgrims from the east lodged themselves in huts through the garden; they sang hymns of praise when Theodora made her daily visits, and the beggars hanging around the gate yelled for alms. She talked with them all, the venerable wanderers and the professional beggars, learning from them each day about happenings in Antioch, and thriving Alexandria, and her beloved Syrian coast.

"Monks from Egypt or monkeys from Africa," grumbled John, the Economist, of Cappadocia, "they all get coin from the bitch. Who provides her with the gold coins? The state. And that means you and I, my brothers."

John did not add that what he took out of the revenues for himself he kept. Already the self-made financier anticipated that he would come to conflict with the smiling, implacable empress. Shrewdly he realized that if Justinian ever had to decide which of the two would have to depart the palace it would not be John of Cappadocia. He ventured to attack Theodora before she could attack him. Her early life, her secretive scheming, and her demands for money—all these lay open to challenge. . . .

Their first skirmish took place after the arrival of Saba.

A shriveled anchorite, ninety years of age, Saba came out of the wilderness of the river Jordan to make a plea for Jerusalem. Justinian welcomed Saba as if he had been a living saint, sending an imperial dromon to usher his ship into the Golden Horn and going afoot to take Saba by the hand and help him into the palace. (John sensed Theodora's prodding in this display of reverence.)

But before Justinian on the throne, the aged anchorite neither bowed his hairy head nor spoke with respect. The splendor of the palace seemed to Saba to be the evil glory of a Sardanapalus. In Jerusalem, he declared, the church of the *Theotokos*—the Mother of God—was falling into ruin; the sick lay in the streets; the people no longer had money to pay Caesar's tax collectors.

Justinian expressed his dismay and regret. Yet Saba was obdurate as a rock of the wilderness. Instead of words, he wanted deeds. Specifically, the anchorite demanded five things: a hospital for the sick of Jerusalem, a year's relief from taxation for the poor, a fine church for the Mother of God, repair of the ruined hostels for pilgrims, and a fort to protect them from the raids of Saracens.

Disturbed by the fiery words of the anchorite, Justinian was worried by the immediate protest of his Economist. John showed him that while he was building his Great Church and waging a war in Italy he could not possibly undertake to make over Jerusalem in that fashion. "There is a point where the possible becomes the impossible, Thrice August. Already you have gone twice beyond what the treasury could afford. A third undertaking will make it necessary for you to stop one of the others. Make the decision yourself—don't let these cavemen and column-sitters persuade you to madness."

In his argument he said nothing about Theodora's allowance or her way of persuading. When he heard from his spies the story of how Saba was summoned to Theodora's court, he roared with delight. It seemed that Theodora stepped down from her throne to kneel before the aged alms-seeker and beg, surprisingly, that he would pray she might bear a child.

At that, Saba was silent long moments, and looked from her to the silk-clad ladies and the gold-sheathed chamber. In answer he said merely, "God will preserve the glory of your empire." And the empress went pale with anxiety.

John's friends repeated the story with gusto. "God forbid," he shouted, "that another such as she should issue from her womb."

John could not believe at first that Justinian agreed to all of Saba's demands. Theodora persuaded him that the distress in the city of Christ was greater than any need in Constantinople. Somehow she could tell him that the roof of the basilica of Bethlehem, that protected the cavern, had fallen in, and how many people slept in niches of the rocks around Gethsemane. As far away as that, she had eyes and ears to serve her.

When he left the Golden Horn, Saba carried with him a guaranty that all the five things he asked for would be done.

After that a great treasure was sent to Jerusalem. Jews of the city besought the emperor to return the golden spoils of the temple. "It is unthinkable that they should rest in any other place than the altar of Solomon." Justinian remembered that when the candlesticks and the table of gold had rested in Rome the city had been sacked by the Vandals; when they had been held in Carthage, Carthage had fallen. In the year 535 he sent them back by the hand of an envoy to Jerusalem.

To ease his weariness at such times the son of Sabbatius would go to the site of the new Great Church. When he approached the stone piers rising skyward in their enveloping scaffolding, he dismissed his retinue and walked among the workmen as a spectator. It was cheering as food or sleep, to see the masses of stonework rising by a fraction each day, and he begrudged the storms that kept Isidore's masons from the scaffolding. Already the outer skeleton of the sanctuary at the east was taking shape. Justinian had asked that the sanctuary be sheathed entirely in silver. When John the Economist complained that it would take two thousand pounds of the precious metal to accomplish that, the emperor said it would need forty thousand pounds to line the sanctuary entire.

More than money, however, was needed to lift the Great Church to a height never before attempted. Anthemius said that the great hall of Ctesiphon where Khusrau held his court sprang to ninety-five feet from the desert earth. But the summit of the crowning dome of the Great Church would be nearly twice that height. Already at the lower levels they had encountered trouble owing to what Isidore the Miletan called the perversity of materials. The weight of incredible masses, and the resulting strains and horizontal thrusts, had been calculated many times; they were known as nearly as mathematics could reveal them—and Isidore had mastered the equations of that other Greek, Archimedes, in dealing with unprecedented forces. His plans, then, were correct; the rising stonework was sound and adequate. Still, things happened beyond their ability to calculate.

Mortar, apparently entirely dried between the stone courses, yielded another fraction of a tenth of a cubit when the courses felt the burden of immense weight laid on them. Green Carystian marble flaked off under pressure that porphyry endured without harm. There came a day after a driving storm when both Anthemius and Isidore reached the end of their resources. Cracks appeared in the two main piers on the east side. These piers were the foundations of the midway vaults upon which the great dome itself would be anchored. The cracks showed when the "binding" arch was being flung from the immense square piers. The ends of the arch curved up from each pier but did not meet as yet. Their two arms curved up into space in readiness to join together, across more than a hundred feet of space.

Work was stopped when the cracks appeared. Critics of the undertaking thronged to see the cracks, and observed that now the mad builders must understand that their Great Church could never have its dome. Justinian haunted the building area, listening to the arguments. Unable to follow the mathematics of Isidore, he asked the master builder if he had made a mistake in his calculations. The harassed Isidore swore that he had not.

His critics pointed to the cracks. "Here is the proof that this Greek erred."

Justinian still questioned Isidore. "You calculated that the piers would take the strain when the arch was finished and in place? You thought they would stand?"

"As I live, Most Magnificent! I did not think. I know."

"Then finish the arch and see what happens."

To quiet the objections of the workmen, Justinian gave them a direct order to join the arms of the arch. After this was done and the side arches flung out from the piers, the cracks ceased to spread; the great piers stood. (After fourteen hundred years they stand as Isidore planned them.)

Theodora persuaded Anthemius to design something for her. Beauty she wanted, and the intimacy of small size. Near the center of the city Anthemius rebuilt the church of the Apostles, where the tombs of the earlier emperors lay, where the lighting was dim and the five domes merely covered the altar and the shrines. Going into it, she was never far from one of the shrines. (It has been destroyed, after nine hundred years, but its likeness survives in St. Mark's at Venice, copied from it.)

Meanwhile Theodora claimed every pound of gold due yearly to the Augusta of the empire. And that at a time when money was urgently needed for the war. "The treasury must melt silver cups," growled John, "but this Augusta of ours calls unceasingly for gold—for what? For more jewels and a fine estate for sluts. This she-devil has genius. She bleeds Justinian to satisfy her whims." And he started the rumor that Theodora had arranged for the murder of the beautiful Amalasuntha, being jealous. But Theodora, confined to the Sacred Palace, was jealous of no unknown Gothic queen. She had not killed Amalasuntha. The Philosopher had done that, to make himself secure upon a throne, when he had thought Justinian favored him.

Unperceived even by John, Theodora was seeking to change the rule of the empire, to turn it away from the Catholic and militant west, toward the tolerant and fertile east. She did not explain that to Justinian, who was so occupied with the war, on top of his other labors. Nor did she explain that she had marked his money-getter, John of Cappadocia, for destruction.

All that summer of 536 the city of Constantinople awaited tidings from the western front more eagerly even than the results of the races now restored in the Hippodrome. The progress of their hero Belisarius excited all the wine drinkers along the Mesé. . . . Belisarius had reached Neapolis . . . he was stopped there by the massive wall . . . why did not the loyal Romans open the gates? . . . The Gothic garrison prevented, and Belisarius could not afford a siege. . . . Where was the Gothic army? . . .

Belisarius was in Neapolis. He had liberated the great port by climbing in through an aqueduct after shutting off the water . . . he had disappeared with his army . . . in defeat? He had never been defeated . . . but where could he have taken an army, to escape the Goths? An army cannot be hidden. . . .

In Rome itself! Before the Ides of December, he had slipped into Rome! Aided by God, Belisarius had conquered!

No one in Constantinople realized how desperately Belisarius had tried to avoid being penned within ancient Rome.

Like a vast brown monument, the older city lay inert on its malarial plain. A parasite, perishing when it had been cut off from the outer world, it maintained feeble life within its shell of skyscrapers, triumphal forums, and vaulted baths. Its population had dwindled and become provincial. Tenement families did their housekeeping on the pent roofs of the Capitoline palaces; grass grew in the Circus Maximus, where the chariot races had become seedy affairs, compared to the games in the eastern Hippodrome. Damp infested the porticoed villas, yet the heat of the sun tormented the streets. Only the clustered basilica of St. Peter on the road outside the walls had vital life in it, being the home of the orthodox Pope.

Belisarius had tried to keep out of this imposing but dangerous monument, by holding the northern roads and hill passes. Procopius, excited by beholding his hero defending the Rome of the Caesars, records their futile attempt to hold the bridge of the last river above Rome. "Belisarius, although he was safe enough, would not stay back in the general's post of command but went into the front rank like a soldier . . . it happened he was riding a gray horse with a white blaze. The Goths began to cry out 'Shoot at the horse with the blaze' and to close in upon him to strike with their spears and swords. Belisarius kept turning from side to side, and his guards held out their shields to protect both rider and horse . . . in this way the Romans escaped and raced back to the fortifications of Rome, with the barbarians pressing them, to the Salarian Gate. But the people of Rome, fearing that the enemy would rush in with the fugitives and get inside the fortifications, were not willing to open the gate, although Belisarius urged them again and again to do so. For those who peered over the wall did not recognize the man calling out to them with his head covered by dust and blood, and they could not see very well, either, because it was the end of the day, about sunset."

Locked out of his city in this manner, the desperate commander tried a bluff. Wheeling the portion of his comitatus pinned against the wall with him, he headed what seemed in the dim light to be a sally against the pursuing Gothic horsemen. These prudently turned back. After that he was able to get the gate opened.

But he was inside with five thousand of his veterans—too few to defend all points along the great circuit of the walls with their fifteen gates and two gaps where the sluggish Tiber flowed through. Outside those walls the main host of Goths gathered in stockaded camps. They seemed to number about thirty thousand armed horsemen with as many more general utility men. Their bright robes and gleaming helmets made a disheartening display to Roman eyes. Promptly they sent in envoys to observe the situation inside, and to suggest that Belisarius surrender the city. It was well enough for a warrior, the bearded Goths said, to show his bravery. But to be courageous was one thing, to be rash was another. And Belisarius would be rash indeed if he tried to defend the city. They offered the Roman commander the privilege of marching his army out, unmolested, with its weapons and supplies, to any port on the sea.

Belisarius must have felt the force of these arguments. Vitigis and the Gothic nobles would have kept their word, if he had surrendered the city. Still barbaric by nature, they held to the old German notions that it was glorious to die in battle and dishonorable to break a pledged word.

He answered with careless arrogance, a fine figure of a soldier among his officers who always made a good showing. "The time will come when you will want to hide your heads, even under thistles, and find no shelter anywhere. As for Rome . . . so long as Belisarius lives, it will never be given up."

With what delight did the tense Procopius write down

these resounding words of his hero! They had the effect of puzzling and impressing the watchful Goths, who fancied that the Roman commander must rely on some support unperceived by them. That was what Belisarius desired, who knew there was no such support forthcoming.

Quickly he rid himself of one danger, by ordering all women, children, and servitors of the citizens to be marched out. As an afterthought he added, all women and children of his own comitatus. For in some mysterious manner his cataphracts accumulated women followers wherever they went. Antonina, however, stayed.

Vitigis allowed this column of helpless folk to pass out. The Goths had not learned the nicety of present-day warfare that attacks the population of cities to weaken a nation's will to resist.

So began the famous siege of Rome, which Belisarius had tried to avoid. He could rely only on the skill, ingenuity, and imagination of civilized humans to overcome the unthinking tenacity of barbarians. The civilized defenders relied on war machines and mental quickness. They easily beat off the massed attack of the Goths with clumsy siege engines (drawn by oxen toward the walls), although at one point the officer at Hadrian's tomb (now the Castello di Sant' Angelo) had to break up the antique statues at a critical moment to use as missiles.

The Goths gave up the attempt to match machines against machines. They broke down the aqueducts that carried water into the city but could not stop the Tiber flowing in; they gave up trying to launch rafts and boats down the river when Roman engineers constructed booms at the river's entrance and exit, with war engines to protect the booms.

Almost from the first, however, the conqueror of Africa had trouble with the citizens of Rome. This populace still remembered—and remembered too well—its glory of the past when it had been the center of the civilized world. Its orators still made speeches, and greeted the surprising reappearance of an imperial army with an enthusiasm that was not entirely deflated by the sending away of their families and the prospect of half rations. Many citizens wanted to enlist in the army, and Belisarius had trouble in keeping them from trying to fight in a battle; he organized them as a home guard, after walling up most of the gates, to prevent enthusiastic or treacherous citizens from opening them.

"The populace of Rome," Procopius explains, "was quite unacquainted with the real evils of war and siege. So they began to be distressed when they could no longer bathe, or have as much food as before, and when they had to lose sleep watching the circuit wall, while the enemy plundered their fields and possessions outside. They began also to suspect that the city would be captured, and to complain because they, who had quarreled with no one, should suffer discomfort with danger added."

The senators, their spokesmen, were highly educated and asked questions that Belisarius could not answer. If he had come by order of the emperor, they asked, why had he brought too small a force to defend the city?

Belisarius, however, was doing his best to keep the conflict outside the mammoth walls. He was doing something never dreamed of by Vegetius—defending a city by mounted cavalrymen. The Goths could never refuse the challenge of mounted enemies riding against them. So he played on their eagerness as an organist plays on the keys of his instrument —planting a detachment of his men close to the walls where Goths charged into the fire of engines mounted above—sending picked squadrons galloping against a Gothic camp, to retire on a full regiment sallying from a gate as the Goths streamed forward in a wild charge.

The size of the city walls gave him one advantage. The encampments of the Goths necessarily spread around a still greater perimeter. His cataphracts could bedevil one camp before another came up to join in the battle. At night his swiftly striking units went out with watchdogs to warn and guide them. By the time the Goths had puzzled out the answer to one such tactical trick, Belisarius had another ready to bother them. The civilized thinker could keep a trick ahead of the barbarian who reasoned from past experience.

The river also served him well. It took the clumsy Goths a long time to cross from one bank of the Tiber to the other, whereas the Romans had bridges inside the city. Belisarius played the game of now-on-this-side, now-on-that to the limit of his imagination, and even risked moving out the Roman citizens as a decoy, keeping them close to the wall with strict orders to run headlong if attacked. When the Goths assembled at this point, he launched his comitatus in a galloping attack on the far side of the river. Some of the citizens made the mistake of trying to stand against the Goths before they ran.

During all this sleight-of-hand maneuvering of cavalry from sheltering walls, the Roman general contrived to get in provisions from the countryside. His enemies could not manage to keep a tight cordon around the city. Small columns of the dreaded gray riders filtered through ravines to outlying towns. They drove off Gothic patrols with volleys of arrows. (The Goths could not or would not learn to use the destructive power bow from the saddle; their archers remained afoot —which was one of the reasons why Belisarius avoided a ranged battle that would bring Gothic bows into action.) Then the flying column of Romans would prepare ostentatiously to defend a town or hilltop; the stubborn Goths would assemble to launch an attack upon the position, only to find that the elusive horsemen had gone off, to circle back to the city with a pack train of precious corn, or a herd of cattle.

The Romans experimented with the Tiber as well. Discovering that small galleys could navigate up the river from the coast to the city, they built wooden shields along the galleys' rails and ran the gantlet of the winding river almost at will.

Yet only small detachments appeared from Constantinople

to relieve the city—their number about balancing the Roman losses.

With all his virtuosity, Belisarius did not break the tenacity of the barbarians. Stoically, they endured their losses, and the Roman garrison could not afford to lose one soldier to five foemen. Summer came, and no harvest could be brought into the city; half rations weakened the soft civilians, who became clamorous in their insistence that he give battle to Vitigis. If he had been so successful in small engagements, they argued, why did he not end the siege and all their misery with one general engagement? What had become of the power of the great Justinian—that the people of Rome should be abandoned to starve?

Until then Belisarius had risked only small numbers of his veterans—and secured some advantage for them in every clash—against equal forces of Goths. Either he was forced by the populace to lead out his army, as Procopius asserts, or he decided to take the gamble.

In the great battle that resulted, however, the civilized army could make no headway against the numbers and physical courage of the German barbarians. Belisarius only saved the bulk of his command by sacrificing the best of his Isaurian infantry.

The real war had begun. And Belisarius wrote to Justinian in the Sacred Palace that he must have effective aid. In the streets he had heard his men called "Greeks" and "Imperialists." He had heard muttering that the Romans in Italy had fared better under the wise Theodoric and the gifted Amalasuntha than under the ambition of the "eastern emperor." The good will of these Romans had been exhausted; the Pope at St. Peter's sought peace for the land, and the time had come when Constantinople must send to the west greater strength than five thousand mercenaries. Yet Belisarius, the soldier, felt guilty in trying to explain this to his emperor in writing.

". . . as to the prospect from now on, I wish it were better, for your cause. I shall never hide from you what it is my duty to explain, and yours to act upon. So, send weapons and trained men to us in sufficient numbers to let us engage the enemy in this war with equal strength. We ought not to trust too long to fortune, for fortune does not go on too long without changing. Do you, Emperor, take this thought to your heart: if the barbarians gain the victory now, we shall be thrown out of Italy and lose the army, and have to bear the shame of our conduct of the war. For we should be looked upon as having ruined the Romans, the men who forsook their safety to aid your empire. . . ."

Strain was telling on Belisarius, as at the first landing in Sicily. Autumn set in; he had held the walls of Rome by mere expedients for nearly eleven months without relief, and had seen his veterans mangled by the Goths. The strain showed in his outbreaks of exasperation—his arrest of the Pope, Silverius, on evidence of an anonymous letter, his sending the faithful Procopius down to Naples to search for reinforcements. Then he ordered Antonina to follow the secretary.

Perhaps he fancied Antonina might go east to beg aid from Theodora. Certainly he brooded over his wife, who complained of the trusted officers who had linked her name to the handsome Theodosius. Seeking to believe both his commanders and Antonina, Belisarius, like many another man, found that he could believe neither. He sensed the stirring of intrigue about him, and hated it. His ablest lieutenant, Constantine, he condemned to execution. Constantine, enraged by Belisarius' disciplining, had drawn a knife and struck at the commander, apparently convinced that Antonina had egged Belisarius on to humiliate him.

Belisarius' state of nervous fatigue was not helped by his awareness that he was being made to serve as an instrument in another conflict that had nothing to do with the war. He could only guess what that conflict might be. No sign of it showed on the surface. In the east, behind closed doors, Justinian and Theodora for the first time were in bitter opposition to each other.

It started when Theodora's friends, Severus, patriarch of Antioch, and Anthimius, patriarch of Constantinople, defied the emperor's authority. Angered, Justinian called a council that deposed and anathematized both patriarchs. (Theodora fought for them with all her energy; Justinian claimed the need of drawing closer to the clergy of Rome now that his army was besieged there. More than that, as emperor, he felt that his authority must prevail over the churches in the east as well as in the west—a feeling that Theodora did not share.)

Apparently defeated by her husband, Theodora threw all her resources into an effort to aid her friends the patriarchs. She worked secretly—so secretly that it is not clear today what actually happened. It seems as if she sought to break Justinian's control of the churches by bringing about an agreement between Rome and the patriarchs of the east. Unable to invoke either council or law to do so, she schemed with individuals. No one knows exactly how.

There was the dubious letter implicating the Pope Silverius with the Goths. (Silverius had first favored Theodora's idea, then opposed it.) Belisarius and Antonina found themselves carrying out the veiled commands of the Augusta, sending Silverius away, then recalling him. There was the appearance in Rome of the deacon, Vigilius, who had spent years in Constantinople in talk with the empress and was inclined to aid her.

As to all this Belisarius could have no certainty. Antonina, corresponding with Theodora, departed in urgent haste for home. It was understood in Rome that Vigilius would be the next Pope. . . .

In Constantinople, to everyone's surprise the original cause of the conflict, the exiled Anthimius, disappeared from sight. Rumor had it that the patriarch might have been killed by some unknown means.

Actually Theodora had smuggled him into her apartments.

There among the ladies of honor Anthimius remained hidden from outer eyes. None of her women gave away Theodora's secret.

The time came when Justinian heard of a ghost that walked Theodora's chambers. The ghost wore no ceremonial robes but greatly resembled the missing patriarch. He took her to the closed gate of the small purple palace, because no one followed them there, to question her as to the truth of this.

"Is Anthimius alive and within our doors?"

Theodora shook her head, as if utterly surprised. One who was exiled and laid under anathema could not be sheltered within the Sacred Palace.

Then Theodora begged something of her husband the emperor. A woman could not understand controversy in religion. She only knew that the revered Anthimius had given her the bread and wine of the Sacrament. It was the old rite of the oriental fathers. Would not Justinian grant one thing to her? Would he not protect Anthimius, who was no longer patriarch but was still a priest able to give the Sacrament?

Justinian could not be persuaded to grant this. He had signed the edict of exile; he could not revoke it. To do so would be to make a mockery of his authority. The former patriarch must go from the city, into exile.

His insistence left her no alternative but to obey. Deeply troubled, Theodora murmured her acquiescence, and cast about her for some sign as to what she might do. It was impossible now to hide the elderly priest within the palace, nor could she bring herself to send Anthimius out like a criminal seeking a road to take him beyond the observation of the prefects of the Roman Empire. In such a moment of frustration she was accustomed to look for a sign to guide her. There was nothing visible out of the ordinary. Below at the boat landing, the emperor's barge waited for his summons as usual; overhead swallows whirled around the pyramid roof of the purple chamber . . . they turned as if at a signal and flew across the water . . . far out on the rocks there was the white speck of Leander's tower, and across the strait, far off, the red roof of her home for prostitute girls. Within sight, yet in Asia . . .

"Justinian," she answered suddenly, "I swear that the good Anthimius will go into exile from your palace."

"That is wise."

At the first opportunity Theodora took the imperial barge to cross the water to visit her asylum that some women called the Penitentiary. Seemingly in a restless mood, she led her escort down to explore the shore until she came to a projecting point that had been made into a garden. It was known as Hieron, and the empress admired it, expressing such delight in it that her chamberlain wondered if she might not build a summerhouse upon it. Theodora said she would call upon the architect Anthemius to design a large dwelling for her on the point.

There, at Hieron, she could quarter herself in a palace apart from the Sacred Palace; there Anthimius could go into exile, no more than two miles from his Great Church, and protected by her.

She was glad that the name of Hieron meant The Sanctuary.

V

War Across the World

IT BECAME CLEAR AT LAST TO JUSTINIAN AND HIS COUNCIL OF war that Belisarius was, in fact, at bay in Rome. Disappointed because his spectacular general had ceased to perform miracles, Justinian grudgingly recalled regiments from the northern frontier to send to Italy. There were so few regiments, to meet so many needs!

By weakening the garrisons along the Danube, Justinian courted new danger. Across that river frontier Slavs were drifting like shadows; behind them tribal Herules looted the forest towns; behind them an unknown force, the terrifying Avars of the steppes, pressed south.

"These Slavs dwell in pitiful hovels, apart from each other," notes Procopius. "Tall and hard-muscled, they all look alike and often lack even a shirt or cloak to cover them. They shift around constantly. For they live in a hard way, without comforts. No one man rules them, nor do they believe in Fate. Instead they worship the god that sends the lightning. In old times they were known as the Scattered, or perhaps the Sowers, because they get hold of a great amount of land to cultivate."

The first reinforcements were small enough. John, the nephew of Vitalian, landed with eighteen hundred cataphracts on the heel of Italy and rode to Naples, as the ill-fated Mundus had been expected to do. There, too, three thousand Isaurian infantry sailed in with a convoy of corn ships. They picked up the delighted Procopius and the relieved Antonina and proceeded by the coast road and the sea toward Rome.

Then Belisarius' famous luck seemed to favor him again. No sooner had they heard of the arrival of the fleet in Ostia at the Tiber's mouth than the Goths asked for a truce to discuss terms. Actually the barbarian encampments, wearied by siege warfare, had heard report of an imperial army and fleet coming in. Upon their anxiety Belisarius played, to bring in his rescuers safely.

The Gothic envoys this time found him amused and apparently indifferent to their anxiety. When they asked the old question, why had the empire, after taking no heed of Vandal raids or Visigoth invasion, suddenly attacked their Gothic kingdom, he gave them a harsh answer. Italy was not a Gothic kingdom but a part of the empire. When they offered to cede Sicily, Belisarius laughed. He held Sicily already, for the emperor. "Should I give you the island of Britain in exchange?" he asked, amused. "It's much larger and has more population."

It upset the envoys of Vitigis to find him so hard and mocking. He barely listened to their feelers about surrendering land in southern Italy and even paying an indemnity in gold. All they could gain from him was a three months' truce, to allow them to forward their offers to Justinian. And they left the truce conference with the feeling that the unpredictable commander saw his way to victory.

That night Belisarius slipped out the Appian Gate with a veteran following to meet and escort back John and the relieving cavalry, and his wife. The infantry transports and grain ships he brought up the Tiber by occupying the strong points along the river abandoned by the Goths during the truce.

When the troubled Goths accused him truthfully of breaking the sworn truce, the Roman commander proceeded to rupture it still more by launching John and the best of the cavalry north in the general direction of Ravenna, the capital city of Vitigis and his people. This cavalry column rode as if expecting battle and looted its living from the countryside.

By then Vitigis and his army began to believe that Belisarius meant to end the truce by attacking them. They heard that the Roman cavalry had seized a fortified town, one day's ride from Ravenna, while still another imperial fleet had been sighted off the coast. So the Goths burned their palisaded camps and started to march back to Ravenna.

Savagely Belisarius launched his forces in Rome after them, striking the rear of their host at the Milvian Bridge where he had nearly been killed a year before. After that, the withdrawal of the Goths turned into a race for Ariminum (Rimini) in the hills where the Roman cavalry column had quartered itself.

Vitigis, with force enough under his hand to defeat all the Romans, seemed to fear that Belisarius was trying to slip into Ravenna as he had managed to do into Rome. Abandoning central Italy, he hurried north to encircle Ariminum. He had been defeated not by a battle but by the truce with Belisarius.

Once he began to retreat, Vitigis never regained the initiative. The imagination of the civilized leader had, in the end, broken the tenacity of the barbarian. After a year and nine days Belisarius was able to leave Rome, and he did so immediately. Nor did he ever willingly return to the monumental, ancestral Rome.

What the inventive Balkan soldier might have accomplished by following at the heels of the discouraged Gothic king will never be known. For Belisarius received an unexpected reinforcement that stopped him in his tracks.

The new imperial fleet that had been reported on the way actually came in, that spring of 538. It brought the surprising strength of five thousand regular infantry and two thousand hired Herulian Huns. With these added to his command,

Belisarius would have had almost the twenty thousand effectives promised by Justinian. The new arrivals, however, were commanded by the eunuch Narses, who had managed to make himself indispensable to Justinian at the palace. He brought to Italy his doglike devotion to his master and his febrile enthusiasm for warfare. In addition he brought a letter of authority that acted like a blow on Belisarius. The letter explained that the new general was to obey Belisarius "in everything that served the welfare of the state."

Read casually, this phrase seemed to put Narses under the orders of Belisarius. Read carefully, it might instruct the eunuch to obey only such orders as he believed fitting for the imperial interest. He had been sent as a check on the veteran leader. Understanding this, the forthright Belisarius wrote at once to Constantinople to ask if he or Narses were to command. Justinian delayed answering.

The advent of Narses ended the remarkable teamwork between the studious planner in the palace and the brilliant soldier in the field.

Civilian intrigue had entered the war. When Belisarius had sailed on that first forlorn hope, to steal across the sea to remote Africa, the great families of Constantinople had not been concerned. Now, with the ancient western empire half restored, they began to consider their own interests. Some of the lords of the court were related to the Constantine who had been executed; some members of the Sacred Senate held long-forgotten properties—or claims to properties—in the west. It was quite easy for experienced orators to argue that Belisarius, who had done nicely in Africa and Sicily, had failed to defend Rome.

The intrigue at home also worked against Belisarius through his officers. The headstrong cavalry leader, John, who had got himself penned up in Ariminum, being a member of the great Vitalian's family, held himself to be at least the equal of a rich but obscure barbarian. The newly arrived officers understood that Narses was to take over from Belisarius at the first mistake, and acted accordingly.

Moreover, the gossip at the Augusteon made much of the scandal of Antonina. Ildiger, the young son-in-law of actress Antonina, had been the first to grapple with the ill-fated Constantine when the general lunged at Belisarius with a knife. Her young son Photius, fathered by another man before Belisarius, had complained of his mother to Belisarius, after Antonina had tried to have Photius sent out of her sight by inciting the other officers to abuse him. Instead of dismissing Photius, Belisarius kept this boy officer with him and exiled his own godson Theodosius, in spite of Antonina's efforts to keep her lover near her.

Procopius, who had observed all these happenings within Belisarius' family, dispensed juicy bits of scandal to eager correspondents in high society at home who made much of him on that account. It flattered the little Syrian to be so treated, and he began to enlarge upon the stupidity of Belisarius as a husband in the pungent style of Suetonius, whereas he had copied the style of Thucydides in his commentary on the war. Actually Belisarius seems to have been devoted to his wife, and intent only on carrying out his duty; but to Constantinopolitan minds it appeared incredible that so dumb a husband could be an astute general of the army.

The first clash between Belisarius and Narses in Italy did no harm; in fact it brought about an unexpected victory. The one urgent task of the enlarged Roman army was to extricate the cavalry caught in Ariminum, against Belisarius' instructions. (John had refused to get out in time when ordered to do so.) To Narses, who had all an amateur's eagerness to end the war with one big battle, it appeared that the combined Roman forces must hurry against Vitigis and the Goths encamped around Ariminum. To Belisarius, who had watched Gothic swords at close quarters slashing above the wall of the barbarians' shields, it appeared certain that his new contingents could not be thrown into such a battle. Yet he knew the erring cavalry must be got out of the fortress.

In the end they did this, as Narses wanted and Belisarius planned. The veteran leader brought separate columns into the hills around Ariminum and maneuvered a fleet in from the sea, to make it appear that Vitigis was being surrounded. Again, as at Rome, the nerves of the Goths gave way before an invisible menace, and their retreat to Ravenna became a route. Ildiger forced his way into the besieged town with cataphracts.

"You have Ildiger to thank," Belisarius told his general of cavalry, "that you are still alive."

"No," John answered arrogantly, "I have Narses alone to thank for that."

This cleavage in the Roman command affected all the army and resulted after a year in the disaster at Milan.

Far in the north, almost under the Alps, the populace of the great city of Milan (Mediolanum) had gone over to the imperialists and had been given a Roman garrison in acknowledgment of its good will. But Milan lay in a far corner of the vast valley of the Po (Padus) that stretched across the base of the Italian peninsula, above the hilly mid-region. This valley of the Po had become the particular home of the Gothic settlers, who naturally retreated there before the slow advance of the Roman columns. Very soon after the Roman garrison appeared in the city, Goths gathered around Milan and were joined by the savage Franks and Burgundians, who had been hovering about the passes of the Alps and had just received a massive payment of gold from Vitigis.

When Belisarius heard of the siege of Milan he was far south clearing the last Gothic strongholds among the hills. Some of them, like Perugia, rested dizzily on the cliffs, and he would not move on into the plain of the Po until these trouble spots had been captured. He ordered the nearest Roman commanders to advance and relieve Milan. A haphazard host of Goths and tribal Franks did not seem to him too difficult to disperse, and Narses had been eager to take charge of the advanced divisions.

One of the commanders happened to be John, nephew of Vitalian, and he replied that he took orders only from Narses. By the time Belisarius could communicate with the eunuch the population of Milan was starving; before Narses managed to assemble a strong force and reach the city the barbarians broke into it, raping the women, herding off the survivors to slavery, and gutting the buildings with fire The flesh of its bishop they threw to packs of dogs by way of burial.

Belisarius arrived only in time to ride through ruins smelling of burned flesh. Narses beheld the effect of the war he was waging. The massacre had come about through their divided command.

Wisely, but too late, Justinian recalled Narses. After the year lost in hesitation Belisarius resumed his solitary task of protecting the populace while driving out the Goths without risking a battle. Patiently he began to form the Italian peasantry into some kind of an army by sending his biscuit eaters into the villages to drill them.

Justinian had tried to ease the feelings of the brittle Narses by explaining that the eunuch was too important to the treasury and the palace to be spared, but Narses' pride had been injured and he spread the report around that he expected only the worst news from the west where Belisarius, intoxicated by authority and victory—although Narses had gained the victory at Ariminum—was preparing to name himself emperor in the west.

This word reached the ears of Theodora through her servants. She said to Justinian, "Have you not cringing souls enough around you, that you try to make your one honest servant into a pattern-patterer?"

Impatiently Justinian shook his graying head. "I've never doubted Belisarius. But he must not fail me."

Curiously she reflected that five years before Justinian

would have spoken of the empire, not himself. Of late he seemed obsessed with a silent purpose that concerned only Justinian.

Then the two thousand Herulian horse, committed to Italy under Narses, reappeared at Constantinople. Surprised, Justinian asked his secretaries why and how these barbarians had left the Italian front. Priscus, the master of the secretaries, explained: the Herulians had been irked by Belisarius' discipline; they had come back to join their old commander, Narses.

Justinian relied on the efficient and deferential Priscus, who could answer questions instantly. Priscus had a way of entering the study with his head bent in rigid attention.

"But how did they come?" demanded Justinian fretfully. "There is no record of their transport by sea."

"As the Most Glorious says. Illustrious Belisarius, Master of the Armed Forces, would furnish them with no ships. After the Illustrious held back their pay, the Herulian cavalry rode around through the land, foraging for their supplies from the Dalmatian mountains to Hadrian's City."

As the precise Priscus put it, Belisarius seemed to have caused the desertion of the valuable but unruly federate cavalry. Having no officer at the palace capable of disciplining the Hunnic horsemen, Justinian was obliged to let Narses do so, and to give them back pay for the time of their long journey overland. It occurred to him that the obliging Priscus might have an understanding with Narses, but Justinian was confident of the eunuch's devotion to himself.

Theodora held a very different opinion of young Priscus, who flattered Justinian by acting like an efficient slave in the presence of an all-wise master. By the reports of her spies, Priscus sold information to more than Narses, and had put his bribes so high that he had been able to buy an interest in the Greek shipping firm handling the Carthage trade, as well as in vineyards and estates in the growing suburban port of Nicomedia. When off duty, this Priscus was accustomed to leave the city by the Bucoleon harbor near her old house. There he entered a sailing caïque as if for a pleasure sail, but in reality to cross to Nicomedia and to change his dress on the way, to land on the Asia shore as a wealthy promoter who was surprisingly well informed of the economic plans of the Sacred Palace.

When she informed Justinian of this double life of his chief secretary, he shook his head moodily. Priscus had become necessary to him. Most officials accumulated money, now that vast sums passed through the Sacred Palace, in spite of the new laws. Unlike Theodora, Justinian depended on his executives. Laboring as he did in his study, he had to trust the execution of his plans to others. During the emergency of the war he could not rid himself of the tools with which he worked. Besides, he understood very well that the empress meant to rid him of the necessary Economist, John of Cappadocia.

"I shall have Priscus' accounts examined," he said, "and the fiscal court will take back his—estates, in fines."

But he put off doing it, and Priscus disappeared.

When the chief secretary entered his caïque one evening, he found strange Greek boatmen hoisting the sail. As soon as they left the harbor lights behind, these silent boatmen brought him, instead of his fashionable businessman's suiting, a coarse monk's robe to put on. They explained, in answer to his questions, that it would be necessary for him to wear it because he was being taken to a monastery on an island. It was not a jest, Priscus discovered, because they began to clip and shave the hair from his head, to prepare him to take the vows of poverty and obedience to the laws of God.

"Who sent you?" Priscus demanded, wondering how much he would have to pay his captors to ransom himself.

"One whose slipper you have never kissed."

Priscus decided to go to the monastery and remain there as long as Theodora lived.

By then Theodora had a flotilla of her own. She needed an

array of small ferryboats to ply between the city and the palace she had persuaded Justinian to build across the strait. A summer palace, she called it—necessary for her health and his relaxation. Since Justinian seldom left the Sacred Palace long enough to venture on a boat, this resort at Hieron became her private preserve. From its marble-paved terraces her people could watch the lights of the distant city, and no one could watch them. Down at the bottom of the garden small breakwaters sheltered her boats from the Bosphorus current, and from observation.

After a while Theodora moved most of her court to Hieron. From Grand Chamberlain to guards, however, she brought over only those she could trust.

So it happened that she saw the comet in the sky that spring from the secluded terrace of her new home. The comet traced a fiery arc across the vault of the sky. "It's like a swordfish," Theodora commented.

Immediately she asked the patriarch, Anthimius, the meaning of the apparition. He had been smuggled across the water to Hieron where he could walk, secure from observation, in the garden at night. Like Justinian, he shook his head moodily. "The sign, my daughter, is of evil to come."

"What evil? And to whom?"

Cosmas had explained to her how the vault of the firmament hung suspended over the flat floor of the earth, and Theodora remembered because it seemed like a circus tent, studded with the stars instead of bangles. The nature of the stars, however, did not interest her so much as the fiery sign in the sky.

After considering the immensity above them, Anthimius agreed that it was like a tent, for the prophet Isaiah had said it stretched out *as a tent to dwell in.* Yet the blessed David said of its Creator: *He that hath founded the earth upon its own stability.* Thus the very earth upon which they sat at the moment rested only upon the staying power bestowed by the Lord. The things of the earth, then, existed in this invisible balance—the fish with water, the birds with the air, plant life with the soil, animal life with the plants, and man in balance with all.

Silently Theodora agreed. You adjusted yourself to life in a precarious kind of balance, and survived.

"Theodora Augusta," added Anthimius, nursing his staff, "this fire in the sky is unearthly. It has broken through the balance of created things, for it is not true fire, nor a star, nor a new sun. We must expect that because of it the balance upon earth will also be broken very soon. When that occurs, earthquakes may rend the ground, or the sea will rage in its depths, or plague may visit the sons of men for their sins. Our poor wisdom cannot foretell the nature of a divine visitation, but I think there is so much sin in Constantinople across the water that plague may appear there."

Theodora reflected that they would be safe in Hieron. But it seemed to her that calamity had already begun with the war.

The war was spreading like a conflagration. In his study Justinian brooded over the miscarriage of his plan. Five years before he had planned simply for Belisarius to take back Italy from the Ostrogoths and their Philosopher. Now, in the spring of 539, hordes of Franks and Burgundians were swarming into the valley of the Po, slaying the inhabitants and dying themselves of disease caused by heat and strange water.

And all the way to the east, other barbarians were moving restlessly toward the wealth of the imperial cities. He had anticipated this, and strengthened the line of forts along the Danube. But Slavic tribes slipped between the forts. The skeleton garrisons could not leave their ramparts.

His secret intelligence brought him evidence that the desperate Vitigis was sending gifts and envoys to all such peoples beyond the borders, urging them to strike against the empire Vitigis was fighting. These savage peoples accepted

Justinian's payments but no longer sought to be hired as federates; they sneaked forward to loot instead.

Then when the grass gave good grazing and the crops stood high, a new power broke through the line of the Danube. Led by an aggressive khan, and yielding to the pressure of the Avars behind them, the Bulgarian Huns swept down into the Macedonian mountains and through Greece as far as the Corinth isthmus, where walled fortification stopped them and turned them aside toward Constantinople itself. This savage clan fed on the country, killing adult people, driving off women and children as slaves; it emerged from the valleys of Thrace and approached the Long Wall built by Anastasius.

The only available field army was in northern Italy, where Belisarius warded off multitudes of ax-throwing Franks while he penned the Goths closer into Ravenna. Justinian urged Belisarius to hasten.

Then he received news that appalled him. Somehow Vitigis had smuggled emissaries through the empire, in the train of Syrian merchants, to reach Ctesiphon, the reigning city of the King of kings of the Persians. After that the tidings from the east were altogether bad. Sittas, the veteran commander there—he who had married the actress Comito, sister of Theodora—was killed; in the Caucasus the Armenians staged one of their periodic revolts. And at Ctesiphon the Persians listened to the arguments of the Gothic spokesmen, that they should not wait for Justinian to regain the empire of the Middle Sea and the west but should strike him now in the east while he was weak. Breaking the perpetual truce on a slight pretext, the Persian monarch prepared to do just that. And there was no semblance of a Roman army in the east.

Faced by catastrophe where he had least expected it, Justinian wrote again to Belisarius to return. Almost with resignation he heard that the Huns were across the Long Wall. That line of stonework offered no obstacle unless tens of thousands of trained men were on it. Methodically the nomads began to glut the towns within sight of Constantinople.

Moving under cover of night, some of the Huns penetrated to the water barrier of the Bosphorus and crossed over on rafts. The imperial troops were bunched up behind the fortifications of the towns, whither the country people fled.

From the roof of the Hieron palace, Theodora and Anthimius beheld the glare of fires where villas burned; refugees streamed into the garden. Both the exiled patriarch and the actress-empress were accustomed to calamity. Theodora had herself rowed over to the private dock of the Sacred Palace and sought Justinian where she knew he would be, in his study.

Sleepless as usual, he was walking about among the piled reports, while the Constable and other members of the strategic council waited outside. He thought the Huns would follow their nature and retire with their loot and multitudes of captives. It was a terrible raid, but still a raid of a few thousand horsemen. The east, he believed, held the greater danger. Not for three generations had the eastern front been broken through. Belisarius must take his army there without further delay.

"The Persians are religious fanatics," he muttered. "If they find a route open, they will fancy their Sun-god favors them, and rush in. If they are opposed they may be doubtful and go away. Belisarius knows how to make them doubt."

"Then why," the empress asked viciously, "did you send him into the west?"

While she watched the puffy, wearied face, he stumbled against a stand and upset a vase that broke. Paul, the captain of the silentiaries, entered without a sound. Clumsily Justinian bent to pick up the pieces, while Paul knelt to aid him. It was ridiculous to watch the emperor and his officer gathering up bits of useless pottery.

In that moment a fantastic thought came to her. Upon the brilliant Belisarius the fate of the empire seemed to rest. Yet the awkward, tired man fumbling with a broken vase was the only staying force in the empire. Of all the thousands in the

Sacred Palace at that difficult time he was the only one who cared nothing about himself.

"Justinian," she said quietly, "you will conquer."

The tide of ill fortune seemed to ebb then. In the autumn the Huns began to withdraw, while their horses could still graze on the crops. The Persians, after assembling a marching host, waited for the heat to lessen in the desert stretches. Belisarius pressed closer to the defenses of Ravenna. And the besieged Vitigis smuggled through Gothic spokesmen, who offered Justinian terms. To gain a pledged peace they would give up Italy south of the Po and surrender half their treasure. (All Germans from the time of the legendary Nibelungs hoarded their gold, jewels, and silver as a treasure instead of spending it like a civilized people.)

At the same time a courier arrived from Belisarius with the advice not to make terms with the Goths, as they were on the verge of defeat.

In his study Justinian could not understand his general's warning. Ironically, the Goths and their king had taken shelter in the one impregnable point of Italy—where the last emperors in the west had sought security. Ravenna, embellished by the great Theodoric—whose victories had been pictured in mosaics on the church walls—lay barred from the sea by shallows, sand bars, and marshes. Its walls rose from the dank encircling marshes, infested by frogs, as mosquitoes infested the air. The very bodies in the cemeteries were said to float away, while living men became inanimate. No army could occupy the swamps that surrounded the walls, where only a single causeway led to the city. So situated, Ravenna had never been captured by assault, and with the formidable Goths inside it Justinian saw no way by which the Roman army could win it.

The terms offered by the Goths suited his plans. Vitigis, humbled and confined to the upper valley of the Po, would offer a buffer to the encroaching Franks. Belisarius, released, could be moved in time to the east.

His strategists agreed.

Without delay Justinian signed and sealed the written treaty of peace, and advised the Gothic envoys to take it direct to Vitigis before allowing Belisarius to see it.

There he made his mistake. If he had journeyed himself to Italy, the result might have been very different. Not since the month of the triumph of the Vandal war had the emperor talked face to face with the master of his armed forces. Inevitably, the Goths accepted the terms and notified Belisarius of the treaty which he was to sign, to end the war.

Belisarius refused to sign it or to end the war. This stirred instant suspicion among the Goths. They had encountered trickery before from Constantinople; they feared Belisarius and lost trust in a signed piece of parchment which he refused to sign.

This had no sooner been reported to the Sacred Palace than an agent who had slipped out of Ravenna arrived on a fast galley with incredible news. The Gothic army had offered its allegiance to Belisarius *as emperor in the west.*

The strategists were aghast at their blindness. Here was the explanation of the mystery! How astutely the commander of the army had misled them, getting them to recall the devoted Narses, ridding himself of the intransigeant Huns! The rest of the army he held, as it were, in the palm of his hand. How quickly Africa and Sicily would hail him as emperor. How eagerly the Roman people in Italy would carry out the orders of their liberator, backed by the familiar military power of the Goths. Of course the Goths would rather share their lands and treasure with Belisarius than to surrender them to the eastern empire. Naturally Vitigis had agreed to become Belisarius' vassal in the north; it would be easier than to remain leader of a defeated and disappointed people.

Fragile little Narses smiled bleakly. They had been warned,

he pointed out, by himself. The triumph in the Hippodrome had turned Belisarius' head. And there was nothing they could do about it.

To Theodora it seemed to be a stroke of genius. She could laugh heartily at the simplicity of it. In it she saw the handiwork of two women. Matasuntha, his Amal bride taken by force, hated Vitigis. Had not Matasuntha burned the warehouses that stored the grain of Ravenna, to deprive Vitigis' men of food? Then, too, Belisarius' wife must have egged him on to it.

Only Justinian remained stubbornly incredulous, muttering that Belisarius would not break faith.

The next courier, early in that spring of 540, came in from Ravenna itself. A young officer, flushed and cold with stage fright, faced Justinian on the throne and laid at his feet a strange old crown. He identified himself as captain in the comitatus of Belisarius. The crown he brought back was the crown of Valens, taken from the emperor's body at the rout near Hadrian's City, eight generations before.

The war was over, the boy officer declared, with Vitigis captive, the Goths disarmed, Ravenna taken without the loss of a single Roman or Gothic life. Belisarius now held all Italy, from Sicily to the Alps, in the name of the Ever August, Ever Victorious Emperor Justinian.

Slumped in his throne, Justinian listened.

Belisarius had tricked the Goths, the boy explained eagerly. Really, he had believed that the only way to overcome the Gothic people was to defeat them utterly—not to make terms that would leave them a nation in arms across a river. So when they offered him an emperor's crown, he pretended to accept it, and discussed it much with his wife, who wanted it done—in order to be overheard. He replied to the delegation of Goths that he was willing to rule over them, and under his rule no man should be put to death or deprived of his home or belongings. But Belisarius thought the public proclamation of his crowning should be made in Ravenna itself, before the old Roman cathedral. To this the Goths agreed.

Then Belisarius called a council of his officers, showing them a copy of the treaty signed without his knowledge in Constantinople. He asked them whether Italy should not be regained entire, instead, and the Goths subdued entire, if it could be done without loss. And they agreed.

It was so simple, after that. Belisarius riding in full regalia along the causeway, with only his comitatus behind him, and riding through the open gate, between the crowds of Goths—where the women, seeing for the first time the small and dingy figures of the Roman soldiers, spat into the faces of their men, for submitting to such poor specimens—riding on to the cathedral, taking Matasuntha under his protection, as a princess of the Amals—and announcing to all that he ruled not as emperor but as commander of the emperor. He said he would take the crown of the dead Valens that the Goths had treasured.

That was all. He put Vitigis under guard. His comitatus held the streets, while the Goths, waiting to greet him as emperor, were scattered and leaderless. The other Roman units were marching in, while ships brought fresh grain up the waterways. Belisarius only had to post a guard over the Gothic treasure. The populace hurried to ease its hunger with the corn from the Roman ships.

Now Belisarius waited to consolidate the conquest, before bringing back Vitigis with his nobles and Gothic volunteers, and the treasure of Theodoric, as he had brought back Gelimer and the Vandal hoard.

When the officer had finished his report, Justinian placed a chain of gold around his neck, named him a patrician, and wrote hastily to Belisarius begging him to come east at once.

For the third time—as once before in Africa, and again in Sicily—Belisarius was recalled before his work could be finished, in Italy. Extricating his comitatus as best he could from the war area, he embarked for Constantinople with it. Disordered Italy he had to leave in the hands of the remaining Roman officers. But precious weeks had been lost.

When he walked for the second time in triumph down the Mesé at the head of his veterans, the crowds of Constantinople roared his name. For he escorted not only the conquered Gothic king and nobles but the standards of the Roman legions that had been lost to the Goths at Hadrian's City. The crowds–Gelimer and the Vandalic nobles among them–realized that this was a greater triumph than the conquest of Africa. Yet the greeting to Belisarius lacked the exultation of the earlier triumph. There was no ovation in the Hippodrome, no display of the great Gothic treasure. Justinian gave order that it should not be shown.

But the crowds in the streets rendered Belisarius a silent tribute. "They took delight in watching him as he came forth from his house each day. His coming forth was like a crowded festival procession." So the admiring Procopius reported. "He was tall and remarkably handsome . . . in desperate situations he showed himself untroubled, and after great success he did not give way to indulgence. At any rate, no one ever saw Belisarius intoxicated."

Justinian's congratulations were brief and cold. Ironically, this should have been Peter Sabbatius' greatest hour, for the Middle Sea had come back to Roman rule, with ancestral Rome and Ravenna. In his signature now, Peter Sabbatius could truthfully inscribe himself as victor over Goths and Franks. He had restored the vital points of the western empire.

But in those last months the empire had been wounded in the east. Justinian showed Belisarius the record of the calamity, the thousands of people lost to the Bulgarian Huns, the total of towns ravaged and villages burned, the crops destroyed and cattle driven off.

That much Belisarius had been prepared to see. It startled him to read on, to the calamity on the Persian front. The

King of kings had broken through, devastating towns that had been secure behind the frontier while Belisarius and Sittas had served there.

"Antioch!" he cried.

The second city of the empire had been overrun by the Persian army. The Persians were through to the shore of the Middle Sea that had not seen an enemy for centuries.

"Khusrau went in swimming in the sea," observed Justinian tonelessly, "to mock us."

To Justinian, the planner in the palace, it seemed as if Belisarius had brought about the catastrophe by disobeying orders. To Belisarius, the soldier in the field, it had been unthinkable to abandon the battle that had gone on for four exhausting years, in the months when he had had the end in sight. The emperor had never been close to the reality of the battle over the sea, while the commander had not understood, because he could not understand, the strategy of the empire.

Again Belisarius was hurried with his wearied comitatus from Constantinople, to meet a much more powerful enemy. This time the strategists in the Sacred Palace did not demonstrate to him how his task might be performed. Justinian would look at no more maps and would listen to no plans of retired generals or intelligence agents. He had gambled on peace to keep the Persian front quiet, and had lost. There was no way to demonstrate how the host of the King of kings could be turned back. He simply trusted Belisarius to contrive some way to do it, with five thousand men.

To Theodora the news from the east had been a stunning blow. Her city of Antioch, with the girls of the Daphne grove and the priests of the venerable Severus, had become a charnel house of blood and misery. She resented the hollow victory in the west, and for the first time she believed that Belisarius could be dangerous.

VI

Justinian—the Redeemer and the Demon

AFTER FOURTEEN YEARS OF RULING FROM THE SACRED PALACE, Justinian began to realize that, while he had succeeded in carrying on the war abroad, he had failed in his government at home.

The wall map in the strategic conference chamber showed him the recovery of the empire in the west. Upon it the names of liberated areas had been neatly marked—although no longer by the skilled hand of his secretary, Priscus. The Dalmatian coast. Tripolitana. The Prefecture of Africa. The Prefecture of Italy. The islands of the western sea. The coast of Visigothic Spain (where his ships had taken in the trading ports like Malaca and Cádiz [Gadira], and had ventured out into the swell of the vast, mysterious Ocean).

In imagination Justinian voyaged himself, out to the limits of his new empire beyond the sea. It was again the Mare Nostrum of the Romans. But he felt a thrill of pure delight when he rode forth in a procession from the Chalké. Beyond that gate lay a new city, his creation.

The burned area, the scar of the Nika revolt, had vanished. That remarkable team, Anthemius the architect and Isidore the engineer, had filled the area with lustrous marble. Wide boulevards stemmed out from the Junction, and the baths of Zeuxippus shone with light at night. Off in the cypress trees rose the lovely St. Irene, dedicated to peace. Close to it stood the asylum for mental incurables and paralytics that Theodora had persuaded him to add to the imperial gardens.

As Justinian rode, wearing the diadem, past the Augusteon, he listened intently to the cadenced cry of the crowds: "Fortunate is thy city, Thrice August! Merciful is our emperor, chosen by God."

Beneath him lay the artificial lake of the great cistern with its columns majestic as the courtyard of a palace—a miracle of construction, flowing with the water of his aqueduct. Secretly he believed that his people should compare him to Solomon the king, who had given the first temple to Jerusalem, or at least to Augustus Caesar, who had found so many brick fronts in ancient Rome and had left them marble façades.

When he dismounted at the portico of the Great Church all sense of pride left Justinian. Humbly he walked into the structure that had been raised for the Lord God. So vast it was, he felt insignificant, moving across its pavement that gleamed with the blue of cornflowers in the grass of earth. . . .

Procopius, returning from the war, had been startled when he first entered it—"more noble than those structures which are merely huge, it abounds in sunlight and in the sun's rays reflected from the marble. Indeed you could say that the radiance comes from within it . . . so marvellous in its grace, yet terrifying in its seeming insecurity. For it appears somehow to float on air rather than rest on its base."

What was the secret of the Great Church? Anthemius, who designed it, could not tell. Procopius insisted that no matter how often you entered it the feeling was the same. It might be that here God loved to dwell.

Secretly Justinian planned an addition to the Augusteon in the form of an heroic statue of himself. He had thought out just how it should appear, mounted of course on a fine horse going forward, the bronze figure steadfast in ancient Roman armor, but without sword or shield. (To suggest that, as a warrior, he sought to wage no battles.) One hand would hold the globe of the world, surmounted by a cross; the other hand would stretch out toward the horizon. Together they would indicate how he sought to bring the world under one empire and one church and one law. So far he had not discussed the heroic statue with his architects because they would tell Theodora about it, and she might try to make it seem ridiculous.

About that time Justinian did an odd thing. He ordered that his portrait, stamped on the medals of the empire, should no longer appear in old-fashioned Roman armor. Apparently he did not wish to appear henceforth as the soldier-emperor of the earlier portraits.

As it was, the patricians who frequented the stone benches of the Augusteon complained of his new buildings. "He spares no expense," they observed, "and spares no property belonging to any of us."

Just then he was sparing no expense in rebuilding Antioch entire, after its destruction by the Persians. By the plans of his engineers the course of its river, the Orontes, would be shifted, and new squares and market places erected on marble paving. The new city would be larger, and he had decreed that its name be changed to God's City—in spite of Theodora's objection that the name of Antioch could not be changed to Theopolis by his order. She had given fifty thousand pieces of gold, her year's income, to buy marble and columns for Antioch.

While he had improved the stonework, as it were, of his dominion, Justinian realized that he had managed to do little for the people. In the eager first years before the Nika revolt he had contemplated a new social order. Liberty, he stated by decree, was a natural condition of man, and slavery an artificial state, contrary to nature. He had planned a new era for the toiling citizens of Constantinople, by raising the inferior classes and lessening the privileges of the magnates. What had he managed to change?

His Praetor of the People sent patrols through the streets to chase robbers, move on idlers, and break up gatherings. His regulation of labor did not prevent the stalls of the Street of the Weavers from laboring after dark by lamplight; children still tended the charcoal furnaces in the Street of the Silversmiths; peasants in the outlying farms still would not leave the fields of their fathers, to work as enlightened laborers. No, slavery and labor existed within the families as before.

He had attempted, after a fashion, to foster individuality among his myriad subjects. He had tried to make an end of the privileges of parties like the Blues and Greens and classes like the magnates. This concept of a subject as an individual came from Egypt and Theodora's lands. It was not understood in Constantinople.

He had made a new code of laws—"to bring about decent order in the state by law"—to put a lawbook, as it were, into the hands of every man and woman, so that they could claim their civil rights. They were still afraid to go into court unless they knew what the judge would decide. "They hold fast," Tribonian commented cynically, "to the right of bribery." Yet rumor related that Tribonian—now named Quaestor of the empire—could only be approached by bribing the officials at his door. Certainly the new Quaestor had acquired a palatial mansion decorated with ivory and gold, and enlivened with a mechanical organ. Living next door to the millionaire Tribonian, Anthemius the Architect—no respecter of persons—had arranged huge mirrors in the sun so that the glaring sunlight was reflected through all Tribonian's windows and the curtains had to be drawn. When Tribonian went to law and obtained a decision against the mirrors, the resourceful Anthemius arranged an earthquake beneath the Quaestor's house.

These new laws enfranchised women, granting them rights in divorce and in holding property. They set penalties for homosexuality and the castration of boys. Yet the laws did not perceptibly change human nature in a dozen years.

Women who appealed to Theodora, however, found that they had no need of a legal court. She had a way of putting male plaintiffs to open ridicule. One of her girl protégées she had married to a young patrician, who had talked about it afterward in the streets, complaining that his bride had proved to be no virgin. Until the day when he was escorted to a public square by strange servitors and made a spectacle by being tossed in a blanket. "Whereby most of the men," Procopius relates, "were very glad to remain silent and escape such scourging."

Observers noticed that this empress who had been a hussy would follow her own judgment in deciding an appeal, while the emperor would listen to petitioners kindly, and try to make them carry out his new laws. "As if," wrote Procopius, envying the pair on the twin thrones, "he had put on the imperial garb only upon the condition that he should change everything else into another form."

Justinian's attempt to revive what had been best in the past was failing. His praetors and consuls belonged to the Rome of the monuments. Their silver gleaming chariots and the fasces carried before them no longer stirred the crowds that shouted when the riders of Belisarius passed with a shrilling of flutes. New nations were taking shape within the old imperial frontiers. An Armenian chieftain of shepherds would not change his treatment of his wife by the Latin warning of a Corpus Juris; an Arab seaman, peering through the heat haze for the white loom of Sinai, would not heed a Roman navigation law.

By the ancient Latin Way of Italy, on the summit of Monte Cassino, the younger Benedict of Nursia was building a cloister on the site of a pagan shrine. Into this refuge men were escaping from the war-devastated cities. They were sheltering themselves in the cloister, raising their food in the fields, in a way of life that would soon be known as the Benedictine.

While the son of Sabbatius failed to understand his Roman people, he had a good grasp of Roman economy. Patiently he had delved into the records of the past to learn when that economy had prospered, and when it had failed—especially in the time of his two heroes, Augustus and Constantine.

Under Augustus the small upper class of patricians had held the posts of responsibility and had contributed most to support the state, while the large lower class of plebeians had kept on with the farming and the soldiering. Matters had gone well enough, despite the extravagance of half-insane emperors and the blight of slave labor, until a change had taken place in the economy itself.

The eastern portion of the new empire began to manufacture most of the things that Rome craved but could no longer pay for. Byzantium and the Syrian coast, for instance, had an abundance of such luxuries as sandalwood, sugar cane, pearls, camphor, and silk. Moreover, the east manufactured the finer textiles, glassware, dyes, and all the stuff of higher civilization. And the ships of eastern ports brought such prized articles to the Tiber.

To pay for all this Rome sent gold eastward, and it did not return. Then a human migration set in toward such affluent cities as Alexandria and Antioch, and it, too, did not journey home again.

So Constantine the Great had merely been following the drift of his gold and people when he moved his capital to the New Rome where stable industry prevailed.

Because of that, the Roman economy remained, more than two centuries after Constantine, the only financial system of the civilized world. Benedict himself could hardly have conceived of the things—taxes and money—that were not Caesar's.

Now in Constantinople taxation was based on property. Every fifteen years a land survey took census of people, crops, belongings—even dogs being listed. After the assessors closed their books inspectors made checks from time to time. Individuals without property paid a head tax (although not in the great cities, which tended to be favored over the country areas). Customs officials collected duties at the ports. Exactors took in a tax in kind for supplying the army—such as corn, wine, oil, meat, and horses.

This heavy taxation caused people to leave their farms and ships—some even burned their trading and fishing vessels—to go to the cities. It also caused the more distant cities like Alexandria and Antioch to rebel against Constantinople where the taxes originated.

Under Anastasius the much-detested *chrysargyron,* or gold-tax-on-profits, was repealed. It had taken a percentage from the earnings even of prostitutes and—so the rumor ran—beggars. The civilian tax bureaus were kept separate from the military administration, and certain classes like teachers or war veterans had exemption from taxation. Another class, however, managed to exempt itself. The wealthiest magnates, with immense landholdings in fertile districts like Cappadocia, had come to hire their own bodyguard armies, staffs of collectors, and even judges. It was not easy for the government bureaus to assess and collect taxes from such powerful nobles, who usually had influence in the senate chamber and the Delphax dining hall. Yet Anastasius left a gold reserve of 324,000 pieces in the treasury when he died.

The state had several monopolies, including the important papyrus reed (to make papyri sheets from which paper was to get its name) from Egypt, and the rare purple dye that came from the seacoast of Syria. It also controlled the salt-works and metal mines. The most vital monopoly was gold. From mining and imports from such coasts as Colchis—of "golden fleece" fame—the precious metal flowed into the treasury. Export of it was forbidden. (Frontier posts maintained a rigid check on articles passing in and out of the customs.) Most of the gold went to the mint to be coined. These Roman solidi were the standard of the world, as then known. Being the currency of international trade, they found their way to the huts of the uncouth Anglo-Saxons, and eastward as far as half-legendary India. The new Frankish kings minted coins with Roman identification on the reverse. Even the cultured Persian *shahinshahs* kept a tacit agreement to use the Roman gold coins, and minted only silver money for themselves. (When Justinian paid gold bullion to Ctesiphon for his "perpetual truce" he stipulated that the gold was to be used for ornaments, not coinage.)

While he had been a free agent under Old Justin, the son of Sabbatius had fallen to wondering why this system, that ground out revenues as steadily as the mills of the ancient gods, failed to fill up the treasury. So much was collected, according to the books. So little materialized in actual coin or goods. He had asked John the Economist what proportion actually got to the treasury, and his financial wizard reported impassively, "One third."

This startled Justinian and roused his indignation. The zealous emperor and the wily Cappadocian worked out together the causes of the leakage and wastage, as follows:

The government bureaus were overrun with personnel. (Numbers should be cut down and working hours lengthened.)

High officials were apt to speculate with the goods passing through their hands. (No official must buy or sell property in bulk.)

Such officials often kept private prisons; they charged fees for documents and even sold jobs to bidders. (Paper work must be cut to a tenth, no fees charged, and no money taken for employment.)

Routine services like the post, with its stations and carriers, had been expanded, to put more individuals on the pay roll.

In similar fashion military garrisons far from the city drew pay for men long dead or deserted. . . .

"More people live off taxes than pay them," declared John.

Justinian and John devised drastic remedies for the leakages of money. John, with his gift for money-getting, also suggested new sources of revenue. By making grain a state monopoly, they could squeeze out speculators and add profits to the treasury. John thought up death taxes to soak the magnates he hated, and a withholding tithe on soldiers' pay. Hence Justinian's exhortation to officials: "Gather in the full total of taxes due."

His aim was the protection of the peasants against the wealthy landlords. Now until then there had been a live-and-let-live climate in the empire, over such vital things as money and taxes. Officials and citizens had adjusted themselves to the mutual need of gathering in money to support their families, if not to accumulate wealth. Justinian's idea disturbed this comfortable climate. It seemed clear to him that the government should economize, while the citizenry paid in full. And he showed great persistence in carrying out an idea, regardless of its effect on individuals. "Pay up the taxes promptly, because our large undertakings cannot be managed without money."

To cut expenditures, at first, he scaled down allowances for army supplies and pay; he asked for a reduction in the livestock kept by postal stations (which resulted—so the story runs—in asses taking the place of the old-time horses and mules). Expensive transport agencies were eliminated, so that peasant women were seen carrying in grain and fuel that had been carted before. In the provinces he cut down government personnel by doubling up duties. In so doing he tried the dangerous experiment of merging civilian and military duties in a new type of official called the Exarch—a sort of general agent. "In certain of our provinces, the civil and military governors quarrel steadily with each other, not about how they can benefit but about how they can more oppress our subjects. So we have thought it right in these cases to combine the two charges to form one office, and to give the old name of praetor to the new governor."

He named the new-era official a *praetor Justinianus.* Promptly the popular voice christened the new executive a "Justinian." So his idea-men came to be "Justinians." These early attempts at public economy, with heavier popular payment of taxes, resulted in the lowering of the spirit of the armed forces, which Belisarius felt, and the near-failure of military supplies, which was not entirely the fault of John of Cappadocia, and the outbreak of the Nika revolt, which Justinian himself experienced at first hand. Nevertheless, since his ideas seemed to be right, he persisted in them.

The Vandalic and Gothic wars—at least as handled by Belisarius—paid for themselves at first by the captured treasure-trove. But the rebuilding of burned Constantinople—especially of the Great Church—became a drain on the treasury. So John the Economist, recalled to duty, was asked to find new sources of revenue, and did so with ingenuity.

Fortification along the now menaced frontiers was intensified, but the army gained little more money or men. Then the raid of the Bulgarian Huns wrought havoc in the harvests as well as the towns, and the Persian invasion destroyed Antioch, while driving off a portion of the people to be settled at Ctesiphon.

In Italy, also, the appearance of the imperial tax collectors, soon after Belisarius left, discouraged the native Romans, who had been under the strain of the war. The chief of them, a certain Alexander, called "The Scissors" for his ability in clipping gold coins, tried to impose the fixed scale of taxation on Goths and Italians who had not known heavy taxation. This resulted in unrest, with which officers like Ildiger and John the nephew of Vitalian could not, or would not, cope. Perhaps the financial blight in Syria, which had not been invaded for long generations, had more vital consequence.

Until then, whatever happened in the west, the revenues from Egypt and Asia Minor and Syria had sustained the empire.

Despite his setbacks, Justinian went on with his building and his new era of government. Time would remedy the damages, he believed, if the revenues came in. "The people must make an increased effort," he declared, "to carry on the war." And he pointed out an untouched source of revenue in the wealthy magnates who had escaped the general taxation. "It is shameful," he announced to the "Justinian" in Cappadocia, "to relate how lawlessly the managers of great estates march about with bodyguards behind them, and throngs following after, on their way to rob common folk of everything." And he accused the Cappadocians truthfully of bribing themselves into ownership of government grazing lands and herds. "The land owned there hitherto by the treasury has become practically all private."

Naturally the foremost Cappadocian was John the Economist, whose estates ran along entire rivers of that mountainous land, whose palace in the city housed a bevy of girls and boys with an imitation forest of jewel-leafed trees upon which mechanical golden birds sang during the feasts.

"Would any but a madman," he roared at his friends, "ask you to keep your hands clean, while you conjure up a new Antioch, and put monasteries for monks on Mount Sinai, with foreign legion forts in Africa? I understand at last why our pious Augusta wanted a madhouse here in these very gardens. Our ever victorious Augustus will have a luxurious cell, with running water and a view over the sea."

Cappadocian John—now "John, Most Glorious Praetorian Prefect of the East, ex-Consul and Patrician"—could fling barbed slander at his sovereigns. As a power in the empire second only to Justinian, he did not fear to do so.

Nor did he try to keep his hands clean. Grim tales were told in the streets, of how he extracted money. A patrician who had refused to report his private jewels for assessment was tortured in the cellars of John's palace, until he walked back to his home, collected his valuables, and threw them at the feet of the Economist without a word. A veteran, assessed a tax of twenty solidi, swore that he did not have the coins to pay. Kept under abusive questioning by inspectors, he said he would go with them to search for the money, which he had mislaid. When they went into his home after him they found the ex-soldier had hanged himself to a beam. Such reports as these were brought to Theodora by her spies.

"The Empress Theodora hated John above all others," Procopius wrote in the history that he kept secretly. "While he gave offense to the woman by the evil he did, he was not minded to conciliate her by flattery. Openly he set himself against her, slandering her to the emperor . . . when the queen discovered this she intended to kill the man, but could not do it because the Emperor Justinian set great store by him."

Justinian, in fact, refused to dismiss John again. No one else, he insisted stubbornly, could keep the treasury from breaking down during the crisis.

The day came when Theodora decided that she or the Cappadocian must fall. She had more than personal hatred for him. As Praetorian Prefect, John now held unlimited power over her eastern homeland; he opposed the rebuilding of her beloved Antioch; he wore the imperial purple. If Justinian should sicken, John could seize the palace, backed by his hired comitatus.

Well aware of his danger, the truculent Cappadocian guarded himself carefully. At night his bodyguards shielded him, and John himself inspected his sleeping quarters closely, waking often at night to look out the entrances. But the woman from the circus never made use of assassins, or poison.

Instead, Theodora invited Antonina to talk with her.

When Belisarius departed for the Persian frontier—"taking the hopes of all Romans with him," Procopius relates—he left his wife in the city. At the moment Antonina must have been torn by resentment at Justinian's cold treatment of the hero of Italy, and by envy of the beautiful Theodora. The two actresses were consumed by ambition; both craved the luxury of their palaces; neither had inhibitions to restrain her. But Theodora was the more adroit in dissimulation, and knew, besides, exactly what she wanted done.

In facing Antonina, across a table laden with nectared fruits, after dismissing the white-robed silentiaries and the graceful girls of the propoloma, she availed herself of a very useful weapon. She told the truth about John of Cappadocia.

Distrusting Theodora profoundly, Antonina felt a familiar stab of jealousy, finding herself waited upon as the guest of the empress. She also felt certain of the obvious truth that, by removing John the archpolitician, she would aid Belisarius, who had no instinct for politics. With John out of the way, Antonina herself would be a step nearer the Sacred Palace when Belisarius returned with the army . . . he would contrive another victory, of course . . .

But how, she wondered, could John be removed?

Theodora explained that John had a weakness. He acted on impulse. If the gifted wife of the Most Glorious Belisarius could persuade him to talk carelessly, Theodora could arrange for witnesses to overhear them.

When she ransacked her mind to discover any harm in the suggestion, Antonina found none. Skillfully, then, she made use of the one person John cared for, his adolescent daughter. The girl was attached to Antonina, and the actress confided in her how brutally Justinian and Theodora had treated her husband. By playing upon the girl's devotion to her father, Antonina brought their confidences to the point where it seemed as if both could free themselves from the domination of Theodora by removing the erring Justinian from the throne. This, Antonina admitted, could not be done by Belisarius alone or by John alone. But what if they agreed to act together? Would it not be according to the will of God, to bring about such a happy release for everyone?

Thrilled by the confidence of Antonina, the girl almost ran to her father. Would he not talk with the wife of Belisarius himself, as she had done? John, who would have believed no one else, believed his daughter's story. Even his alert suspicion could not trace Antonina's rather foolish proposal to Theodora. In any conversation Antonina would incriminate herself equally with him. Besides, John was very curious to learn how far Antonina would go. It would be something new to hear of the white knight Belisarius in the role of a court conspirator.

With the adolescent girl acting as go-between, Antonina set an evening for the conference, in the garden of Rufinianae, a new country villa of Belisarius. Thither she would go herself on the pretext of preparing to journey on, to join Belisarius.

"It was perfectly done," Theodora assured her. "And our gratitude will reward your devotion."

Before the day of the rendezvous, Theodora approached Justinian with one of her customary sarcasms about the exactions of his Economist. The man was capable of stealing the throne!

Justinian, as usual, wanted the name of her informant.

"The wife of the Illustrious Belisarius."

"You would discover a plot in every whisper."

"Perhaps." Theodora seemed to dismiss the matter, which was not characteristic of her. "In any event, Caesar will discover if there be truth in it."

Her departure left some uncertainty in Justinian's preoccupied mind. After making inquiries, he sent a warning message to John through a mutual friend. "Under no conditions hold any secret talk with Antonina."

This intrigued John, rather than deterred him. It seemed desirable to hear what the emperor did not wish him to hear. But he had his bodyguards follow him to the meeting.

Theodora had chosen her witnesses with inspiration—Marcellus, a guard captain whose thoughts did not stray beyond duty, and Narses. They had an armed following and her authority to arrest John if they heard treason discussed, and to kill him if he resisted.

So, as if upon a theater stage, John made his entrance to the dark garden where the two officers waited behind a trellised wall, with John's swordsmen concealed behind him. Antonina played her part well; John spoke his mind freely; the listeners heard sufficient treason to bring them out with a rush. In the free-for-all that ensued in the dark, one man was wounded—Marcellus. When he heard Narses' voice, John broke away and escaped with his guards.

If he had gone straight to Justinian he might have escaped entire. In his excitement he remembered the emperor's warning with new dread. If Antonina had baited the trap for Narses, he decided too quickly, Justinian must have ordered the trap set. And he fled to sanctuary in a church.

With the testimony of Narses, and the wound of Marcellus, and the flight of John to act upon, Justinian could only strip the Praetorian Prefect of all rank and confiscate his property as belonging to a traitor. In sanctuary, John was ordered to accept priesthood—he refused to be ordained as a bishop—and exile to a church outside Constantinople. Probably Theodora suggested it.

Very quickly Justinian showed signs of relenting. Much of the culprit's wealth was restored. Since John had as much more concealed, he began to live luxuriously as a priest—he had refused to perform the offices at the altar, and so had kept open a way of return to his civil eminence. Wagers were made in the city that the Cappadocian would shed his robe for a cloak again.

Sheer luck prevented this. A fellow priest who disliked him intensely was murdered by a band of youths, and John was suspected of arranging it, although he had not done so. Stripped of his robe and his belongings again, he was compelled to stand naked as any felon, to be beaten with scourges by strange inquisitors who paid no heed to his whispered offers of gold.

Between scourgings they demanded all the details of his misspent life. Writhing with pain and humiliation, John could not think up answers to satisfy his examiners.

"Who sent the extortioners after the twenty solidi of the ex-soldier . . . who ordered the skull compressor for his torture chambers . . . why did the Ephesian dancer drown herself in the garden pool of the Praetorian Prefect of the East?"

Only one person would have sent such anonymous questioners with scourges in their hands; Theodora alone could have uncovered so many details of John's past life.

She had not finished with him. By due sentence of the judges in his case the property he had gathered back during his exile in church was confiscated again. One robe, a coarse garment worth only a few obols, by Procopius' estimate, covered his nakedness. So clad, he was escorted to a vessel by new and unnamed guardians who did not reveal his destination. At sea he was obliged to beg bread and water from the crew. Then, put ashore at a port in Egypt and given a beggar's bowl, he was allowed to glean scraps of food and copper coins in the streets before being shut up for the night in a cell.

So the beggars of the waterfront where Theodora had starved beheld the daily spectacle of the ex-patrician, ex-consul, ex-Economist competing with them for charity. This ended the career of John of Cappadocia but did not break his spirit. Before long he made an attempt to regain favor with the treasury by reporting how a clique of Alexandrine businessmen escaped their tax assessment.

Antonina had played her part so well, and had received such evidence of favor within the portals of the Sacred Palace, that she went with great anticipation to be given her reward when a messenger of the empress announced that a rare gift awaited her in the Daphne court. There she found Theodora seated in state, with the Mistress of the Palace, the Chamberlain, and the coterie of patrician girls attending her.

When Antonina made her formal prostration, she decided that Theodora had never seemed more piquant and benign. Even upon the throne seat the empress conveyed a sense of sly intimacy between them. Actually, she spoke as if in discreet jest. "Dearest patrician lady, yesterday a single pearl came to my hand, such as I had never seen before. Do you wish to see it? If you do, I shall show it you—nay, I shall not begrudge it you."

The solitary pearl, Antonina reflected swiftly, must be magnificent, if Theodora would exhibit it before the court. And surely Theodora meant to offer it, or she would not have hinted at begrudging it. Of course! It would be a queenly gesture, when the wife of Belisarius admired the pearl, to make a gift of it. "Indeed," murmured Antonina, "if it please Your Clemency to show it."

Theodora nodded to a eunuch, who went to draw back the curtain from a door. Out stepped Theodosius.

A splendid chlamys covered his familiar figure, eagles of woven gold shone on his cloak, emeralds gleamed in artificial leaves of ivy around his notable blond hair. At sight of the man with whom she had been too intimate, whom slander had named her pretty golden boy, Antonina was speechless.

The silent dignitaries of the court watched her. Theodora waited. (The empress, it was learned later, had summoned back Photius, the son of Antonina, who had been protected by Belisarius after his accusation of his mother; questioned at Hieron, Photius had disclosed where Theodosius hid himself in a monastery; the order of Theodora had brought the nearly desperate godson of Belisarius from his hiding to the Sacred Palace unseen.)

Theodora waited. Rigid in the too massive jewels of her

court dress, beet-red with humiliation and surprise, Antonina forced words from her lips. "I thank—my benevolent Mistress, the ever merciful Augusta."

No one answered. Perfumed and anointed, Theodosius was tongue-tied. When Antonina turned blindly and stumbled out, he followed.

After receiving her gift, Antonina hurried out of Constantinople to journey as fast as carriages could take her to Belisarius in the east. She did not dream again of advancing herself in the Sacred Palace.

Having heard of her scheming against the Cappadocian and her public appearance with Theodosius—for rumor ran more swiftly from Byzantium than couriers could travel—the downright Belisarius was angered and resentful. For a while he kept Antonina shut up like a culprit. But she appeared more devoted to him than before, and she no longer nagged him about his lack of ambition. Procopius says she practiced magic arts on him, but the Syrian historian had begun to write with a venomous pen of the great ones above him. Before long Antonina resumed her place at Belisarius' side. She never forgave Theodora, but she never tried again to match her wits against the empress.

The troubled Photius and the unhappy Theodosius were held in loose confinement. Apparently at liberty in the city, Theodosius discovered that he could not leave it. Drinking too much wine in the heat, he died of dysentery soon thereafter. Antonina took no observable notice of his death. Her son Photius found that he could not leave the walls of Hieron, where he served Theodora as hostage and informant. That is, he escaped twice to neighboring sanctuaries, only to be brought back by her servitors. The third time he got away to Jerusalem, and there took the tonsure of a monk. Either Theodora was content to have him in that distant sanctuary, or she was too preoccupied to bother about him at that point.

Those who feared her—and their number increased daily—whispered that the cellars of her summer palace at Hieron engulfed unfortunates who crossed her will. The cellars had been made into cells. Yet it was a strange prison from which everyone managed to escape. It was a strange torment they endured there, from which they emerged without scars on their flesh but with new personalities . . . so "Theodora's punishments" became proverbial in the city, with the emperor's new "Justinians."

With the passing of the Swordfish comet, a fresh phenomenon appeared. It was in the water this time, a monster from the mysterious outer Ocean. Invisible most of the time in the depths of the Marmora and Bosphorus, the great monster emerged to disport itself around rowing caïques or pleasure barges, often overturning the small vessels and drowning their occupants. Natural scientists from the university said it was a leviathan known as a whale, which must have strayed from the deeper seas.

The whale could not be wounded by arrows or javelins. The Constantinopolitans christened it Porphyrius—either in memory of the famous charioteer or after a famous philosopher. By some illogical process of thought, gossip connected the misdeeds of Porphyrius with the unpredictable attacks of the mistress of Hieron across the water. Then, as tragedies seemed to multiply throughout the empire, many reflected that the fire of the comet in the sky and the leviathan emerging from the deeps must be tokens of the Revelation foretold in the Scriptures in which the great Harlot should come to land riding upon the Beast, to judge all men.

This popular concept of approaching doom was based upon an actual fact. Until then Justinian and Theodora had appeared to oppose each other readily enough. In consequence the different factions and suppliants had appealed to the sovereign favoring them. Those sentenced by the emperor felt sure of a hearing before the empress. This dualism of control had brought about a healthy political climate, clear of clouds of oppression. Now it began to appear that the exquisite woman who spent so much time resting her body in bed and refreshing herself in scented baths—or so it seemed—really controlled events. Theodora had become more implacable than Justinian, who spent eighteen hours a day in judging and deciding.

And that was true.

"In their trickery," Procopius relates, "they pretended openly to take opposite sides, but secretly they were in full agreement with each other . . . this tyrant who seemed so good-natured and Theodora who was actually most harsh and exceedingly difficult."

Now cunning, by Constantinopolitan standards, was a virtue. To have been hoodwinked by the distinguished couple on the throne would have amused and pleased the sophisticates of the city. But to realize at long last that Theodora had become a force behind Justinian's tearing down and rebuilding of the state made them afraid. What was her ultimate purpose?

Apparently she had merely the venial sins of Augusteon society—ambition, lust for power, avarice for gold. Yet Vigilius, her confidant of earlier years, had become the Pope in Rome; contrariwise the patriarch Anthimius, exiled by decree, was her confidant just across the water; the powerful John of Cappadocia had become a beggar in Africa. More than that. Pillar-sitting saints of the east came to Constantinople at her bidding. A hermit, Zooras, stalked through the Sacred Palace to the very thrones of the sovereigns, calling them sinners who gave no bread to the starving folk of the eastern deserts. Neither of the imperial pair tried to hush the hermit. Theodora listened without emotion, but Justinian fainted—or fell into a coma. "What can you do with such an overbearing man?" he asked when he recovered.

"Theodora's monks," they were called. They took their stand at the Venus statue in the square of the brothels, and harangued the aristocratic clients; they pulled their lice-infested robes over the clean red garments of prostitutes; they sat in their dirt at the Baths of Zeuxippus, calling upon the bathers to take thought for their souls; they appeared like skeletons at feasts in Chrysopolis, spoiling the taste of the spiced pheasants.

What was the woman after, the feasters wondered, who already possessed everything that a human soul could desire?

In that spring of 542, Theodora was more than forty years of age and certain that she would never give a son to Justinian. It was fantastic that she should have a young grandson, the child of her daughter in Alexandria, who could never be brought to her side, even at Hieron. At the same time she felt that she was losing her influence over her husband, who had begun to treat her as a rival. In her anxiety the woman of the circus found only two things to consult, her mirror and Anthimius.

More often now she crossed the water to escape from the palace and the sight of the Hippodrome. In the garden of Hieron she could rest, while the old Anthimius put aside his books to listen to her. Being still exiled and under anathema, he had no one else to tell him of happenings outside the garden. Oddly enough he had become greatly interested in the obscure happenings close to him, like the rising of the constellations at night.

"Must one thing be destroyed," she asked, "to give life to another? Must that always happen?"

"My daughter is too wise to believe that."

"Your daughter is too stupid to believe otherwise, at this moment."

But the patriarch could never cease to think of her as the empress who sought for guidance. There were four angels of destruction, he declared, who visited the earth—bringing invasion, war, pestilence, or famine. "Invasion has come and passed. War has come."

"Does not one bring the other?"

At every question, Anthimius fingered his beard or glanced longingly at his Scriptures, from which he longed to quote. "One may follow the other, at God's will."

There was hunger enough in Italy, where the stubborn Goths had taken up arms again. Yet Justinian urged his generals to press the enemy.

Philosophers in Greece had argued such questions, she supposed, since the time of Aristotle. Justinian had closed the ancient School of Athens, because it was pagan, and seven philosophers had fled from the empire to refuge in Persia.

If he could be kept from enforcing his will. But he believed that the will of the emperor must prevail over other powers. Having created the new laws, he confiscated the property of lawbreakers, and in so doing put himself above the law. Justinian persisted in keeping within his walls. Confined in that manner, his tiring mind could not always sift out flattery and lies from the unceasing reports and petitions brought in to him.

Always she had one question to answer. Was Justinian so pent up with his thoughts that he lost his grip on realities? (He issued so many decrees that could not be carried out.) Was he a prey to megalomania? Did he imagine, now, that he could shape the minds and control the actions of the Oecumenon, the known world? Watching him in the Sacred Palace, she often thought so.

Or had he become like an ascetic of the desert—taking so little food, burning from his mind all qualities except imagination alone? The imagination that pictured a world united under his hands, vivified by one religious faith, obedient to one law? When he sat motionless in the Great Church where the dome rose above him like the vault of the night sky, it seemed to her that this was the case.

She did not know the answer to the question. It was only certain that, visibly weakening, he would not alter what he imagined must be done.

"The pestilence," she told Anthimius one evening, "has begun."

Reports of it came first from the Red Sea shores, then from Alexandria. It seemed to move inland from the coasts, so it must have been carried by ships. It passed down the Nile, then jumped to the Palestine shore, entered Jerusalem, and advanced up the Syrian coast.

Superstitious tales ran before it. Invisible specters, the people said, entered the streets striking down one human being after another. The deaths made no pattern. In their secluded gardens, the rich would be touched by the specters; devoted souls in prayer before the altar might be stricken by the pain and swelling.

"Men became mad and attacked each other," a refugee from Syria told Theodora. "And they went out into the mountains to die."

Anxiously Theodora asked the opinions of physicians. They could only shake their heads, pointing out that since nurses and the buriers of the dead usually escaped, it could not be contagious. The plague seemed to move upon an invisible transit of its own. The physicians added that Constantinople was well protected against disease.

Refugees, however, were coming in from Alexandria. In her anxiety, Theodora sent to Egypt. There the daughter born to her before her marriage had matured and given birth to a boy, now a half-grown child. When the pestilence increased, instead of lessening, Theodora sent her servants for the boy.

It was simple enough to have an unknown youngster transported with other fugitives, to an island near the city. No one, in Constantinople as yet, knew Theodora's secret.

She confessed it all to Anthimius, who considered it in silence. There could be no place, they both knew, for a child in the palace who was not of Justinian's blood.

"Because of its sins," he said, "this city will not escape. The pestilence will not cease until it has come within these gates.

What happens then will be according to the will of the Lord."

The first consequence of the plague, however, was the change in the war in Persia.

This war in the east, to which Belisarius had been summoned, was no more than an episode in a conflict of eleven centuries. It was really not so much a war as a meeting of peoples.

In almost legendary times the first onrush of the Iranian nomads had carried them into the west, over wealthy Croesus, on the shore of the Middle Sea. These formidable Iranians were an "Aryan" (Iranian) people like the Greeks who held that sea. In the ebb and flow of conflict and trade between them, the Iranians easily assimilated Hellenic culture and became known to the Greeks as Persians after the founding of their far palace city, Persepolis. There had been efforts of one antagonist to crush the other—the Persians under "Xerxes" penetrating once as far as Salamis, the Greeks under Alexander of Macedon sweeping through the Persian domain as far as India. Under the Parthian dynasty the easterners sorely troubled the early Roman emperors with their Parthian arrows.

After the emperors moved to Constantinople, and the Persian Shahinshahs to Ctesiphon by the Tigris and Euphrates, the ebb and flow intensified. Religion divided the antagonists when the Romans became Christians, the Persians remaining Zoroastrians. The unfortunate Julian tried to reach Ctesiphon and died in the deserts after the breakup of his army; another emperor, Valerian, became captive to a victorious Persian. But neither antagonist had been able to master the other for long. The military conflicts had been no more than episodes in the long clash and mingling of the two human entities.

"We are like two lighthouses," a Persian ambassador once declared in Constantinople, "that illuminate the world."

So it was. Did not the three legendary Magi, the "kings of the east," journey to Bethlehem? The laws of the Medes and the Persians became proverbial before Justinian's Code. A Persian prince designed Theodora's house—and sons of reigning monarchs had been sent to the rival court for an education. Even the Vandals copied Persian dress. In the Sacred Palace the staging of visual splendor imitated similar effects at Ctesiphon, where the carpets were woven of silver ornaments upon a gold ground, and emeralds gave color to artificial lawns, and strings of pearls formed streams. From Diocletian's time, emperors had clad themselves in Persian regalia. Their courts adopted the prostration of the land of the Magi. Insensibly, in so doing, these eastern emperors had assumed some of the semidivine attributes of the "King of kings, companion of the stars, brother of the sun." The emperors had become something more than human. The very crowds of the Hippodrome, with nostalgic memory of a vanishing democracy, saluted them as "chosen by God."

At the same time Roman culture penetrated the east. It was carried thither mostly by refugees. There the self-exiled Nestorian Christians followed their own way of life and built their churches patiently through Asia—exerting an influence on the Asiatics as great as the conquest of Alexander. They could do so because the Zoroastrians were, in the main, tolerant of other religions. Khusrau himself welcomed to his court seven of the pagan philosophers, fugitives from the School of Athens, closed by Justinian. With them the Persian monarch debated the ethics of Aristotle, and when the fugitives became homesick he sent them back with honor to Justinian, requesting his rival not to persecute them. (Justinian agreed not to do so, and kept his word.)

The chivalric, impetuous Khusrau differed entirely from the cautious, stubborn Justinian. The Roman was defensive, the Persian—who spent his life in the saddle—aggressive; the Roman was monarch of an empire built upon ancient democracies, clinging to the coasts of the sea, sustaining itself laboriously by trade; the Persian, greatest of a dynasty, the Sassanian, ruled by sheer ability a feudal dominion, agricultural, intensely religious, confined to the inland continent. The Sassanians declared, "There can be no power without an army, no army without money, no money without agriculture, and no agriculture without justice."

Khusrau Anushirvan Adil was called "The Just." And he was the son of a philosophic reformer king. He had accepted the "perpetual truce" with Justinian to put his own house in order by purging Mazdakean communist cults internally and driving the dangerous White Huns eastward. While thus engaged he jested with Justinian, who did not appreciate jests. "Surely you owe us part of the Vandal treasure, because without our aid in keeping hands off, you would never have got it."

Justinian sought earnestly to keep the peace along the stabilized frontier between them, and to keep trade circulating. But Khusrau turned to war in the Caucasus, and rode to Antioch. There, magnanimously, he left one gate unguarded for civilians to escape, and he sent back a captured relic, a fragment of the True Cross. He said this was no use to him, and the Christians revered it. Besides, he meant to ride to Jerusalem himself, very soon.

Behind his gasconades, however, Khusrau the Just had a purpose well understood by the son of Sabbatius. The Persians were attempting to break through the Roman frontier cordon to the seas—to the Euxine itself—by forcing the passes of the Caucasus, and to the vital Middle Sea at the Syrian coast. Khusrau's bath in the Middle Sea had been symbolic of his intentions. At the same time he mocked the Romans by building two suburbs near Ctesiphon which he named "Antioch" and "New Rome" while he populated them with captives taken in the war.

Then Justinian sent Belisarius east to stop Khusrau. There was nothing else he could send.

The champion of the Romans returned warily to the shattered eastern front in those years of decision, 540–542. As usual, he faced a seemingly impossible task.

Ahead of him, the frontier itself stretched from the no-man's land of the far northern steppes where roved the Hunnic tribes, through the Caucasus mountain barrier, with its restless Armenians and Lasgis, down through the foothills of the great trade routes, into the southern prairies and deserts—six hundred miles of geographical difficulties. Only in the foothill region did the Romans have forts like Daras to guard the roads.

To defend this vast terrain Belisarius could dispose of barely twenty thousand men, who could be counted on to stand against the Persians only behind walls. Against him the Persian *Asvaran* or noble-born knights might send horsemen in overwhelming numbers, who could ride around fortifications.

As usual, he could rely entirely only on his veteran comitatus. The Vandal and Goth volunteers—good swordsmen in a stand-up affray—sickened in the eastern heat, and drank heavily to ease their sickness; they could not be prevented from plundering and killing off the native population, at a time when Belisarius was trying to rally support from Arab tribesmen and Armenian villagers.

Perhaps Belisarius lacked the inspired decision of his early years. Before moving at all, he delayed to call the leaders of his motley command into council, to explain what he wanted done. It was seldom done as he wanted. A flying column of tribesmen that he sent into Persian territory vanished with its loot. When he concentrated around the key forts of the Daras-Euphrates mid-region, a strong Persian army bypassed him, to forge through the Caucasus heights and capture the port of Petra—"The Rock"—on the vital shore of the Euxine. The loss of Petra alarmed Justinian.

Once Belisarius showed a flash of his old skill. Crossing the Euphrates, he maneuvered and tricked a Persian stronghold into surrender. (This success caused Khusrau to return to the Caucasus.)

But at Constantinople Justinian heard complaints that Belisarius remained inactive and afraid to face the army of the Sassanian king. The loss of Petra rankled. When Belisarius continued to hang back from the enemy, Justinian summoned him to the palace for consultation.

Early in the spring of 542 the sun telegraph flashed its warning from the river Euphrates to Constantinople. The mirrored flashes spelled out their message: Khusrau was on the march up the river, with Jerusalem as his objective.

At the time, Belisarius was in conference with Justinian. The emperor ordered his general to safeguard the Holy City. There were no troops in Palestine.

Immediately Belisarius started back over the six hundred miles of post roads to the Euphrates. Through the Bithynian hills he raced, changing horses as he reached each station. On the highlands by Ancyra (Ankara) he changed to chariots drawn by picked teams. Leaving the forested valleys of Cappadocia, he sped southeast, through ancient Armenian towns. Then he came out on the post route made centuries before by Persian kings for their own convenience.

In the foothills he met a courier from Buzes and the other army commanders. They reported that Khusrau was advancing up the Euphrates in great strength; since they did not know where he would strike, they were concentrating around the defenses of Hierapolis, between Edessa and Antioch, where they hoped that Belisarius could reach them without being cut off by the Persians.

Now Hierapolis lay along the defense line of the foothills through which Belisarius was hurrying. Far to the south, the Persian army could swing west across the great plains, grazing on the fresh grass not yet killed by summer heat. By following a caravan track to the south it could reach Damascus and enter Jerusalem unopposed.

To check Khusrau's march at this point, Belisarius would need to drag his mixed command out of its defenses, down into the Mesopotamian plain. That might well be the end of his field army of twelve thousand men. To do so at all, the anxious generalissimo would need to cope with the apprehensions of his officers and the dread of the still unseen Persians that permeated the small army.

Under the circumstances, he must have pondered carefully the wording of his answer to the commanders at the Hierapolis base—to cajole them and sting them into action. "If Chosroes [Khusrau] were moving against another people than the Roman, your plan would be well chosen for the greatest possible safety. But since he is advancing against a territory of the Emperor Justinian that is without defense, you will accomplish nothing except to save yourselves without a fight. And that would rightly be called not salvation but treason."

Belisarius added that he was proceeding direct to the caravan town of Europos on the lower river, where they should join him by forced marches. Whether the commanders were reassured, or stung, by his irony, they hurried after him.

Picking up contingents of armed men as he rode, Belisarius reached the desert junction point of Europos before the Persians. By then he had his veteran household troops with him. But scouts brought in the worst possible news. Khusrau had crossed the river below them. The Persian engineers, it seemed, had demountable bridges in which the wooden portions fitted together on iron hooks. The host of many tens of thousands was on the Roman side of the river. No obstacle, not so much as a canal, remained between the invaders and Belisarius.

The situation being as bad as it could be, Belisarius put a bold face on it. By sending a mounted regiment to maneuver along the far bank, he made a pretense of closing in on the Persians—the one thing he could not do, in reality. Then he waited to see how the Persians would react. (Meanwhile the regiments from Hierapolis were coming in hourly.)

Khusrau was younger and more impulsive. With the Romans showing themselves at Europos, he could not turn aside toward the coast. Not, at least, without learning something of their strength and purpose. Why were they marching heedlessly into the open, instead of staying as usual behind their walls? When he discovered that Belisarius awaited him at the caravan junction, he became more thoughtful. He longed to know what kind of a man this legendary Roman might be, and what he meant to do in his peculiar situation.

Quickly enough Khusrau's royal curiosity impelled him to send an envoy to find out. Selecting an experienced diplomat, Abandanes, he instructed him to make some excuse for a conference, to study the Roman commander face to face, and to observe the equipment and spirit of this odd northern army.

With a spasm of hope, Belisarius agreed to receive the Persian. Then, rapidly, he arranged his stage as he had done at Rome with the Goths, to bewilder a diplomat-spy. Hurrying out a way from Europos, he set up a festive pavilion on a rise, and gave careful stage directions to his veteran but varied followers.

When Abandanes was led within the Roman lines he beheld no military formation at all. On one side of him dark horsemen cantered about, making test of their bows. What would they be? the envoy of Khusrau asked. Moors, his guides informed him, from the farthest corner of the earth. On the other side blond young giants clustered about packs of dogs, trying out their javelins. And what were these? Vandals they were who, like the Moorish riders, had been conquered by Belisarius and had come to serve him. What were they all doing? Why, preparing to hunt gazelles and hares.

No one except the guides paid any apparent attention to the Persian. When he neared the pavilion on the hill, Abandanes found himself in the midst of other hunters, and athletes pitching the stone and wrestling. He learned they were Goths, Balkans, and Dalmatian Slavs, at their usual games. All seemed physical giants—Belisarius had picked them for size—heeding only their sports.

Fierce-looking riders on shaggy ponies swept near, tossing a ram's head from hand to hand—the only game the Herulian Huns knew. Climbing the hill, Abandanes could not guess the number of soldiers because they extended to the sky line. There might be a thousand of them or a hundred thousand. Not a helmet or breastplate could be seen, except on Belisarius.

In silvered cuirass, pleated satin kilt, and plumed half helmet the celebrated general amused himself with his staff over fruit and wine. Courteously but without great interest he greeted the Persian, who studied every line of his face. When Abandanes assumed a herald's portentous tone, to declare that his lord the King of kings had failed to receive ransom and tribute payments of gold from Caesar (Justinian) and so, therefore, had entered the dominion of Caesar with his armed strength, Belisarius interrupted as if not wishing to be bothered by official business.

"Then Choesroes doesn't act at all like other men. If they have a dispute with a neighbor, they discuss it first, and if they aren't satisfied, then they go to war. But he comes into the midst of the Romans the first thing, and afterward begins to suggest a peace."

"He has said no word about peace."

"Then why did you come here?"

The shrewd Persian, not caring to explain that, wondered audibly why Caesar's illustrious general should occupy himself with trifles, instead of the vital matter of the safety of his land. At this Belisarius laughed. Why shouldn't he and his men amuse themselves? The Roman Empire lay safe within its encircling forts; it was Khusrau who had endangered his state by venturing himself among the Romans.

The bluff succeeded. Abandanes reported to his king that he, at least, had never seen such soldiers, and their leader surely had courage and sagacity. Moreover, the Romans made such display of heedlessness, they must have great strength at hand. If so, then Khusrau had really endangered himself by advancing among them. It might be well to delay while doing as Belisarius suggested, sending terms for Justinian to accept or not.

The upshot of the comedy of the Roman-army-on-holiday was that the Persian army disengaged itself and retired slowly down the Euphrates. Belisarius, who had no least wish to prevent it, followed warily. Recrossing the river, Khusrau abandoned the campaign, taking a hostage from the Romans as pledge for the truce interval while he negotiated with Justinian. He also sacked a Roman town on the far bank, an incident that had its consequences later at Constantinople.

Procopius, who was very glad to be still alive on the bank of the Euphrates, asserts that this maneuvering of Belisarius was a greater triumph than the victories in Africa and Italy. Jerusalem was saved. While Belisarius' prompt action undoubtedly turned the Persians back with the wreckage of only one town, the actual cause of Khusrau's withdrawal must have been tidings that the plague was spreading through the Roman lands.

It entered the province of Syria. By trading ships and highways the pestilence moved inexorably toward Constantinople. (The rats that slipped from the grain ships at the docks of the Golden Horn carried the bubonic germs into the streets of the city; the lice and fleas of the caravans infected human beings along the roads.)

Waiting on the Euphrates frontier, for once relaxed and reasonably free of care, Belisarius was surprised to receive a peremptory summons to return with Buzes and other commanders to conference in the Sacred Palace. The order had the familiar signature Justinian Caesar Imp. traced by a woman's hand. The couriers who brought it said the plague had seized the capital and Theodora Augusta was issuing orders.

Belisarius discussed it with his staff and then obeyed the order.

"The disease reached Byzantium in the middle of the spring when I happened to be there. It seized on people in this manner: they felt a sudden fever, when just wakened from sleep or even when walking about. Being of a languid sort, this fever roused no suspicion of danger at first in those afflicted, or in the physicians attending them. But sometimes on the same day, sometimes on the day following, a bubonic swelling developed in the groin or armpit, or beside the ears or on the thigh. There followed either a deep coma or violent delirium. Those under the coma forgot their friends and seemed to be sleeping. If they were cared for, they would eat without waking; if not, they would die at once."

So Procopius records the symptoms of the most terrible plague for a thousand years of history.

"Those who were delirious could not sleep, and those attending them suffered from exhaustion. They could not easily take food, and if water chanced to be near, they wished to fall into it. If neither coma nor delirium came on, the bubonic swelling decayed and the sufferer died . . . suffering came without warning, and recovery was due to no external cause. Only when the swelling rose and a discharge of pus began, it happened that many escaped.

"At first each man attended to the dead in his house. Afterward, people shut themselves within their doors and would not answer calls. The dead were carried to the edge of the sea and flung down. Slaves wandered about without masters, and masters lost the service of their slaves. Nay, those who in the past delighted in baseness, shook off their unrighteousness and zealously practised the duties of religion. Then, if they had the disease and rid themselves of it, they went back to their former baseness, feeling themselves safe.

"During this time you seldom saw a man in the streets. Within this city, so provided with good things, starvation was running apace. For those still alive kept sitting within their houses. Nor would you see one wearing the [official] chlamys, especially after the emperor became ill. Yes, in the city that held dominion over all the Roman Empire, men wore the clothing of private citizens."

While he was able to do so, Justinian had tried to check the spread of the pestilence. Physicians could suggest no remedies—or rather each one had a different thing to try. Military patrols were sent out from the palace, and funds were allotted for food. Supply ships no longer put in. For a while trenches outside the walls served for graves; then the officer in charge of burials had bodies thrown into the towers of the fortifications across the harbor. When the wind blew from that quarter it brought the stench back into the city. After a time the soldiers reported that they handled five thousand bodies a day.

It seemed as if the pestilence must diminish after that, but it took its toll for two months more, and in the end perhaps half the inhabitants came down with it. Yet in spite of the urging of Theodora and Narses, Justinian refused to leave his palace.

Hieron, secluded in its gardens across the water, escaped with few deaths. But the thronged labyrinth of the Sacred Palace became a nightmare abode. A lamenting crowd pressed against the brazen Chalké to beseech aid from the emperor. The marble benches of the Augusteon were deserted. In the corridors guards strained their eyes to catch a glimpse of the elusive demons that seized upon their victims and passed on.

Justinian discovered that it quieted the throngs to see him close by. Always the emperor had been visible only as a withdrawn figure, robed and raised above them. Not that the throngs had any knowledge of the human being, Peter, son of Sabbatius. They recognized only the wearer of the diadem, resplendent as an archangel.

Understanding that, he sat long hours in the hall of audience; daily at a fixed hour he moved in procession out of his doors through the crowds to the wailing mass at the portico of the Great Church. He walked afoot without his diadem, with incense swinging, beside the patriarch to his seat in the church, to the chant of the Trisagion. He heard the agony in voices below him: "Give bread to thy people . . . drive out the demons of Hades that have entered thy city . . . let the saints witness, we have suffered enough . . . Thrice August, give aid!"

By sitting there, hour after hour, Justinian gave the only aid he could.

The days disturbed Theodora. Leaving the palace after the long ordeal in the Great Church, she entered her canopied barge, to be borne to her own house. There the lowered voices of her women, the touch of massage, the fresh smell of growing things relieved her exhaustion. The messengers from the island assured her that her young grandson was vital with health, and safe from contact with fugitives from the city. It seemed as if in crossing the water each day she escaped death. She hated to go back.

Yet in Hieron, shaped by her will, with every flower bowl and brazier made to suit her taste, she began to feel narrowed within herself. She could not understand her malaise. It was like the feeling of the earliest days in the Hippodrome when no man protected her or wanted to hire Theodora the mimic.

Anthimius only shook his head. It mattered not at all where she might be, he thought. In the desert, water could flow from a rock, a cloud might give covering, and a fire give light in the night.

When the messenger came from Narses to inform her that Justinian lay ill with fever, she went to her sleeping chamber to sit alone for a while by the alabaster screen of the window. In the soft blued light from the gossamer curtains she relaxed in the quiet that she craved. Then she called her handmaidens to dress her for public appearance without diadem, jewels, or veil. She told the Mistress of the Wardrobe that they would move into the Daphne.

There she took her place by Justinian's bed.

After the third day of vigil there were signs that Justinian would recover. He had fallen into the coma of the pestilence; the swelling discharged and his flesh became wet instead of dry with the fever. Narses, who had waited like a grieving dog in a corner of the chamber, curled up and slept.

Each day Theodora took Justinian's place in the procession to the Great Church. As he had done, she listened to the exhortation of the people. So long as they had sight of the imperial power, they held to an irrational hope, although the bodies were still carried by the thousands across the harbor to the deserted suburb.

Justinian came out of his coma too slowly. It was evident that his speech and memory had been affected. Although only the silentiaries of his chambers, the physicians, and officials like Narses had been allowed knowledge of his sickness, the news seeped out into the streets.

There the rumor became connected with the presence of Theodora. Gossip had it that the empress called in a mad hermit who laid a spell upon Justinian, depriving him of speech and thought. "She who has given birth to no child," women added, "must have the curse of God upon her."

When the death toll for a day dropped below three thousand, Theodora sent announcers through the streets, to cry that the pestilence was ceasing and Justinian recovering. She had the Hippodrome thrown open, with choruses, dancers, and mimics to perform.

The day came when she went with Justinian to the imperial box, taking the throng in the Hippodrome by surprise. During the tumult of rejoicing few observers noticed that Justinian said nothing, barely moved, and was led out very quickly.

"He will take the salutation of foreign envoys, commanding officers, and some petitioners in the morning audience," she assured the anxious Master of Offices. "Then, between us, we will hear their urgencies. We will promise that the Augustus may pass upon all questions, and the next day we will return the answers ourselves."

It was possible to do this, because Justinian needed only to be seated on the throne, which could be obscured with clouds of incense, during the silent prostration. Then the veils could be let down before him, while he was carried back to his bed.

On her part Theodora had little sleep. Never before had she been called upon to play so many roles, and to pretend so much. Within the hours of an afternoon's sitting in the Triclinium she might have to flatter the pride of an ambassador of the beastlike Avars, who brought silver talismans and expected to be laden with bar gold; she might show herself implacable to the revered priests of the Franks, and then listen sympathetically to missionaries from Colchis who protested the waging of the war Justinian would not cease, or match wits with a silk-clad satrap of Persia, who took any refusal as a slight to his King of kings, while he schemed for advantages.

Then there were the anxieties. Peter Barsymes, the clever Syrian who had taken the Cappadocian's place, complained that the generals in Italy were using their troops to seize local property claimed for taxes by the Economist, Alexander the Scissors; at Alexandria, after the passing of the pestilence, a mad revivalist drew mobs after him by preaching the end of the world.

There was the horror of starvation setting in. . . .

One face that peered up at her in awe seemed faintly familiar. Middle-aged and plump, it was still the face of Cosmas the Merchant, who had nursed her in her wanderings. She cut short his labored salutation. "Good Cosmas, did you ever find the mountain of the sun?"

Surprised, he stared at the beautiful empress. No, he had

not managed to do that, Cosmas explained; but he had fared to the mountains of the river Nile that flowed out of Paradise; his eyes had beheld uncanny giraffes, and dragons of the sea. Evidently he did not recognize Theodora. And Cosmas himself now wore a monk's robe. "Lo, I have discovered," he cried, "the hidden shape of the earth."

"Where did you see that?"

"Here in the treasury I beheld its form. For the earth hath a *Christian* shape. Verily it is flat as the golden table of the temple of Jerusalem, and the stars light it from above, like the flames in the candlestick.

"And the wavy line around the edge of the holy table," Cosmas added triumphantly, "is the sign of the Ocean that surrounds us."

In the evening, when she had bathed, Theodora would sit by the sick man, telling him what turn events had taken, while Narses listened closely. Although Justinian could speak only a word at a time, he seemed to have his old memory for details. By degrees she learned to sense his thoughts from his intonation.

"Petra," he repeated over and over. The Rock. The seaport of the Caucasus. It must be recaptured and the passes of the Caucasus freed from Persian control. And this at a moment when Peter Barsymes had made excuse to hold back the pay of the army posts on the Italian front.

"St. Vitalis," Justinian whispered, pointing to the mosaic pattern of the sky on the ceiling. The church of St. Vitalis in Ravenna. It was ordered to be stripped of the mosaics that pictured the religion of Theodoric and Arian Goths. Justinian wanted portraits of himself and his empress to be set in the walls.

Slyly he touched her face with his plump finger, murmuring something about a gift. Some gift for her? He persisted in saying the word, until she understood. It had been years since he had called her "My Gift."

As time went on, both she and Narses realized that, while

Justinian was recovering his physical strength, his mind had altered. Although it seemed tenacious as always, some intensity had gone from it. He did not leave his sleeping room willingly. Instead of reading voraciously as he had been accustomed to do, he liked to have her read to him.

"What if he had died?" Narses dared to ask once, when Justinian slept. "Would the senate and the army have supported you, or Belisarius?"

That night Theodora signed the order recalling the Master of the Armed Forces and his generals from the east.

No other man in the empire had served Justinian so unquestioningly, or had less mind to conspiracy. That very integrity made Belisarius dangerous. With Justinian gone, or incapacitated, the victorious soldier might listen to new advisers who would find him an ideal figurehead to set upon the throne. Ironically, the very wars begun by Justinian made it necessary for Belisarius to succeed him. Nor would Antonina have the least mercy for the widowed empress.

Theodora struck swiftly. Upon the arrival of the commanders, she had Buzes escorted to Hieron and confined, for her questioning. Evidence had come to her, she assured Buzes, that he, a soldier of an old aristocratic family, had talked in the east of a successor to the Caesar of the empire. Of what successor? And what had been planned by whom?

The startled general insisted that he had merely talked about the pestilence, and what might happen in Constantinople. After a while he admitted that he and several others—but not Belisarius—had agreed that they would not accept an emperor chosen in the city during their absence.

With this one detail confirmed, Theodora kept Buzes out of communication (to release him after two years, a silent and cautious man). To her court in the Sacred Palace, with Narses at her side, she summoned Belisarius.

There she played the part of a judge, cold and implacable. Belisarius had been the one man she admired—once, in the

House of Hormisdas, she had thought of him as a husband. Knowing him to be courageous, and having no valid evidence against him, she struck at his pride, and took from him what he valued intensely, his hold upon the army.

She denied the rumor that there was a charge of treason against the Master of the Armed Forces. Yet there remained the facts that he had hesitated to take action in the east, had allowed the Persians to break through the Caucasus, had looked on while Khusrau laid waste a Roman town, and had talked foolishly with his staff officers.

All of this Belisarius denied instantly. If the empress, he demanded, had doubt of his courage she should allow him to return to his duty and he would satisfy her.

In answer Theodora showed him an order from Justinian, depriving him of his eastern command, confiscating his property, and taking away the comitatus of veterans that had followed him for twenty-four years. Upon Belisarius himself no direct punishment was inflicted. Thereafter, he might go where he wished and do what he pleased.

Perhaps the most savage blow was the loss of his household troops. The famous comitatus was to be divided among the high officers—even the eunuch commanders—in Constantinople by lot. Theodora made certain that Belisarius could not muster again the personal army he had trained for a generation. Acting as she did, with Narses at her side, most spectators would conclude that she had been influenced by the eunuch.

Without protest, the conqueror of Gelimer and Vitigis accepted his demotion. In the desolation of the epidemic's end, there was no public outcry. People merely wondered at seeing the first general of the empire going about the streets without escort or fife-playing.

The grieving Procopius, however, had much to say, behind barred doors. His hero had been made a victim of the hatred of the wanton Theodora, who had cast a blight on the empire. Had not the evil demons of the plague appeared where Theodora had sinned unspeakably in those early years of wandering over the very track of the plague, from Alexandria to Constantinople?

Perhaps because Belisarius accepted disgrace without complaint, but more probably because she had planned it so from the first, Theodora appeared to relent. An imperial messenger walked into his house and handed him a written decree. "You are the best judge of your actions of the past. Now all charges against you are dismissed. Your life is safe. Let your actions show what your feelings are, in truth, toward us."

At once Belisarius asked to be restored to command in the east. This Justinian and Theodora refused. They returned two thirds of the soldier's property—the equivalent of six thousand pounds of gold, by tally of the assessors. With that he was allowed to go back to the army. Not, however, as Master of the Armed Forces, but as Constable. This, being little more than a court title, gave the brilliant soldier no direct command.

Because the conflict in Italy had gone from bad to worse, Belisarius was ordered to go there to raise an army. His comitatus that had been the spearhead of his campaigns was scattered over the map. No amount of gold could restore the matchless body of men.

As she had meant to do, Theodora had broken down the legend that surrounded Belisarius, and in so doing she had made an irretrievable mistake.

The Roman strategy of defense, sharpened by Justinian, relied on barriers of fortified posts, with a fleet in readiness to transport a small mobile army to any danger point. Belisarius had been the brains of that striking force, his comitatus the veteran nucleus of the army.

When he left the presence of his master and mistress, the single-minded soldier must have realized that Justinian was a sick man, no longer the architect of predestination. Perhaps, also, he wondered if he had not caused calamity in

Italy by refusing to agree to Justinian's peace with the Goths; perhaps for the first time he saw himself as he really was, a gifted commander of a single army who had never been able to bring a war to an end.

Theodora had not finished with him. Before he embarked, uncomplaining, for the western front she invited him to talk with her, alone upon the canopied roof of the Daphne.

Never had she made such an appeal as this to Belisarius. What she confided in him and what he may have objected, we do not know. In the end she drew a pledge from him, knowing that he would keep a pledge. Between the two of them, his young daughter Joannina was betrothed to Theodora's grandson Anastasius, to be married when they came of age. Belisarius had no other child, nor had she.

With the end of the summer the plague lessened in Constantinople. After it came the hunger.

From all the outlying provinces except Africa and the far shores of the Euxine appeals poured in from the exarchs and prefects for the basic foods—bread, salt, olive oil, and wine. It was strange to hear the cry of starving people in the wealthiest of the world's domains. Gold could not buy bread where no grain had been harvested.

The mechanism of supply had broken down. The delicate apparatus by which crops were bought, to be distributed by ships and transport trains to the cities, had ceased to operate. More barbaric communities where each village produced its own grain and livestock fared better. Thronging the forest lands, Goths, Herules, Bulgars, and Slavs suffered less than the multitudes pressing into the cities.

Theodora found it hard to believe some of the reports that reached her, telling of districts changed as if visited by an earthquake. No shipping moved from the docks of Ephesus, because no crews remained to sail them. The streets of Pelusium lay deserted by the people, who had fled into the desert haunts of Sinai. Looms in Bithynia had been abandoned for lack of wool. Irrigation wheels turned steadily in the Orontes River, but they watered fields where no seed had been planted.

"The world is accursed," a refugee cried at her, "for foxes fatten in my village, while my people dig roots in the wilderness."

The breakdown in human relationships was the greatest evil. Children survived without parents; the men of a family had been lost; mills lacked owners to operate them; soldiers released from the fighting fronts wandered in search of their families. . . .

Theodora felt her helplessness. Justinian's mind could no longer grasp what suffering went on, far from the city. Their private reserves of coin had been spent. Impatiently she challenged Peter Barsymes to find stocks of food. The new Logothete had promised her to accomplish more than the Cappadocian; his dark eyes admired her covertly, even when he excused himself—which John had never done. He needed money, vast sums of it.

Fleetingly she wished to hand over her caskets of jewels to him, but she would not part with the precious stones. "Man," she cried at Peter, "do something!"

Inclining his head as if he had expected her words, he hinted that there was a way to double the amount of coin in the treasury without adding any gold.

"We are not sorcerers, to turn lead into gold."

No, Peter admitted, they were not; but she had power to do so by recoining the old gold into twice as many solidi—if she could coax Justinian to do it.

To Theodora it appeared as if they were being punished for their attempt to change the natural order of life. Clearly enough the deserts of the hermits, the remote islands of fisher folk, and barbarian mountain villages had been spared. Justinian, struggling against his weakness, fancied that the forces opposed to him had been strengthened by the pestilence.

Magnates who had kept their bodyguard-armies seized what they needed, and enforced their own laws. Peasant farmers rebelled against paying taxes for devastated lands. Peter Barsymes put his fears into blunt words. "We are impoverished. We cannot bring back wealth, because years must pass before normal crops can be gathered in—or taxes."

Justinian longed then for the mad genius of John of Cappadocia, to ward off the poverty of the treasury. For Peter insisted that they could stave off disaster by lowering the gold content in coins, to possess more expendable money during the crisis. This Justinian would not do. Only by one sixth did he allow the Economist to lessen the gold in a solidus. Nor would he reduce the tax scale, except to allow a captured city or a devastated district a year's exemption from taxes. Meanwhile government agencies bought what supplies they could by requisition——

"The Caesars of old," he muttered, "cheapened the gold aureus to one half its worth, and by so doing they cheated their people."

"As Caesar says."

That evening Theodora was walking with him along the bridle path by the hospital of the sick in mind.

"The hunger will end," Justinian insisted, "but if we cheapen the coinage—that will go on and on."

Over them passed the night breeze from the Bosphorus, toward the glow of sunset. Lifting her tired head to the breeze, Theodora heard a burst of song in the dusk on the water.

"What are the seamen laughing at?" demanded Justinian.

"They do not see us, Caesar. No, they are singing, not laughing, and I think they are from the Ionian islands." By force of habit she interpreted the voices to him. Of late he found it hard to understand them, and he became suspicious of shouting. Theodora laughed herself, and explained. "They are singing—'Why did you break the statue by the fountain, Old Man? Into pieces you broke it and something alive flew away. Old Man, something flew away on the wind toward the stars, and you did it by breaking the statue in pieces.' "

"A pagan song!"

Yes, a pagan song. Something young and alive rising from the dead, broken statue. Catching her breath, she appealed suddenly to the man at her side. "How many are the statues of the old Caesars, the Julians and the Constantines! Why do you bind your thoughts to them? We've never set eyes on Rome. Peter comes from my land, and Narses from the Armenian mountains. What if we should break the old statues—and go away ourselves!"

Remembering that his consort had never liked statues, even of herself in purple stone, Justinian said, "I have ordered your portrait to be set in mosaics against gold, within St. Vitalis at Ravenna, to celebrate our triumph."

"We could go there. Justinian"—the eagerness in her cried out—"we could ride out to the rivers, to let the people of the villages see our faces."

He muttered that it was impossible.

"I am afraid of these walls. Here, death touched you, Justinian."

She sensed his eyes searching her face in the dimness. She should not have mentioned death.

"Theodora, where would we go?"

"Oh—to your home. You've never gone back to Skoplye, and the river." When he was silent she wondered how to persuade him. "The people would rejoice and hold festival at the coming of their Caesar."

"I have provided for them. The town now has the name of Justiniana Prima—the first to bear my name, because it is my birthplace. I have ordered the wall to have four towers of Carian limestone."

How many Justinianas were there? Eight, or ten? Silently she decided that they would not keep their names of honor long. No, they would become Skoplyes again. But now Justinian would not consent to leave his palace——

Still he peered at her suspiciously, aware that she had set her will against his. "They will honor Caesar's name," she murmured placatingly, "for that."

Against the sunset glow the familiar pyramid roof of the purple chamber took shape. They had never carried her there to give birth to a child . . . her daughter's son would be wed to the girl of Belisarius, so the pair of them would have hope, and wealth and rank, after the passing of the wars and famine . . . with the thought came resentment of the man at her side who would not turn his face to the outer world. Did he live now only to plan monuments to his name?

"Yesterday, Justinian, I talked with Jacob the bishop of Edessa——"

"Jacob Baradaeus—Old Clothes?"

"Old Clothes." Deliberately she challenged her husband, because this wandering bishop was of her faith, protected by her. "He slipped past your road guards, Justinian; they have not found him to arrest him. Now he has journeyed out to the Jewish king Abu Nuways, who dwells in tents on the far Arabian shore they call the blessed. Christian priests of Edessa are going there to the pagans." She lifted her face to the tired stooping figure beside her. "I hate these walls of the palace and want to leave them. Give me leave to depart on the journey with the priests. Truly there is need for me to go, Justinian."

His head turned away, and he leaned heavily on her shoulder, so that she felt the wrench of his breath drawn in. His words faltered, and he stabbed his finger at the twin flames of the lamps at the palace door. Something he said about safety in encircling darkness. So he did not mean to let her go.

"As Caesar has said." Turning back up the path, she led him toward the palace.

Then a strange thing happened. Justinian began to hurry; his breath rasped as his feet, in the stiff half boots, slipped over the pebbles; his arm, weighing down her shoulder, pushed her forward, as they passed the dark façade of the purple chamber. Then she realized that he was afraid of the empty darkness behind them where the fishermen's song had ceased. That fear, in some manner, he connected with her. Although he sweated and gasped, hurrying to escape invisible presences, he clung to her.

"Justinian," she said, very quietly. In that moment she felt the hopelessness of what she was trying to do. She had planned for Hieron to be the true foreign office and the final court of appeal, while her husband served as the figurehead of power, in the Sacred Palace she hated. Yet if Justinian became afraid of her, she would bring about disaster by carrying out her plan. Hieron could not supersede the Sacred Palace. And she must abandon her plan, to support him, instead, in following out his blind determination. For if Justinian became afraid, the servitors around him would realize it instantly.

"Justinian"—she sought for something to relieve his tension, and found it—"you have not told me what you are building in Justiniana Secunda."

It pleased him to explain that. "By the river there will be a great church to be consecrated to the Theotokos."

As he spoke his tremors left him; his head came up as he told her how green Carystian marble would be set into white limestone in the walls of the church; his arm linked loosely in hers as they approached the lighted entrance where the two guards lowered their silvered spears like automatons. In the glare of the flaming oil Justinian and Theodora passed by, a truly imperial pair. . . .

The silentiaries and the guards of the corridors had noticed the change in Justinian, who took no heed of them but talked into the air. Out in the streets star gazers and prophets of the boulevards furnished them with an explanation of his conduct. Unseen by them, a *daemon,* a malignant demon, must accompany the emperor now. Obviously Justinian talked with his demon-companion.

When this rumor was brought to Theodora by her spies, she made a habit of walking with Justinian during the evening while people were still about. In so doing she had to abandon Hieron for the palace.

Germanus, of all people, brought the first warning from the frontiers.

The tidings affected Justinian the more because he believed anything his handsome cousin chose to say. Not a soldier by nature, Germanus, a nephew of Justin, possessed the wealth of his mother—one of the patrician Ancinii of western Rome—and accepted willingly enough the hard duty of frontier service. In Africa he had kept good order; at Antioch he had failed to make a stand against Khusrau; but he was popular with the Germans and federated Huns of the north, and because he was generous with his gold they talked to him freely.

"There's a storm brewing over the steppes, Cousin," declared Germanus. "You know how birds wing to tree growth when they feel the wind rising. Well, the German tribes are moving into the peninsula of the Euxine. As far down as Mount Olympus in Greece the Slavs are cutting poles to make huts. They all feel a wind behind 'em. That's truth."

The yellow-maned commander had his uncle's way of blurting out facts. Disliking horse racing and court intrigue, he relished the harder game of playing barbarian chieftains against each other, paying them not to raid, or driving them off if they turned themselves from allies into plunderers, which they frequently did of late. Since Germanus was the emperor's closest kinsman, with a bevy of mature sons to back him, Theodora distrusted him, as the logical heir to the throne. Thus she had taken care to keep the Roman patrician on duty far from the capital.

Now he had noticed a new spirit among his barbarian neighbors. As he expressed it, they were digging in. After the plague, he stumbled into a freshly built town of the

Bulgars next door to Justinian's old home at Skoplye. Their kral refused to take orders from the local prefect. "They say you hired 'em to cart limestone down for the building. Did you?"

Justinian nodded, and protested that the laws forbade barbarians to organize under their own leaders.

"The laws are well enough, Cousin Caesar, but it takes a numerus to catch a cutpurse in the forest. It would take a regiment to disorganize those particular Bulgars."

"How did they pass the watch posts?"

"Some posts haven't a dog to bark."

"The castles?"

The *castella,* or castles, had been Justinian's idea. Scattered behind the frontiers, they walled in hilltops large enough to shelter the people of a village with their cattle. The idea was that the villagers could defend themselves there against raiders until relieved.

Considering his cousin, Germanus smiled. "The barbarians are moving into them. Herds and all. Very convenient."

Germanus had the failing of his breed. The task of holding a long front with skeleton armies had become a game to him and his sons. They played it loyally enough, without having anything at stake themselves. Merely the honorary title of consul, handed down from father to son. That meant nothing, nowadays. Better if Justinian could give them a province to rule. But Theodora, who had contrived to destroy the Praetorian Prefect John and to belittle the name of Belisarius, would never allow Germanus to become prince of a province.

Abruptly he exclaimed, "The honorary title of consul will be abolished. There will be no more consuls."

"What?" Germanus looked his surprise, and then laughed. "Well, it was more of a nuisance than an honor. I'll tell my son he's the last of the Roman consuls. But he takes titles seriously, Cousin."

Like Belisarius, Germanus was content to serve without

honors. They had made their homes in the encampments; they had ventured with a handful of lancers into masses of mutineers and wild barbarians; Germanus had taken the leader of a mutiny in Africa into his own bodyguards, to lull the man's suspicions, until he could be seized and impaled safely. Such physical courage he, Justinian, had never known.

"I take your accomplishments seriously, Germanus," he said quickly. "There is no man living who has done more for the empire than you. I can bestow no title so honorable as the name of Germanus."

His words had the effect he anticipated. The careless, wealthy patrician was uplifted emotionally.

"I will tell my sons the commendation of the Ever August Emperor."

"Do so. For they share the glory of Germanus."

The simple-minded prince actually reddened with delight, and glanced around instinctively to discover if any servitors had heard him praised. Justinian had been careful to banish listeners. Now, pretending to relax, he probed for what he wanted to discover himself—some means of meeting the new danger on the Danube front that Germanus sensed without analyzing too clearly. This illegal grouping of migrants behind the frontier must be broken up, by some means, or the new villages might link themselves together and become kingdoms too strong to be subdued.

"You can give the new villagers some pay—call it a gift—as allies," he suggested. "Then enlist the best of their fighting men."

At this Germanus shook his head. "The plague did the damage. They've dug in—settled—set up their altars or pagan shrines. I've told you, Cousin, they'll only obey their own tribal krals and bans and khans."

Remembering how Germanus had suppressed the mutiny in Africa, Justinian said, "Then hire their krals and bans and khans. The tribes will follow their chieftains into your service."

"And I will lose more sleep at night. It's not so easy to become shepherd of a pack of wolves. We've never enlisted barbarians by clans and towns before. Will you take this risk?"

"Yes," assented Justinian, "so long as Germanus commands."

No sooner had he made the decision than it troubled him. At night he turned to his silent counselors, the ancient books, for guidance. Without Germanus' robust presence, his imagination pictured the silent inscrutable barbaric peoples stealing past his guards, refusing his payments, making their way toward his city . . . somewhere Augustine had mentioned such small kingdoms of people, and the empire.

Anxiously Justinian searched the pages of *The City of God* until he found the place: ". . . is it well for good men to rejoice in extending an empire? If human affairs had been happy, without war being waged, all kingdoms would have remained small. Many kingdoms of nations would have rejoiced and agreed together, like neighbors within a city."

But there could not be *nations* within his empire, like the houses that made up his city. There could only be the empire itself, protecting all and ruling all. . . .

Nations were forming, travelers said, in the lost island of Britain. Angles and Saxons obeyed only their kings, and the surviving Romans wore the neck rings of slaves. No officer of Justinian had fared to that farthest island and returned alive. . . . Procopius said that ghosts were ferried thither by fishermen. . . .

"Men who fish with nets or carry on trade across the narrow sea say that they also have to ferry dead souls across to the island. As soon as the dark of a day comes on, they retire to their huts, to sleep and wait. Late in the night a knock comes on their door and they hear voices indistinctly, calling them out to their task. They rise from their beds and go down to the shore, compelled to do so by something beyond their understanding. They find skiffs waiting, but not their own skiffs. In these they sit and take up the oars, aware that the boats are weighed down by a large number of passengers. The oarlocks sink to the water's edge and are wet by the waves. However they themselves see no one. Yet when they put in to the shore of Brittia, their boats suddenly become light. They say they hear a kind of voice from the island, calling the name of each of the passengers. If the passenger is a woman the voice calls the name of the husband she had during life. When they depart, the fishermen find their skiffs risen high above the waves, so that they can go at speed."

Surely that was no more than a legend, told along the shore of the Franks that had once been Gaul. Yet it held one truth in it. Britain had become lost to human knowledge, except for the fishermen and traders who ventured there as fearfully as if visiting the underworld of hell. That same fate might befall Justiniana Prima, or even Ravenna. Or Constantinople itself . . .

Justinian gave orders to cut all government expenditures to the bone. He demanded that the war in Italy be pressed, until the rebellious Goths were subdued, and the armies released to defend other frontiers.

Then as if Fate itself mocked him, frightening news came from the east in the summer of the year 544.

Again Khusrau led the Persian host up the river Euphrates, with no army and no Belisarius to stand against him. Forging westward, he reached the battlements of Edessa, the city that had known the Apostles of Christ. There, for ransom he demanded all the portable wealth of the city and the Edessans resolved to defend themselves. Justinian could only hope that some miracle might discourage the temperamental Sassanian. Because he could not send an army to relieve the city.

The reports that reached him, however, told of savage assaults by the Persians—one surprise attack being turned back because an unknown farmer happened to give the alarm where he was resting on the wall. A certain Peter, a Christian Persian, took command of all the desperate defenders, even children.

Khusrau erected a solid mound of tree trunks, timbers, stones, and earth. As it rose, the Persian engineers extended it nearer. It would soon meet and overtop the wall, and Edessa would suffer the fate of Antioch. The people of Edessa could build their wall no higher, nor could they sally out against the mass of Persians.

Instead, a nameless engineer showed them by drawing a plan how to sink a shaft and run it beneath the artificial ramp of the enemy. It would accomplish little, they all understood, to make some timbers and stones of the mound collapse into their shaft. No, the engineer had a different thought. When the shaft reached the towering mound, he extended it into a square chamber, shoring up the roof with timbers. Then he made the Edessans pack the tunnel chamber with cedar wood, sacks of bitumen, and lumps of sulphur, and pour oil of turpentine over all.

When they fired the chemical fuel of the tunnel chamber, the conflagration rose to intense heat; the shoring timbers collapsed, pulling down part of the Persian structure and letting in the air. This resulted in the timberwork of the mound catching fire.

When the mystified Persians beheld smoke rising through the holes in their shaken mound, the Edessans tricked them by throwing out fire pots and torches—to make it seem as if the smoke came from the missiles. Khusrau himself inspected the smoldering mound and understood what was happening. By his command thousands of men brought up water from the river to pour over their structure.

"Then was the King of kings confounded in his mind," related the courier who brought word of the city's deliverance, "for the water did not quench the flame of the chemicals. Nay, a choking steam arose, driving away living men. The great work fell into charred ruin, while poisonous fumes hung over it. The King of kings was enraged. During several days he ordered his sun-worshippers to attack the walls, but they were defeated by burning oil that peasants and women and children helped pour on them. After that the host of the enemy went away."

It seemed to Theodora that Edessa had been saved not so much by military force as by the spirit of a Christian Persian, the watchfulness of a farmer, and the skill of a city engineer. But to Justinian it seemed as if his great plan was vindicating itself. Had he not fortified Edessa, and had not Edessa in turn protected him? Hurriedly, on the strength of the victory, and helped by the ravages of the plague through the east, he bought another five-year truce from Khusrau. All such happenings on the far frontiers he now related to himself—to the helping or harming of his unalterable Idea.

It pleased him that Theodora no longer opposed him with argument. In fact she had come to accept his plans as finalities. "I am only a woman, and I do not understand controversies," she explained. "But I will not forsake the teaching of my spiritual fathers, as long as I live. I'm no longer young, Justinian. Suffer me to do as Euphemia did, and give aid to my church."

Willingly he agreed to that. More than once he spoke of her as his empress sent by God. Nor did he anticipate how much Theodora might accomplish in aiding her patriarchs of the east.

His stark determination to restore the old empire began to frighten his people. In the estimation of patricians and commoners alike the emperor ceased to be a human being. He became a force defying the realities of plague, hunger, and defeat, driving them all toward the illusion of victory.

"Some who were with the emperor late at night," wrote Procopius in his secret notes, "seemed to see a sort of phantom take his place . . . his face became featureless flesh, without eyes . . . then his face would become again as they knew it."

It was as if his companion, the malignant demon, now possessed him. What he did henceforth might be the demon's doing.

After Edessa, Justinian received aid from another source. From across the sea his ships came in again, to repair the destruction of war and plague. Or so he thought.

Actually venturesome merchants brought relief to distressed Constantinople by resuming trade over the sea as soon as the plague loosened its grip on the ports. From Visigothic Spain and Gaul beyond the mountains—where no Roman army could penetrate—they shipped back iron and silver as well as slaves. Jewish and Greek traders established their own communities beyond the frontiers, in Cadiz or Marseille (Massilia). From inner Africa Syrian speculators transported cinnamon and ivory, to barter for the timber and salt of the Adriatic shores. The barbarian kings preferred to deal with these independent traders—who were not bound by Roman monopolies—and as far north as Tanis at the mouth of the river Don (Tanais) they filled entire vessels with furs, wool, and silver in exchange for handfuls of Ethiopian emeralds, which the Hunnic chieftains craved.

Wedged between the seas and fairly upon the land route leading from Europe to Asia, Constantinople served as entrepôt for this trade. When it revived after the epidemic, ships began to line the Golden Horn again. If he visited the mosaic-setters in St. Irene's, Justinian could see their sails passing beneath him.

Then from the far end of the earth he gained unexpected hope. This was nothing less than the discovery of the secret of silk.

For a long time the Logothetes had labored to open up a trade route to the place of the sun's rising, the Land of

Silk. It lay beyond the maps, even the world map of Cosmas the Monk, who fancied the mount of paradise to be there. There was a road by the north thither. It passed through the steppes of the Huns and Avars; from the river Don it led to the Volga (Rha), beyond which it vanished into a limbo of People of the Cold (Hyperboreans). Some furs came back along it but nothing from the Land of Silk.

Now the main caravan routes to the east were blocked by the Persians, who acted as middlemen, selling Asiatic goods to the Roman merchants at high prices. (And Khusrau's advance into the Caucasus had endangered the otherwise hazardous northern route over the grasslands.)

Justinian had pressed hard to open a southern route by sea around the Persian dominion. From Alexandria daring traders, Ethiopians and Arabs, went by the canal to the Red Sea. They crossed that to the Land of Incense (where Theodora's missionaries were journeying out to King Abu Nuways) for frankincense and myrrh. From this Arabian shore, called the blessed, sea traders found a wind that took them over to the shore of India. There they obtained vital copper and woven cotton and pepper, as well as the pearls and tortoise shell of Ceylon. But the sea route thence to the Land of Silk was too hazardous for them. The Persians, who controlled the supply of the finer oriental textiles, damask, carpets, and splendid tapestries, also controlled the supply of silk.

How silk was made, and of what, remained a secret carefully guarded. The precious stuff did not seem to be woven of the fibers of any plant or the hair of a known animal. Invisible looms fabricated it, in the Land of Silk.

Then two Nestorian monks arrived from the far east, to swear that they knew the secret. The threads of silk, the monks said, were spun by worms that fed upon mulberry leaves. No human hands could manage to do what the silkworms did. They offered to try to bring eggs of the worms to Roman soil. Justinian ordered that money be given them without stint, to enable them to make the attempt. If worms could be bred on the warm Syrian coast, silk might be spun and woven in the factories of Beritus.

Doggedly intent on these trade routes, and hoping for the silk culture, Justinian fancied that the ravaged and beset Roman Empire was strengthening. Those who talked with him now took good care to say so.

Unperceived, however, other human entities were growing. Within the Balkans the Slav and Bulgar migrants were cohering into clans. In Spain, the Jewish merchants settled in Cartagena; fugitives from the Hunnic penetration at the Adriatic's end took refuge on close-lying islands among lagoons that would be the lagoons of Venice. In the deserts by the Red Sea—where Khusrau's forces tried to drive the Romans from the ports—pagan Arab tribes came into contact with Sassanian and Roman armies, and learned their way of war. By no plan whatsoever, but by their urge to escape the devastation of war, increasing throngs sought sanctuary in St. Peter's basilica, or on Monte Cassino.

Justinian's plan was failing. His world of imagination, the ancient world of Alexander and Augustus, was coming to an end. The Middle Ages were beginning.

VII

The Bequest of Theodora

AN INEXPLICABLE CHANGE HAD COME OVER ITALY. NO TIDINGS of victory arrived with the courier vessels from Ravenna. It seemed to the counselors in the palace that Belisarius had lost his secret of victory. With the spring of 545, he wrote to Justinian.

"We reached Italy, most mighty of emperors, without men, horses, arms or money. All those things are necessary for anyone to carry on a war.

"Although we combed Thrace and Illyricum for soldiers, we managed to collect only a pitiful following, unseasoned and without weapons. On the other hand we found the men left in Italy dispirited by many defeats. As for revenues here, we found them taken over by the enemy. Our men, being unpaid, refuse to carry out orders; our debt to them has taken away our right to command. You should know, my master, that many serving in the armies here have deserted to the enemy.

"If you wished only to send Belisarius to Italy, that has been accomplished, for I am here. If, however, your will is to overcome these enemies in war—then send supplies sufficient to accomplish that.

"A general can't do much without men to aid him. I need

above everything to have back my own spearmen and guards [comitatus]—next to that, really great strength in Huns and barbarian fighters, who should be paid immediately."

Belisarius had not changed. His message to Justinian has the old touch of irony, and the quizzical questioning. But the new errant Constable did not receive the massive reinforcement that had been sent to the old Magister Militum at Rome. Manpower was lacking, of course. Narses journeyed north to try to raise a volunteer force among the Herules. But at the same time something rather odd happened to the messenger of Belisarius.

This spokesman, John the nephew of Vitalian, was entertained delightfully by Theodora and her ladies. John, headstrong and not at all inclined to take orders from Belisarius, had a habit of making mistakes with the best intentions. Now he told the persuasive Theodora all he knew about Italy. Pleased by such a flattering reception in the Daphne banquet halls, he lingered on at the capital. Conceited, he saw his way to gain prestige by marriage with the daughter of Germanus, cousin to the emperor. The girl was young and attractive, yet no suitor had claimed her because the house of Germanus—a courageous and not too bright nobleman—rested under the displeasure of the empress. (With John of Cappadocia and Belisarius out of the public eye, the stalwart Germanus had become the most popular figure in Constantinople.)

Theodora opposed the match but Justinian consented to it. John, the commander, returned to Ravenna eventually without the new forces Belisarius needed desperately but with a new sense of importance since he had become kinsman, by marriage, to the emperor of the Romans.

Whatever Theodora may have instigated, John proceeded to disagree with Belisarius' plans and to depart overland with his own command. Thereafter he gave no aid to the Constable.

Bitterness had eaten into the Roman command like a

canker; the general shut up in Rome, Bessas, sold back to the population the grain he had requisitioned; soldiers, unpaid, deserted to the Goths, who now had money to pay them.

It was all due to Totila. This new leader of the barbarians acted with more humanity and piety than the Romans. Benevolent and handsome, Totila assured his people that they had almost lost the war by their evil disposition in the past; now, with nothing more to lose, he called on them to keep the commandments of the Lord and to fight. (Totila did not make the mistake of fighting in the way that suited the Romans, at siege-and-defense; he kept his growing host together, mounted and moving, and the Romans could no longer stand in the open against the swords of the German riders.)

His prayers and humanity alike won over many wearied Italians. Neapolitans yielded to Totila's paternal good will, when he furnished them with food and wine respectfully; the wives of Roman senators taken captive at Cumae marveled at the rude chivalry of the victorious Goth, who refused to allow them to be plundered or violated. To the senators who still clung to Rome, the Gothic champion wrote to ask why they had abandoned the cause of the Goths and a united Italy—at the command of a peasant-born Greek across the water. Had they prospered, he inquired, under Justinian as under Theodoric the Great and the queenly Amalasuntha? In the streets of Rome his placards appeared, to ask other questions. How had the citizens liked the accounts of Alexander the Scissors? How long would they bear with the corn speculations of the hired general, Bessas?

Undoubtedly Totila had a canny way of appealing to men's longings. (He could be savage enough in a conflict.) Passing along the Cassino road, he climbed the hill to kneel before the saintly Benedict and humbly ask for guidance.

The barbarian leader, in the fullness of his physical strength, knelt to the frail saint who was near to his death. "You have done much evil," Benedict told him, "and you do evil now. From this hour abstain from unrighteous deeds." He said more. "You will go upon the sea, and you will enter Rome. Nine years you will reign, and die in the tenth year."

It seemed to Totila after that that he should try to bring about a peace.

Totila sent an offer to Justinian. In it he declared that he had regained Italy, but would hold it only as the great Theodoric had held it, as viceroy for the emperor. Justinian did not answer the offer.

His refusal left no basis for peace in Italy. Apparently the Goths—who resented Belisarius' treachery to Vitigis and the old army at Ravenna—had only the alternatives of complete victory or extermination. Holding the open countryside, they pent up the remaining Roman commanders in the strong northern fortified cities. Behind their walls the generals of Constantinople maintained themselves like feudal lords on the populace, extracting what money they could for themselves, paying their men as little as possible.

All but Belisarius. Taking his skeleton army to sea, he kept it in ships, moving down the windswept Adriatic in rowing barges, dromons, and merchants' transports, relieving or recapturing ports like Otranto (Hydruntum). Only on the water could he protect his men from the Gothic riders.

The war became a duel between the Christian, tolerant barbarian and the cultured soldier who could count on nothing except his imagination in his loyal effort to carry out the command of the sick emperor in Constantinople. To do that Belisarius had to bring relief to Rome, where the defenders were at the point of starvation, owing to the encirclement by the Goths and Bessas' hoarding of the last corn reserves. There the survivors of the populace were stealing out of the city, to be caught or killed for the most part by the Goths.

With all his old skill Belisarius went about the task of bringing food into the despairing city which he could not approach by land. There was only one way by water, up the narrow winding Tiber.

Collecting what grain he could from Sicily, Belisarius assembled all his shipping at the Port, off the Tiber's mouth, and worked out a way to move his small navy into Rome. The river itself he knew only too well from past experience; his spies brought him accurate details of the defense that Totila had thrown across the upper Tiber. This was a rather effective imitation of his own river block of ten years before—a chain slung across the current, a palisaded boom above the chain, with twin log towers to guard the ends of the boom. It was necessary to destroy this barrier without risking his small force ashore. His biscuit eaters of the early great days could have stormed such wooden defense works, but his sleazy regiment at Portus would not go against the long swords of the Goths.

Since the river itself was too shallow and infested with mud flats to be navigated by the larger dromons, he selected two hundred of the smaller sailing craft—which did not need to be propelled by long oar banks—and built wooden palisades along their rails. Archers in the sailing craft could shoot through holes in the wooden parapets. Then Belisarius contrived an odd sort of fireship. Two broad barges were lashed together and a tower of wooden beams built on them. The height of this tower had been calculated to be slightly greater than the defense works of the Goths. Atop the tower a small boat was roped to a slide and filled with a Roman fire mixture—pitch, sulphur, pine resin.

When all this was ready, Belisarius got word through to Bessas in Rome—urging the besieged general to sally with his force down the river on the appointed day, when he sighted smoke rising from the Goths' barrier.

As he had done when approaching Carthage, Belisarius gathered his leftovers of men, ships, and stores into the walls of the Port at his rear. In this base he left Antonina and yielded its command to a certain Isaac the Armenian. "Whatever happens," he ordered Isaac, "stay inside these walls."

"I understand."

"If you hear that Belisarius is killed, what will you do then?"

The Armenian was not to be tricked. "*Whatever* happens, I shall stay within the Port."

"Then do it."

The insistence of Belisarius showed that he was under strain. And the energetic Isaac was left with the impression that he had been ordered to hold the Port *if* Belisarius were killed. Veterans of other years, like Mundus or Ildiger, would have understood what Belisarius meant, and thought nothing of the words.

Luck seemed to favor Belisarius on the day of the attempt to force the river. A breeze from the west drove his flotilla against the current. The Goths assembling on the lower shores seemed more puzzled than disturbed by sight of the sailing craft with clattering wooden walls escorting what looked like an oversize funeral pyre, and followed by harmless food ships. Although a stone tossed from the bank would have fallen on the decks of the makeshift fleet, it reached the barriers without casualties.

At the chain, the fire of the shielded archers kept the enemy back long enough for the iron links to be broken and the ends of the chain let go to sink. The flotilla bore down on the main barrier where Goths manned the bridgework across the boom, and the two flanking towers. The action became intense when the barges with the poised boat were pushed against a tower at the water's edge. Into this tower the Gothic commander pushed with his guards.

Then the combustible-laden boat was let go down the slide, with its chemicals fired. This boat did its work, overturning upon the men on the tower summit and discharging sulphurous flames down the timberwork. Immediately the structure burned with intense heat and stifling fumes, incinerating two hundred of the elite of the Goths. At this apparition of flame, those on the boom-bridge ran.

Belisarius led his most dependable men on the bridge, to

cut and burn it through, protected by discharges of the arrows from the small craft which now filled the river from bank to bank. As they labored, Goths poured down from nearby encampments; Totila rode up. While the boom was demolished the fighting intensified, in the choking smoke.

There was no sign of Bessas coming up in support from the city. The wind pushed the clumsy vessels against the barrier, while the current bore against the severed bridgework. This had to be hacked apart, to clear a way for the sailing craft. Missile fire from the banks took toll of the workers.

When a channel was cleared and Belisarius started the first boats through, he could observe only reinforcements of the Goths along the river. Bessas had not sallied out.

A courier came in with a spoken message for the anxious commander. "Isaac the Armenian is dead, and all of his men lost."

So much the courier repeated. What had happened at the Tiber's mouth was that Isaac heard the rumor that the Romans had broken through the barriers. Perhaps he had fancied that his orders did not bind him in that event; perhaps he sought a share in the victory himself. In either case, he sallied out with a hundred mounted men to pillage the nearest Gothic camp, where he was caught and killed.

Not knowing that the Port, and his wife and reserves, were still safe, Belisarius took the message as meaning that his base was lost. The long strain told on him. Observers say he lost the power of speech and signed for the flotilla to turn back.

For the first time in twenty years of combat the Roman champion made the mistake of retreating when he might have pushed ahead. Medical indications are that he suffered a stroke at the barriers, because fever set in that night at the Port and he seemed unable to speak clearly.

Rome was lost very quickly after that. Some of the Isaurians of Bessas' command made a profit for themselves by letting the Goths into the massive walls. Bessas fled with his mounted men, leaving his hoard of gold. When this was re ported to Totila, he said it made pleasant hearing.

Urgently, his officers begged to be allowed to pursue the vanishing Romans, but the eccentric Goth shook his head. He did not wish to divide his command while Belisarius was close by. "What could be sweeter for a man," he observed, "than a flying enemy?"

Some patricians, who had horses, escaped across the Tiber to sanctuary in St. Peter's. Thither rode the Gothic chieftain with his guards. From the bridge of Nero to the grilled gates of the basilica, his attendants killed twenty-six soldiers and sixty of the populace—for the Gothic swordsmen would take no prisoners at a battle's end.

Out to him came the deacon Pelagius bearing the Scriptures in his hands. Wealthy and courageous, Pelagius had done more to defend Rome than its commander, Bessas. "Master," he said, bowing his head before Totila, "spare what is now yours."

And he pointed behind him to the bell tower and the cloister packed with refugees.

"At last, Pelagius, you have made yourself a suppliant before me."

"Yes, I have, because from this moment God has made me your slave. Master, will you not spare your slaves?"

Whereupon Totila gave orders against killing and any violation of women. When the refugees in the churches were counted, they numbered no more than five hundred. To that remnant the population of Rome had diminished. The city itself was thoroughly looted. The remaining patricians and their wives put on the rough clothing of slaves and begged food, knocking at the doors of the Goths. "A very remarkable example of this change of fortune," Procopius adds, "being Rusticiana, who had been wife to Boethius, a woman accustomed to give her wealth to the poor."

Presently Totila made use of the courageous Pelagius, sending him with other envoys to Constantinople, to inquire if Justinian did not believe that the Goths would make valuable allies, as they had been in the time of Anastasius and Theodoric. If not, Totila was prepared to raze the walls and monuments of Rome and to carry the war eastward along the Dalmatian coast.

Justinian returned the answer that he had given full command to Belisarius and the Goths must address themselves to him.

Instead of doing so, the angered Goth broke down some sections of the outer wall and prepared to burn all the historic structures of Rome. Before he could do that he received a letter from Belisarius, who lay ill at the Tiber's mouth. "Only civilized men can create beauty in a city; the destruction of such beauty could only be carried out by men without understanding. So posterity will judge them to be. Of all cities, Rome is the most notable. It was not built by the ability of one man; a multitude made the city such as you behold it, little by little.

"Be sure of this: one of two things will happen. Either you will be defeated by the emperor in this struggle, or—should it so happen—you will triumph over him. If you preserve Rome you will make yourself by so much the richer; by destroying the city you will gain no benefit but will make certain that no plea for mercy will be left you.

"You will have the reputation, among men, that accords with your acts. It rests with you to decide what that reputation will be."

With his shrewdness, Totila had his vanity. And the more he pondered Belisarius' letter the more he wondered who, except himself, he would harm by destroying Rome. Indecision tormented him, and he had to end it by action. Without doing any further injury to the city, he marched off to resume the war elsewhere.

No sooner had Totila reached the north than he heard that

Belisarius was in Rome, piling stones into the breaches in the walls.

Swiftly the angered Goth rode back, expecting to throw his forces through the dismantled gates and breaches. It seemed certain that he would catch in the ruins the elusive Roman who had plagued him from the sea.

By day and by night the Goths rushed the barricades of stones and beams under the sting of arrows. Broken stonework was toppled down on them, flame and arrows spat at them, platforms gave way beneath them. They drew off and hurried away again, to make the accursed walls vanish behind the horizon.

The year after that Justinian rewarded his general, who had regained the Rome of the Caesars. From his ships landed slim columns of reinforcements, three hundred Herules enrolled by Narses, under a chieftain who stayed drunk, eight hundred Armenian peasants from the Caucasus—and one thousand veterans of the old comitatus. Going out the Appian Gate to greet his comrades, Belisarius understood that Justinian and Theodora were sending all the reinforcements they could scrape together. After the end of the plague, in 546, no greater manpower would be forthcoming.

Still avoided by John and separated from the remaining Roman garrisons, Belisarius resorted to slipping from fortress to fortress, while moving his supplies and skeleton commands by sea up and down the coast. Totila held the balance of force. Procopius, who no longer looked on Belisarius as a hero, reported laconically, "He did not succeed in setting foot on land except where some fortress was; he kept visiting one port after another."

There was nothing else he could do. The city of Rome lay prostrate. The temple of Fortune gaped empty; stunted pines and thistles began to hide the mosaic pavements and baths of the Capitoline palaces. Imperceptibly the darkness of the Middle Ages was settling upon the Rome of the Caesars.

Its population began to seek refuge at the sanctuary of

St. Peter's basilica, where the Pope Vigilius—who had been the friend of Theodora—wrote in gratitude to Justinian.

During the next month Belisarius had urgent letters from Theodora. The letters reminded him of his pledge to her. By now his daughter Joannina and her grandson were of age to marry, or almost so. Would he not announce the betrothal?

These missives Antonina pondered intently, seeking the hidden purpose of the empress. Weary in mind and body, Belisarius would not hear to leaving Italy. An order from Justinian would be needed to recall him—but what order would the emperor give that Theodora had not approved? Hating the woman of the circus who wore the diadem insolently, Antonina persuaded Belisarius to answer that he had not forgotten his promise, yet he believed the betrothed pair were still too young and the wedding should await the return of Joannina's parents.

In reply Theodora requested that it take place without delay. Anxious to be within hearing of the machinations of the court, Antonina nagged her single-minded husband. The cruel empress who had snatched gold from them, she told him, must intend to shame Joannina by tossing the girl to her bastard's brat; Procopius, the secretary, swore that from childhood Theodora had picked up the black art of sorcerers. She—Antonina—could not sleep from worrying, and by returning to the palace she might beg Justinian for more regiments and supplies——

Unable to deny his wife, Belisarius gave permission for her to return, with Procopius. By fast courier galley she hastened back. But she was too late.

"She treats her body with great care, more than is needed. She enters the bath early, and after bathing goes direct to breakfast. Then sleep lays hold of her for long stretches, by day and at night until sunrise." Procopius made hurried notes of the change in Theodora. "Nothing will she do by persuasion of another person. For she sets her stubborn will to everything and carries out her decisions with all her energy."

Her face had thinned, and her eyes became luminous under the long, darkened brows. When she arose from resting she became vital, feverish, until her strength failed. The pain in her breast was eased by sleep and the numbing medicine of the physicians.

"No one dares intercede for the victims of her wrath. For her passion seems beyond any power to quiet."

To the Pope Vigilius in Rome her words went: ". . . fulfil the promise you made of your free will, to recall our father Anthimius to his office. . . ."

And when, as Pope, Vigilius would not lift the ban of anathema pronounced against the patriarch of the east, Theodora ordered an officer, "Seek the Pope and if you find him at the basilica of St. Peter, spare him. If you find him elsewhere, take him to a ship and bring him hither."

The officer found Vigilius at a festival in the streets of the city and bade him go to a vessel in the Tiber. So Vigilius was brought back to face Theodora, on Anthimius' behalf.

In the land of Colchis, in the pass of Daryal, Khusrau the Just mused over one of her letters seized by his spies. A letter to a Christian of Persia, praising him, trusting him to work toward a peace between Justinian and Khusrau——

"What kind of a state is this of Rome," Khusrau demanded of his counselors, "that is administered by a woman? Have we anything to fear from it?"

Throughout the Roman state in those months, secret orders passed; unnamed agents rode with the couriers from Sivastopole to Cádiz. Those who served her then did not leave their names in the records.

"For if she wishes to conceal a thing, that thing remains unmentioned by all. Yet there is no chance of concealment for one who has given offense. She would summon the man before her, even if he be a notable, and give him to the charge of one of her ministers. At a late hour of the night this man would be put on a ship, bundled up and shackled—to be delivered to another agent who would guard him until the empress took mercy on him, or he ended his days."

Black market dealers in silk, who bought their stock in Persian markets and sold it for more than the price fixed by Justinian, of eight gold pieces the pound, had their ships seized and paid the value of the cargoes in fines. Keepers of new and prospering brothels were escorted across the frontiers.

Augusteon society no longer made a jest of Theodora's monks. When lean figures emerged from the House of the Monks, ladies who wore embroidered eagles listened to them. It became fashionable to have such a monk at a feast.

Ladies of yellowed hair and hennaed nails rode warily in their carriages, pausing to whisper warnings and listen to conjectures. Where were Theodora's messengers hurrying now? What had the woman planned for the morrow?

This society, which Theodora had fought, discovered that her whims now made and unmade marriages. The indolent and popular Germanus sought a match with Matasuntha, refugee queen of the Amal dynasty. Theodora claimed that Matasuntha was hostage to Justinian, in a time of war. (And so Germanus did not gain in popularity among the barbarians by marriage with kingly Gothic stock.)

Artabanes, the tall and mannerly Persian-Armenian, was the rage with the ladies of the Augusteon. (In the Caucasus, he had killed Sittas, husband of Theodora's sister.) A veteran of Africa, honorary Master of the Armed Forces, he had raised his eyes to Praejecta, the niece of Justinian. The emperor did not know how to refuse Artabanes his bride. Theodora's agents were set to trace out the past of the affable foreign commander. After months they brought back with them an elderly woman of the Caucasus. She appeared more aged than the striking Artabanes, because her years had been spent in a woman's labor; she was his wife, and she had not known of his rise in fortune. The splendor of Constantinople and the gentle welcome of Theodora the empress rejoiced the heart of the old woman. Implacably, Theodora called upon Artabanes to give up Praejecta and take back his wife. Furious and complaining, he did so.

The days passed too quickly for Theodora, while the pain increased. Never had she worn more bewildering regalia. Deftly her women drew the folds of spun gold across and around the fragile shoulders, arranging the long lappets of emeralds and pearls to hide the rouged cheeks and to keep the secret of the empress.

Then there was the secret that came out. Almost beyond belief, the implacable empress who had given birth to no child in the purple chamber acknowledged a grandson.

He bore the name of Anastasius, like the emperor who had favored the eastern churches. From an island in the Marmora he was landed at the gardens of Hieron, where he was guarded from questioners. . . .

There the sixteen-year-old boy seldom came face to face with the empress who kept so much to her bed. When she talked with him, questioning him about Alexandria and his mother, she kept her face veiled, and there was a strangeness about her brilliant dark eyes behind the gossamer silk. He told her all that he could remember, and she seemed pleased with him, although she sent him away quickly, saying that this house and its garden would be his home until he married. His new servitors assured Anastasius that she wished him to be married soon.

That seemed to him as incredible as the fine house thronged with people who made way for him. At times he felt that he merely imagined the face of his mother's mother in the shadowed room. Since he had amused himself on the waterfront at the island, he turned to the reality of the boats at Hieron. His attendants allowed him to take out a skiff and row out to search up the wind-whipped strait for a glimpse of Porphyrius, the sea monster of which he had heard during his stay on the island. Interested in all the craft that sped down the Bosphorus before the wind, the boy did not notice that he was followed by another boat. During his stay at Hieron his new companions took him hunting, keeping him apart from the throng of courtiers.

Then the empress led Anastasius into the adventure that drove thought of the sea and Constantinople out of his mind. Sitting with him alone in the garden, she confided in him that he would meet a girl who had been pledged to marry him.

After that they took him across the water to a pillared palace near the Golden Gate, where servants waited upon the girl called Joannina, no older than he. Being shy, and uncomfortable in the strange house, Anastasius could say little until the ordeal was over. Afterward, when the Most Noble Joannina came to offer her respects to the empress, there was no more discomfort. For a while Joannina waited upon the Augusta in her chamber; then they had a lunch of rare things from the sea. The girl Joannina ate sugared fruit eagerly, licking her fingers like anyone else.

Without any objection she went with him to look at the caged peacocks, and the ducks in the garden pool. She said there were swans in the garden of Belisarius. . . .

". . . they say," Procopius wrote, "the empress secretly made her offer herself. So after the girl had been compromised the wedding was arranged, so the emperor might not interfere with her machinations. Still, after it all had been accomplished, Anastasius and the girl found themselves passionately in love."

Theodora no longer ventured to her old home that had become the House of the Monks. Secluded in Hieron, she heard how her people went out from there to far places. John of Ephesus wrote to her that the church had entered the Carian mountains; on the Nile the bishop of Memphis journeyed east to pagan people. But most of all Theodora followed in imagination the wandering of Jacob who was called

Baradaeus ("Old Clothes"). On past Sinai, and the desert, on to the blessed shore and the Himyarite Arabs who had not known the mercy of God. He asked for a patriarch, and a patriarch was sent into the desert after him, with a throng of deacons and priests.

He was restoring her eastern church that Justinian had tried to outlaw.

Jacob moved so swiftly, so surely. His words were hard demands and she obeyed them, thankful for his swiftness. There was so little time to do so much.

"The name of Jacob," old Anthimius told her, when she rested, "is a fragrant perfume over all the empire."

She thought of the bit of cedarwood she had kept in a box beside her bed, because of its fragrance. Remembering Cosmas, who had once journeyed to find paradise, she smiled at the patriarch. "Cosmas did not venture as far as Jacob."

When the Pope Vigilius reached the Golden Horn he talked long hours alone with Theodora. No one wrote down what they said. In the end Vigilius declared for all to hear that the anathema against Anthimius need not endure, nor did blame rest upon the churches of the east. There could be a reconciliation of minds, so long as belief remained steadfast.

It was a triumph for her when, after twelve years, she could go to where Anthimius waited with his books and tell him the ban of anathema had been lifted.

His fingers drew through his white beard and lifted to make a sign in the air. She bent her head, at his sign of blessing, and she felt the pain burn in her throat, growing when she coughed, while the strength went from her shoulders until she cried out with fear. "I'm frightened."

Patiently he sat at her bedside, waiting. Taking the bit of cedarwood from the box that Jacob Baradaeus had sent, he held it in his thin hand and said, "The tree is dead, but the fragrance will never leave this wood. Can the hands of men make anything so sweet and everlasting? The Lord God made it so. And if this be true of the wood of a tree, is it not true of the life in our bodies? Smell of it, my daughter."

She did so to please the patriarch, who had become so old that his thoughts at times were childish.

After that Theodora did not cross the water to the palace except when foreign ambassadors came at the ten o'clock hour to bow before the emperor and the empress. . . .

Now Procopius could not gain a close sight of the dark-eyed implacable beauty who ascended from the boat landing to the garden gate of the Sacred Palace. Silentiaries supported her by the arms, for she came full robed at the summons of Justinian. The organ notes sounded when she moved up the steps, slowly, so that the maids in waiting could lift the gold border of her train clear of the stones. Resentfully, the writer listened to the adulation of the throng of commoners around him. "The glory of the purple, the joy of the world." The words they were forever mumbling.

When Theodora had passed, he took his way stubbornly by the statue of imperial purple stone on its pedestal among the dug-over flower beds heavy with the dampness of early spring. He told himself that if the figure had been carved from plain white marble it would never have appeared so remote from its surroundings. If the woman were stripped of her regalia, what would be left but a perverse little thing, craving luxury?

In the dusk of an evening when the lamps were lighted over the bakeries on the Mesé, Procopius encountered a ghost whispering at his side. It bent over, in a patched chlamys, to conceal its height; grease streaked its beard; its eyes shifted watchfully, but it had the voice of John of Cappadocia, muttering that he could show evidence that the Grand Logothete, Peter Barsymes, had raked in monies from Alexandria by fining honest merchants who had rid themselves of army goods at a loss rather than have their stock requisitioned by Peter.

Over the bowls of a wineshop Procopius heard John out and spread his hands helplessly. "No one can touch Peter

Barsymes. Don't you know he is beloved by the empress, because he comes from her land?"

Mention of her stirred embers of hatred in John's eyes. Passion lifted the gaunt body of the exile. How many men had she not loved? he demanded. Was there a city in Asia where she had not offered her body, to pay her way?

It stimulated Procopius to hear his own thoughts echoed. Sensing his eagerness to draw closer to the shamelessness of Theodora, the Cappadocian whispered, "She plied a trade which I could not name without losing forever the compassion of God. Didn't you know how she contrived not only to use her body but to draw men into shameless deeds? Did you never wonder why they turned away from her, meeting her in the street afterward by day?"

Bending closer, staring at the wine-stained table, the writer of history felt exhilaration at hearing the wantonness of Theodora, whose eyes had never taken notice of him.

At the end of spring of that year 548, Theodora did not come as usual to Justinian's study, although the dampness had gone from the air and the gardens were in bloom. It was told from the Chalké to the Mesé's end that the emperor walked sleepless through the nights. When the rumor of her death came over the water, few believed it at first.

They said she had not been touched by the pestilence; they had seen her not long since in the highest spirits, and the report must have been circulated by her spies. Antonina, landing at the Magnaura docks, thought it was some caprice of the willful woman.

But Theodora was dead, of cancer. The actress of the circus had played her last part well.

Even then, when her body lay between the two candles at the altar of the Apostles near her old home, there was something unlooked for, almost fantastic, in the scene. By the body stood an old man, a patriarch of the east, Anthimius, whom everyone had believed to be dead for a dozen years.

VIII

The First Byzantine

AT SIXTY-SIX YEARS OF AGE, JUSTINIAN WAS LEFT ALONE. HE had endured defeat and sickness, and now he set himself to the task of carrying out his gigantic plans without the help of his wife.

The Grand Janitor observed that the emperor made no change in his work hours of the night; promptly, on the minute of the turn of the water clock, he appeared to advance to the veiled throne for the ten o'clock morning audience. But something fierce and unquenchable had forsaken him; something gay and inflexible had passed beyond his reach, leaving him alone in the courts of the palace. Until then, from those early years of their arguments in the House of Hormisdas, Justinian had always been able to go to Theodora's chamber or to look for her in the garden when he could not decide a thing in his mind. Those who had wondered, like Procopius, which of the two had decided their final problems now understood that it had been the woman. Without her, the abstracted emperor reasoned as before but could not come to a firm decision. Or if he did, he might brood over it until he saw it in a different light.

People noticed that he liked to hear them speak her name. When he was deeply stirred, he would make a pledge in the name of Theodora—"our best-loved empress"—and if he did, he would be apt to keep his word. Moved by some strange fancy, he ordered all her rooms at the Daphne or Hieron to be preserved as they were, with toilet articles in place and the songbirds fed in their cages. More than that, he continued to employ her people, from doorkeeper to Grand Chamberlain, bidding them perform their daily duties as before and to report to him.

Justinian even went to her hall of audience at times. There he found unusual petitioners waiting. Prostitutes no longer wearing the once obligatory red mantles bent to kiss his scarlet half boot; religious women waiting, in their gray body-garment with black sleeves, beggars from the docks, and caravan drivers from the Taurus roads bespoke him in awe. Some of them had journeyed for months to bring a petition to the feet of Theodora, and he did not wish them to be turned away unheard. But it was difficult for him to understand their throaty dialects, and he could not trust his interpreters to repeat truthfully what they asked of him. He heard one of Theodora's ladies of honor whisper, "*She* could never resist a really unhappy person."

Outside the palace, relationships changed in the year after Theodora's death, as if a kaleidoscope had shifted.

Within a month the vindictive Antonina tore apart the two young lovers, Anastasius and her daughter Joannina, in spite of their efforts to hold to each other. As Belisarius' wife, the Lady Antonina now had few superiors at court, and her influence virtually annulled the marriage. Perhaps by her urging to protect his interests but more probably because he felt himself useless in Italy after his collapse at the Tiber barrier, Belisarius sought his master's permission to return and Justinian gave it. Strangely, the originator of the Italian war appeared to have lost interest in it.

Germanus carried out his plan to wed the Gothic heiress, Matasuntha. By doing so he set himself in line for leadership

FX 050/31

MESSAGE FOR

MR. RATCLIFFE

Contact MR. Dubois at
Whitehall 8474 Ex 500,
when you arrive at
Airways Terminal.

of the barbaric masses between the Danube and the Po, among whom he was already popular. More swiftly still, after the death of the empress, the violent and fashionable Artabanes freed himself from his aging wife. "She is repugnant to me, to touch." Yet by so doing he failed to gain Praejecta, the aristocratic lady of his dreams. Willingly or not, this niece of Justinian had been wed to an unambitious man, Marcellus, commander of the excubitor guards. Not being a man to restrain either his thoughts or his words, Artabanes fumed against the sovereigns who, he said, tried to play God. When Justinian took no action against such an outburst, Artabanes lent his ear to conspiracy.

The conspirator was an Armenian who had a grievance, and his proposal was to kill Justinian now, and to eliminate Belisarius after the generalissimo's return from Italy. Such dual assassination, of course, would leave Germanus the only powerful prince in the empire. Would not Artabanes avenge himself, and earn both honor and security for himself by boosting Germanus to the threshold of the throne? Surely the militant Thracians and Dalmatians would rally to Germanus, who had tied himself also to the Goths through the Amal, Matasuntha. By way of precaution the assassination should be carried out before Belisarius came back to court.

Artabanes, still vindictive, shrugged his shoulders. For all of him the Demon Emperor could die. But Germanus, he objected, would never agree to such a stroke.

Here the Armenian showed his cunning. It was perfectly true, he admitted, that the favored Illustrious Germanus could say no word for it or act openly to further it; yet this man of the hour might consent to profit by it, so long as he was not openly involved.

That Artabanes doubted.

The Armenian remarked then that Germanus had a son, a boy with his first beard—yet already honored as consul—who would long to behold his father raised in the world. And this son, in his eagerness to aid the plot, confided it in Marcellus, Master of the Excubitors, chief guardian of the life of the aging Justinian——

All this round of conspiracy Marcellus himself related to Justinian, standing at rigid attention. He was a man who would not do things for money, who seemed to relish the austerity of his duty.

Listening, Justinian asked wearily, "How did they intend to kill me?"

"May it please Your Clemency, they said a man need hardly fear to murder one like yourself, who sits unguarded late at night in some alcove intent on unrolling the Scriptures with priests who are even more aged."

For a moment Justinian considered this portrait of himself. "Germanus, not you, should have spoken to me."

"Thrice August, he believed that I could tell Your Mercy the entire case better than he."

With a grunt Justinian let that pass. When he gave his instructions to the officer, Marcellus hesitated and begged him to repeat them.

"Punish the Armenian with forty cudgel blows, not heavy ones; then parade him through the streets on a camel. Confine the Magister Militum—Artabanes—in his house under guard. Send Germanus to me. Finally, repeat this story wherever you go."

The whole thing may have appeared to Justinian as a bit of garden-party chatter. There were greater values involved —he was recalling Belisarius, to replace the Thracian with Germanus, a commander without taint of failure. Artabanes he needed to co-operate with Germanus . . . after he talked with his cousin, he sent that officer to the north to organize an army of barbarians, while he ordered the moody Artabanes to the field in Sicily . . . the crowds watching the artful Armenian set up on camelback for their edification, after the public broadcast of his story, came to the conclusion that Justinian had dealt with the would-be assassins in a way unheard of before now. Narses might have suggested it.

Another phenomenon held their attention just then. Like the Swordfish Comet, the monster of the deep sea came to his end. "It was in the river Sangarius," an eyewitness related. "The great whale Porphyrius came in from the sea, chasing a school of dolphins. We all ran away, because he churned after the dolphins up on the muddy shore. There he became caught in the mud. Some soldiers on rafts struck him with axes, but he did not die until long after they towed him up on the shore with ropes."

Astrologers of the Mesé arcades pointed out that the death of the monster coincided with the passing of the empress. Sailors of the docks remarked that earthquakes had shaken the towns of Asia, while the Nile flooded its banks. The conjunction of these signs indicated a change about to take place on the earth, and the crowds waited to learn what it would be.

Already a change was taking place, heeded by Justinian and his advisers, in his old homeland of the Balkan highlands. The new barbarian peoples who had intruded there, across the northern frontier, were pressing slowly south. Slavs, Hunnic folk, and formidable Lombards were inside the old frontiers to stay.

No longer could the emperor in the Sacred Palace set one khan or kral against another by a bribe of gold or a clever barb of deceit. Definitely the balance of force lay with the newcomers. So Justinian—with Narses counseling him—sent Germanus to try to enlist them all in a new army.

In so doing he bowed to the inevitable and departed from the Constantinopolitan policy of recruiting only Romanized and Christian fighting men. He also gambled on the integrity of Germanus, a Thracian by birth and a moderator by nature. Germanus was not a soldier by instinct, like Belisarius; he merely gathered men about him and conducted himself bravely in the front rank with a sword. But he looked well and inspired loyalty. Moreover, by allowing Germanus to marry Matasuntha, Justinian had conceded to the popular prince a claim to both eastern and western thrones—to the old and the new Rome. Germanus had energetic sons alive, and would have others of the Amal blood. His dynasty might well succeed Justinian's. Theodora had set herself against that.

In these years after Theodora's death, 548–550, the crisis intensified. Justinian ordered Germanus, with the new army of barbarians and Matasuntha accompanying him, to enter Italy and crush Totila.

Belisarius, arriving in the Golden Horn that first September, aided Justinian with his advice. Totila, who had retaken Rome as soon as Belisarius left it, was behaving with a new humility, and that might be a sign of weakness. The moody Goth actually was making some attempt to repair the damaged monuments of the imperial city, while inviting fugitive Roman patricians to come back to their homes. Beyond expectation, Totila was trying, pathetically, to revive chariot racing in the Circus there, to cheer up the Romans. It seemed that he believed in a prophecy of Benedict the Abbot that the time of his death was near. Justinian agreed that was a sign of weakness. Totila even attempted to build a fleet, out of reeds bound together and green wood. His Goths were neither shipbuilders nor seamen.

But Germanus never reached Italy. Starting thither with his great host, strengthened by Lombard allies, he was turned aside—by Justinian's demand—to drive off a raiding army of Slavs. Falling sick in the campaign through swampy lowlands, Germanus died of a fever. His personality had been the keystone of Justinian's plan.

The danger of which Germanus had warned him seemed to grow with each month. While war intensified in the Caucasus, savage Avars appeared from the steppes, moving toward the Danube. With their new fleet the Goths attacked Sicily.

Justinian called on Narses to take Germanus' place.

Narses had a way with the barbarians; for some reason the fierce and realistic clansmen trusted this highly artificial figure. There was a touch of fantasy in sending forth the eunuch, more than seventy years old, who as Grand Chamberlain of the Court wore the imperial eagles embroidered on his skirtlike robe.

"Whenever you go out of quarters," Belisarius warned him, "have march music played. Sound off the trumpets, pick up with the flutes. Never let your soldiers see you hesitate. Do your worrying inside a closed tent."

Ironically, after sixteen years Belisarius had won his long argument with Justinian—for Narses' benefit. In this gamble to end the war Narses was to have the unlimited funds in gold coin that Belisarius had never been given; he was to command the great army for which Belisarius had begged.

Generously, out of his long experience, Belisarius gave advice to the eager eunuch. "You have strength enough to give battle to Totila. Do it at the first chance. Your barbarian federates will do well enough if they can see an enemy massed in front of them. If you try to maneuver, they may wander off or wait to see which side is gaining the upper hand. Keep them always together, facing the Goths, with the strongest of them on your flanks, so your array can't be turned."

The prospect of a mighty battle stirred the spirit of the old man.

"As for the Goths," the victor of Tricamaron counseled him, "they will rush to attack, like all Germans. Let them. If you can beat off their first rush—and you must do it—they will fall into hesitation, and each Goth will begin to think what to do next. Some will probably form into shield rings, to sing about their bravery in dying that way. Others will run back to their camp. Then you must attack their leader and kill him as quickly as possible. But keep the music playing all the time."

So Narses rode out of the crowded Golden Gate in a horse litter shining with silk and gold; he rode ahead of the standards of the eagles and the cross of Constantine, with the flutes trilling behind . . . an insignificant sexless man, but carrying the authority of an empire.

Watching the new army parade out the gate, Belisarius saw the survivors of his biscuit eaters pass and heard their chant, the Trisagion: "Holy, Mighty, Immortal Lord . . ."

It was strange for Belisarius, a gentleman of leisure—Justinian had named him First Citizen of the Roman Empire—to dismount at the Augusteon where the new marble statue of Justinian was being raised within its scaffolding, to wait for news of the battle fronts.

The first tidings hinted at a change for the better. In Sicily the thwarted assassin, Artabanes, held the forts against Totila, who retired hastily to the mainland on hearing of the Roman army assembling in the north; at sea John, nephew of Vitalian, found the ill-made Gothic fleet, and the Goths, helpless on the water, hastened to beach their vessels and escape to the familiar earth.

Autumn came, and the storms of winter. Through the mountain ways Narses led a growing army. Lombard mailed knights and servingmen, Herulian riders with their bows, hired Goths and Saxons, thronged around the comitatus of the dead Germanus. With gold and food in plenty, they followed after the litter of the wizened servant of Justinian, who wheedled them all. The old man with his music playing seemed to be some strange instrument of fate. Twenty-five thousand hardened men followed him, and the ships of John joined him on the coast, so that he waded and marched and rowed forward along the shore, avoiding the inland valleys where Goths and Franks waited uneasily.

The battle was fought near the ancient Flaminian Way.

It ended in the breaking and destruction of the Goths. "The king fled with five men, after dark. Of those who pursued Totila, the rider closest to him was a Gepid with a spear. The pursuers did not know that they followed Totila, galloping through the darkness. Then one of the king's esquires reined in and shouted at the Gepid. 'Are you a dog, to attack your master?' After that the Gepid understood that Totila rode before him, and he hastened on, to thrust him with his spear. Totila did not fall, but in a little while he died and they buried him there in the earth."

By way of proof, a courier offered the shirt and the mantle of this last champion of the Goths, showing the bloodstains on them. Totila had gone upon the sea and had died in the ninth year, as Benedict foretold.

Gothic bands struggled on as partisans, but a second battle broke them, until their leaders agreed to depart forever from Italy. Some of them joined the watching Franks. That happened in the year 552.

Then, like a flood racing down from a broken dam, the barbarian Franks rushed in from their eyrie in the north. Pagan and Christian, blending with drunken Burgundians and desperate Goths, they filled the roads to the south with their tens of thousands, snatching at the loot of churches, feeding and drinking off the impoverished country. Narses and his commanders had the good luck or wisdom to take refuge in the cities while this human flood raced by.

The Franks quarreled among themselves, sickened in the heat, weakened themselves with dysentery that came from the wine they tried to brew in the grape season. When Narses' army assembled, the headstrong Franks threw themselves at it, their axes flailing, in a human wedge. The wedge thrust deep into the Roman-commanded regiments and never got out. Legend relates that only five of the axmen survived the disaster; actually the scattered survivors fled north, over the Po and back into the passes of the Alps.

Again the discipline and planning of the civilized command had destroyed a barbarian army. At seventy-five years of age Narses found himself a victorious generalissimo. After nearly twenty years the war begun by Belisarius' sailing to Sicily had been ended by Narses at the Alps.

Beyond the Alps the Franks stayed put in what had been Roman Gaul; but not even Justinian, at this point, imagined that they could be driven elsewhere and the province of Gaul restored to the empire. Instead, it became the embryo of France. Isolated beyond the Channel, the island of Britain remained in the hands of the Anglo-Saxons.

Almost as far away, the Spanish peninsula was coming back more firmly into the hands of the courageous Visigoths, who kept up a raid-and-trade relationship with the imperial merchants' stations and garrisons along the coast.

Such gradual transmutations did not show at all upon the mappa mundi in the Sacred Palace. In Italy, Narses had to pay off and flatter the powerful Lombard contingent and send it home. These blond giants in armor, with their esquires-at-arms and rude notions of chivalry, proved too hard to handle. He could never be sure whether, at the start of a battle, these Long-beards might not take it into their thick heads to join the other side. Their peculiar sense of honor impelled them to fight for, not against, any blood kin; their fondness for loot turned their eyes on the imperial coffers rather than the mean war chests of the barbarians. Belisarius' warning had served the eunuch well.

The Lombards, however, had seen much of Italy. Under a more aggressive king they would return to the northern plain of the Po, the future Lombardy.

Narses himself was ordered to stay on—as Belisarius never had been allowed to stay—in Italy. Supreme authority rested in his aged hands. A Praetorian Prefect came out as ostensible governor, with a bevy of rectors, but behind this façade of officials the eunuch ruled as Justinian's servant.

To Italy returned the exiled Pope Vigilius, who had been brought to Constantinople by Theodora. With him he brought Justinian's Act for the government of liberated Italy. This long and legal Act was humane—persons enslaved during the war of twenty years were released from bondage, and even nuns who had been dragged, or had departed, from the cloisters were restored to the service of sanctity. It made no effort to punish war crimes; but it brought with it a host of new judges and tax collectors. It imposed the yoke of officialdom on the liberated but long-suffering survivors. And Narses was the very man to carry out, through this Act, his master's will.

There were too many in Italy who had died or wandered from their homes in search of food. Some of the remaining patricians availed themselves of Justinian's suggestion and moved eastward to Constantinople. Their ancestral land bore too many scars.

A twelve-year-old boy came back to Rome to live among the scars. Sensitive and imaginative, he prowled the palaces of the Caesars restored on the outside but littered with dirt and the droppings of animals within. Son of a senator, when the senate had ceased to be, he had tradition as his guide through the ruins, climbing the tiers of the Colosseum when tumblers, gypsies and bear-baiters performed for pence in the arena, sitting atop the cracked marble benches of the Circus when the last races of the chariots given by Totila were run.

Steeped as he was in the past, this boy Gregory found his greatest comfort in the brown brick basilicas of St. Cosmas and the St. Maria in Cosmiden, by the empty Forum. There the mosaic pictures had been kept clean, and he studied the mystical splendor of the Apocalypse, the quiet expectancy of the Annunciation. Like Justinian, but with very different aspects to influence him, he grew up among imagined things.

Gregory, who was to be Gregory the Great, must have read the carved words of the old-time prophecy:

> While stands the Colisaeus, Rome shall stand;
> When falls the Colisaeus, Rome shall fall;
> And when Rome falls, with her shall fall the world.

The Colosseum still stood, although empty. Gregory longed to restore the life of his city and to free it from the trammels of the easterners, the men of Byzantium. The imaginative boy would not admit that these easterners could be *Romans.* In his uncompromising thought, they remained Armenians, Persians, men who chattered Greek and obeyed slavishly the commands of an Autocrat of a hybrid city beyond the seas.

Yet in spite of his longing, Gregory the Great would never manage to restore his native city of Rome. The Colosseum still stood, but the Rome of Julius Caesar and Trajan had fallen. Gregory, as a monk and the first of the authoritative Popes, would upbuild the basilica across the Tiber, the church of St. Peter.

In another particular the ancient prophecy erred. The civilized world had not fallen. A remnant of it survived in Constantinople.

"Practically the whole Palace is new, and was built by the Emperor Justinian. We know the lion, as they say, by his claw; and so we know the impressiveness of the Palace from its entrance, the Chalké . . . where the whole ceiling boasts of pictures inset with beautifully colored cubes of stone—pictures of war and battle with many cities being captured, some in Italy and some in Libya, where the Emperor Justinian is winning victories through his General Belisarius, and the General is returning to the Emperor with his whole army intact and he gives him kings and kingdoms as spoils.

"In the center stand the Emperor and the Empress Theodora, both seeming to rejoice. Around them stands the Roman Senate all in festive mood as they bestow on the Emperor honors equal to those of God because of the magnitude of his achievements. . . .

"On the side toward the sea, white marble gleams with the light of the sun. There also the Empress Theodora stands upon a column, which the city dedicated to her in gratitude. The statue is indeed beautiful, but still inferior to the beauty of the Empress; for to express her loveliness in words, or to portray it in a statue would be, for a mortal man, impossible."

So Procopius wrote, hating the words. His latest book, *The Buildings,* needed to bestow fluent praise upon Justinian, who would pay for the book. And no one in his senses would put into writing anything but reverent esteem for Theodora—so greatly did the mad emperor dote upon her memory . . . at times Procopius was disturbed by a nagging thought: what if, after all, he wrote the truth? In life, Theodora had been lovely, and surely Justinian demanded buildings that were like dreams in marble. . . .

Alone now in his sanctum, Justinian kept track of them all. Over the dark arches that Constantine had put above the cavern of Bethlehem a lofty basilica was rising; cisterns collected rain water in the deserts; a new aqueduct brought pure water to Antioch, the city of Theodora. In Ravenna her face had become a portrait in stone——

After the crisis that followed her death some good news came. Petra, the port at the far end of the sea, was stormed and captured, in Roman hands again.

Unexpectedly, just when Peter Barsymes had to take over the silk industry as a state monopoly to keep it from dying out, the far-traveling monks returned from the Land of Silk. They had nothing in their hands but bamboo staffs. Within the bamboos they had eggs of the mysterious silkworm hidden and ready to hatch. A few morsels of eggs that might breed worms, to be fed on certain leaves in the heat of Syria, to begin in time the manufacture of silk at home . . .

Among the many volumes lying in rolls, pigeonholed along the walls, were the massive Body of the Law, now completed with a handbook to help students understand it. Nowadays Justinian hardly turned to it. There in parchment and papyri lay the Law, fixed for all, digested and commented upon, but never questioned. At times he glanced at his own name, written there so long ago—"Flavius Justinian, victor over the Goths, Franks, Germans, Slavs, Alans, Vandals and Africa itself—the pious, happy, renowned conqueror in triumph, always August."

Had it not become truth? His analytical mind probed at the sonorous Latin words and decided that most of it was now true.

Out in the Augusteon, his statue in gilded bronze would wear eternally the regalia of Constantine, with feathered plumes. Was he not greater than Constantine, who had had to share his authority with the bishop of the Church, as Augustus himself had had to conform to the opinion of the senate? After long meditation, Justinian decided that one of his hands—in the effigy—should hold the world-and-cross, while the other should be raised high as if in the act of giving an order. For a legend to be inscribed in words he fancied something brief and simple. It should mention glory. Perhaps two words might suffice. *Gloriae Perennis.* The glories of his reign would last forever——

When he meditated, far-off sounds disturbed him. The cries of the boatmen and vendors were never still. Their shouts and songs reached him in unknown dialects. At times he lifted his bald head with its fringe of gray hairs to demand of Theodora what they said. . . .

There was no one to tell him that his Act in Italy could not restore the past. The human beings there would never be a nation under such an Act.

He had no way of knowing that the mighty Code of Law left no room for argument, no easement for local customs, and no place for future theory. It spoke with the single voice of authority, and it said what he, Justinian, had said: "There is nothing more sacred than the imperial majesty."

He had built roads for vehicles, aqueducts for human beings, and great churches to cover sacred places. But humanity itself had escaped him.

There was no longer anyone to tell him that.

In imagination, then, the son of Sabbatius looked upon the empire as regained. At last, he believed, it was governed again by one law. There remained the task of uniting the Church.

That must be accomplished also if his herculean labor of restoring to the world one empire, one law, and one Church was not to fail. Compared to it, the laws and wars and reforms had been minor matters, to be decided—at least in Justinian's mind—by the will of Caesar. But there were things that were not Caesar's. There was the mystery of life, and the providence of God.

True, Justinian's inflexible will had closed the last pagan School of Athens, and had created the Great Church, to serve all his empire. And from that empire heretic Arians and Nestorians had become barred almost as effectively as the Manichaeans and Zoroastrians of the east. Yet what could his people believe, concerning God?

That was the question, so simple and still vaster than the Ocean itself. It waited, he believed, for the Emperor-Basileus to answer. Without an answer, there could be no universal Christian Church. Throughout the five years after Theodora's death, Justinian applied himself to his last task. He labored alone, because no ordinary mind could aid him. Because he was then seventy years of age, memories beset his mind with the force of actual happenings. The years merged together. Reality faded into fancy, and inevitably the memory of the dead woman intruded upon his reasoning.

For Theodora had never yielded to him on the question of religion. He had been made to promise that he would protect her patriarchs of the east . . . when he closed his eyes, remembering her casket in the church of the Apostles, there stood the unyielding Anthimius. . . .

So many visions thronged into the concept of one Church. There were the words of Jesus Christ, the teachings of the Apostles, the writings of the Fathers, of Augustine himself. There were the memories of the earliest churches. Jerusalem, Antioch, and Alexandria looked back to the days of the Apostles. Their eastern patriarchs held fast to hallowed ritual —resenting the primacy of Rome and Constantinople—stirring separatist tendencies and national feeling.

There were the questions forever arising. Of the nature of Christ, whether human being or God incarnate; of the nature of the mother, whether mortal or divine. Could a simple man of flesh and bone bestow salvation upon all mankind? Could a mortal woman be also Theotokos? Did salvation extend to pagans who merely understood the truth? Would faith alone redeem a soul?

What multitudes had parted and followed after those who answered the questions, each in a different way—Nestorius, Arius, Augustine, Origen, Basil, and Cyril? Every generation had seen a new parting . . . yet in each one the populace had demanded of its leaders to proclaim the truth. Echoes of the cry of the people lingered in Justinian's memory—"Holy, holy, holy. The Trinity has triumphed. We are orthodox brethren, with one soul—with one faith and one soul. The faith of the orthodox prevails."

So they had greeted his uncle, Justin, in his city. Of them Gregory of Nyssa wrote: "In all places, cloth merchants, money changers and grocers alike argue unknowable questions. If you ask a man how many obols you owe him, he expresses his ideas about the begotten and unbegotten. If I inquire the price of bread, the baker answers that the Father is greater than the Son. If you try to find out whether your bath is ready, you are told that the Son was made out of nothing."

In the previous century an oecumenical council of the world, meeting at Chalcedon across the water, had decided such questions. The creed of Chalcedon, announcing the two natures, united in Christ, had become the orthodox creed.

Instead of healing the unrest, Chalcedon seemed to intensify the antagonism. For the eastern patriarchs clung more firmly to their belief in the one nature of Christ and cried out against "those who divide and confuse." It seemed at times as if all the energy and thought of the people had been driven inward, in quest of salvation. Hermits left the cities to meditate. Monks isolated themselves in cloisters, to labor with their hands while freeing their minds from the clamor in the streets. From the deserts of Libya to the convents of Edessa these easterners believing in the one nature of Christ, the Monophysites as they were called, rebelled against the decision of Chalcedon.

Their intensity of belief produced a cleavage in the empire, with Monophysites opposing orthodox. It divided the circus factions and brought with it the danger of civil war. It tended to form ideological nations within the empire, for Egypt followed the belief of Alexandria, and the Syrian coast held to the belief of Antioch . . . Theodora's belief.

He could not reason with her, although he understood all the different viewpoints. "I am only a woman, I do not understand controversy." Her faith was curiously blind.

Yet Augustine said, "Understanding is the reward of faith."

Theodora would not study the written words. Let the churches stand as they are, she said, in the lands where they have been from the first. If you change them, you will harm them.

But the cleavage could not be allowed to go on. At every turn, like a basilisk, it faced Justinian . . . stirring Vitalian, in those first years, to rouse up the orthodox in rebellion . . . grouping the Arians together, to form an iron ring around the Middle Sea. . . . Justin had tried to bring about reconciliation with Rome . . . when Belisarius went there, orthodoxy marched with his armies . . . yet the orthodox west would not agree with the patriarchs of the east.

There could not be an orthodox church and a Monophysite church antagonistic to each other. Justinian had tried to force them to agree, saying to Agapetus the Pope, "I shall force you to agree with us, or else I shall send you into exile." On the persuasion of Agapetus, he had exiled Anthimius instead.

He had tried to reconcile them, by pointing out flaws in three chapters of the canons of the council of Chalcedon, hoping to satisfy the easterners by attacking the canons of the west. His attack on the three chapters aroused a new storm of anger in Africa, Egypt, and Syria. It seemed that the bishops of those eastern dioceses preferred to let the canons of Chalcedon, whether right or wrong, go unchallenged.

Do not change what is gone by, Theodora begged him. He remembered her words clearly because that was the only time she begged of him, anxiously. Let people believe what they will, she asked, because all of them hold to their beliefs. He knew she was begging for her friends of the east but he could not refuse, because she was ill . . . at the time when the priests went out to the far Arabian coast, and the missionaries to the Hunnic tribes where the armies could not go . . . he had been forced to weaken the armies, to pay the cost of the missions . . . when Jacob Old Clothes walked forty miles a day to escape his road police, and the monks from her house outdistanced his ambassadors to the Caucasus and the Nile . . .

To find a way to end the cleavage, Justinian had studied the doctrines of the easterners, of Basil the Great of Caesaria and Gregory of Nyssa, seeking to identify their writings with his own. He had tried to make a confession of faith, to agree with them: ". . . and when we say that Christ is God, we do not deny him to be man; and when we say that he is man, we do not deny him to be God. . . ."

These carefully reasoned words did not convince the men

of the churches. And Theodora asked for the praetor to fetch the Pope Vigilius from Rome to Constantinople for those last talks. Vigilius agreed that there could be an understanding and issued his Judicatum, supporting Justinian's attack on the three chapters of Chalcedon.

It seemed then as if Justinian had prevailed, and ended the cleavage of belief.

Then, after Theodora's death, the disputations began again. In Justinian's presence the bishops and deacons agreed with his arguments; when they left him they talked among themselves and opposed him. Vigilius himself no longer assented, and refused to affirm his Judicatum.

In anger Justinian lashed out at the Roman, who could not leave Constantinople. The struggle between them went on in written words, Justinian demanding that his captive sign approval of the condemnation of the three chapters of Chalcedon, and Vigilius announcing instead that the decisions at Chalcedon were infallible in every detail. Their minds could no longer meet.

The struggle left stark memories—of the harried Pope shutting himself up in his palace, then fleeing to sanctuary from Justinian's threats, hurrying past Theodora's house, to the altar of St. Peter in the adjacent church of the two Apostles. A praetor, ordered to arrest him, entering the church with soldiers and a throng following: the Latin deacons pulled by the soldiers from the pillars—the stout and powerful Vigilius wrapping his arms about the pillars of the altar, clinging to them until pulled by his beard and hair—the slender pillars giving way until the altar canopy fell, to be grasped by anxious priests. And then the roar of the crowd, shouting sacrilege and shame, until the worried praetor went away with the soldiers, without Vigilius. . . .

Then the flight of Vigilius over a wall by night to a waiting boat, and across the water to sanctuary again in St. Euphemia, in Chalcedon . . . Belisarius sent after him to persuade him to return, and Vigilius, refusing, writing the story of his stand for all to read—until Justinian gave way and pledged him immunity from interference.

Justinian made his decision, then, to invoke his supreme power. As emperor of the Roman state, he summoned a world council, to unite the divided churches. The fifth oecumenical council, to assemble at his city of Constantinople, obedient to his command. . . .

Then, in the spring, the prelates from the far corners of the earth, listening to his written advice and exhortation, sitting in the corridor of the Great Church . . . Pelagius, who had faced Totila, coming to speak for the brethren of the west, Jacob Baradaeus speaking for those of the east . . . Vigilius refusing to be present, refusing agreement with his emperor . . . Justinian, quoting Scriptures and precedents, claiming that his council could agree on unity, without Vigilius . . .

And in the end the sense of failure, after disputation. Justinian allowing the Pope to return home with the Act for Italy, hearing of the death of the ailing Vigilius, proposing Pelagius as his successor . . . Narses writing from Rome that the Latin clergy would never change their views, suspecting Pelagius of being intimidated by the emperor and his Greeks . . . until Pelagius faced them at the altar of St. Peter's, raising the Scriptures above his head to swear that he would adhere to all that was held sacred in the west . . . Narses confessing that, in Rome, the eastern clergy were called Imperialists and were not admitted to be orthodox. "Most Magnificent Emperor, believe thy servant when he declares that the human mass here will never suffer its pope to be under the order of emperor or patriarch in the east. The space of the water between us is not so great as the gulf between our minds and theirs."

Narses had used a Greek word, *humanoia,* for those distant human beings. Humanity.

Justinian would not admit that the gap between west and

east had grown too great to be ever closed. It seemed to him that the people, the folk in the street, had become the mute antagonists of his plans.

They had no voice in the Fifth Oecumenical Council; they did not appear before him with their petitions now. They followed after obscure priests, worshiping saints of their own choosing and looking for miracles to relieve their misfortunes. Armenians had their catholicos and, because they were Armenians, claimed that the catholicos could not be subject to the emperor in Constantinople. Orthodox Egyptians disputed with orthodox believers in his city because their church in Egypt had been a sanctuary before the Great Church was built. They said Justinian should carry out the commandments of God, instead of disputing about them.

While he brooded over the problem, Justinian had his Prefect of the People arrest astrologers and would-be prophets and parade them around the streets on camels. But others appeared to prophesy in their place.

What bond held them together, as groups, uniting here, dissolving there? Not tradition, for they were fast losing memory of the empire as it had been. Belisarius claimed that recruits drilling in the Strategium no longer understood the shouted Latin orders; they obeyed the intonation of the commands, not the words. And certainly birth did not unite his people, for even in the palace he was surrounded by Africans, Armenians, Saxons, Herules, Syrians, or Thracians.

No, there was only one amalgam that held his people together. Their religion. Diverse, speaking all the tongues of Babel, they still looked to the emperor as their protector by divine providence. Had they not greeted him, twenty-six years before, as "Our emperor, chosen by God"?

He was their Basileus, the agent of the Eternal. . . .

In how many ways had he fulfilled his obligation, building the new churches for old sanctuaries, poring through the collected volumes of Christian lore, passing judgment on the bishops of the dioceses? In war he had defeated the encircling Arian heretics and pagan Persians.

Yet he had failed to influence the servants of his Church, in the council within sight of him, at the Sancta Sophia.

Why?

Justinian could not answer his question. His wearied mind could only believe that he had been close to a solution and it had eluded him.

There remained the possibility of force. He could exile dissidents, execute Samaritans, Manichaeans, Jews, and compel Arians and Nestorians to accept orthodox doctrine or lose their property and liberty. In the earliest years he had attempted to do much of that—with the consequence that misery increased.

Brooding until his mind sickened with vertigo, he thought he could enforce orthodoxy through the armies, bidding Narses seize and imprison Pelagius. But he remembered the groan of the crowd that had watched Vigilius gripping the altar pillars with bleeding hands.

The months went by and new years came. There was no one to tell him what to do.

Perhaps Justinian never made his decision consciously. He yielded to the will of his people. He did not make use of force. No Pope of St. Peter's was summoned again to board a dromon to be taken to the court at Constantinople. The dissenting churches of the east were allowed to follow their doctrines, under his protection, even though in Syria and Egypt they tended to become national churches. Pilgrims came and went unhindered at the House of the Monks. No other council was summoned. In his mountains the Armenian catholicos separated further from Constantinople. In Asia Jacob Baradaeus organized his dissenting Jacobite church. In their deserts the Arab tribal people followed their paganism, blended now with the Christian concept of One God.

The embryos had formed of a Catholic Europe and an Eastern Orthodox dominion.

But if there was no longer a single universal authority obeyed by all peoples, then the Roman universal state had ended. Paradoxically, the empire that Justinian had sought to restore through his armies had been lost at the council within his own Great Church.

He could not have imagined that his dominion henceforth would face toward the east, speaking with the tongues of the east, and would in time be known by the old name of the city buried beneath his palace, Byzantium.

He had been the Caesar-Pope of what he still believed to be a world dominion. Only involuntarily, and after bitter effort, had he renounced his authority as a Caesar. He had, as it were, given up the sword held by Augustus and Theodosius the Great.

What remained to him?

At seventy-five years of age, immured within his palace walls, he no longer dreams of the Rome of the Caesars; he searches, instead, for inward meanings; he studies the kaleidoscope of the outer world, seeking some means of safeguarding his city, by plotting, by drawing upon the brains and the strength of other men, or even by planned treachery. He still has inner conceit, and, measured by the western code of chivalry, he is a coward; but he has an unquenchable will to survive. He refuses to be another man's slave. His civilization has become his life.

No longer emperor and Caesar, he has become the Autocrat and Basileus of his people, a despot dependent upon their approval in holding to his throne. From his palace he goes only to his Great Church, where he can rest in a golden haze of memory.

So Justinian the First has become the first of those remarkable men we know as Byzantines, who—apparently doomed to eradication as rulers—preserved their city, its culture, and the population within its gates for exactly nine hundred years.

But he would not have been Justinian if he had renounced his competence to solve the religious questions. With fresh eagerness he returned to his study of the writings of the Fathers and the canons of the councils. Somewhere in Christian lore, he fancied, lay the solution that had escaped him—the one universal creed for all churches.

So, with the eagerness of a pilgrim finding his way to a shrine, he searched among parchment pages through the hours of the night. The mighty imagination of his early years had decayed to fitful fancies. He found relief in his new quest, sitting in an alcove of the palace.

Never had that melting pot, his city, been more alive with people than in the beginning of the year 557. By the statue of Theodosius on University Hill, professors hurrying in gray robes to their lectures sniffed the balsam and spice from the market below. Riding through the Strategium, Belisarius exchanged gifts and stories with war veterans who, lounging on the sunny side of the barrack, watched critically the drilling of new recruits. Daily Belisarius went to glance at the news bulletins in the hall of the Chalké—not oblivious of the mosaic replicas of his battles on the wall above . . . it seemed that only his victories had been immortalized in this way. He seldom saw Justinian, who avoided him now.

On the benches of the Augusteon and among the canopied caïques that carried them out to the island resorts, patrician ladies made much of Justin, nephew of the emperor. A handsome man, Justin, kind to his family—in a word, a second Germanus. He had married well—the daughter of Comito, sister of the pious Augusta Theodora. So they agreed, and discussed the new mechanical fan on sale in the Galatian arcade, a fan that worked by a hidden spring, needing no effort of fingers or wrist.

Down the steps from Theodora's house to the small harbor the jewelers showed a stock of garnets with the fire of rubies, imported from Samarkand-way and marked down in price because they had paid no duty to the gouging tax collectors. Along the stone quays of the harbor Greek naval seamen had souvenirs of the Italian wars to barter for strong Cyprus wine. The sailors wore brown tunics and kilts, the colors of the sails and hulls of their small, swift scout vessels. This camouflage of color protected the scout boats from observation at sea. Massive dromons, being battleships, needed no such disguise of coloring. The dromons were the queens of the sea, fearing no enemy.

Within the Hippodrome the four-horse chariots raced again on festival days, when silk awnings billowed over the great arena. The first woven silk was coming in from the Syrian coast, with the purple dye reserved for imperial garments, and the herbal medicines for the physicians. Within the treasury the new Economist had restored the gold reserve of 324,000 pieces left to it by Anastasius of beloved memory.

The Mesé hummed with activity. With the revival of trade there was work for every man; idlers were sent to the fields beyond the Long Wall, where peasants, for the first time, could keep more than half their harvests.

Constantinople was showing the effect of protection from the dangers that beset the outer world. The terror of the pestilence was almost forgotten; the burned area had been hidden long since under the magnificent new government buildings.

In the map of the world drawn by Cosmas, the explorer, the sea was named "The Roman Gulf"—so entirely had the Middle Sea come back into the hands of the emperor.

Drawing near the end of his last book, the secretary-historian Procopius took note of that . . . "And at Gadira [Cádiz, beyond Gibraltar] on the right side of the Pillars of Hercules and the strait there had been a fortress of the Romans in early times. Because the Vandals neglected it, time had almost destroyed it. Our Emperor Justinian made it strong with a new wall and made the wall safe by means of a garrison. There, too, on the threshold of the empire he dedicated to the Mother of God a notable church, protected by the fortress. . . ."

Turning his attention to the eastern threshold of the empire, Procopius wrote into his record, "A barren land stretches far inland here without water. It was called Arabia and is known now as the Third Palestine. Above it a steep and fearsomely wild mountain rears, by the Red Sea. On this Mount Sina [Sinai] live monks who spend their lives rehearsing for death. Their solitude is precious to them. They crave nothing else, so the Emperor Justinian built them a church to pray in —not on the summit of the mountain but lower down. For no man would dare pass a night on the summit, where crashes of thunder and manifestations of divine power are heard. It was there, they say, that Moses had the laws from God and published them. By the church below the mountain the Emperor built a fortress, to keep barbarian Saracens from stealing into the lands of Palestine itself. . . .

"So much for these matters. Concerning them there can be no dispute. It is clear beyond question to all mankind that the Emperor Justinian has strengthened the empire, with fortresses and garrisons from the edge of the east to the very place of the sun's setting—these being the limits of the Roman dominion."

Concerning the protection of their dominion, then, there was no question in the mind of the aging Procopius, luxuriating in a good salary, although he would dispute readily enough concerning the character of the man who ruled it. In that very year Constantinople was making an end of the long-drawn-out conflict in the Caucasus. The Persians agreed to another five-year truce, sweetened by gold and oiled by diplomacy. In Italy, Narses, viceroy and Grand Chamberlain, had the situation well in hand.

There seemed to be no cloud upon the horizon. An unaccustomed tranquillity extended through the lands, when the first manifestation of divine power came in the form of an earthquake along the shore of the Euxine. In one city the roof of a church fell upon a throng seeking refuge. It was like the thunder and lightning flashes on the summit of Sinai.

Once the signs had been manifest, the dangers were observed approaching. Like fire rising from old embers, the plague reappeared after the earthquake. It did not pursue a direct course as before; it claimed isolated towns and spread through stricken Italy. A new famine followed there, because crops had not been gathered in or properly seeded for so long.

"As time went on, only portions of the crops took root again. It happened in Aemilia that the inhabitants left their homes and went to the sea shore, supposing that some supplies must be there. In Tuscany, they went to the mountains to grind up acorns of the oak trees for grain to make bread.

"Those who were to die at first became thin and pale; the skin became dry and fastened on the bones. Their faces always wore an expression of amazement, while they had a dreadful sort of insane stare. Some died from eating too much when they found food. Most of them were so overcome by hunger that if they happened upon a growth of grass somewhere they rushed to it and tried to pull it from the ground. If they found themselves too weak to do so, they would lie down on the grass with their hands outstretched on the earth."[1]

Another observer, Paul the Deacon, said curtly, "You would behold there a land fallen into the silence of primeval ages."

As the months passed, Justinian heard of the pleas in distant churches: "Thrice August, give bread to thy people!"

This time the famine could be fought by shipping grain from untouched Africa and Egypt. But unrest rose with hunger, and the demes, the old factions of the Blues and Greens, revived their meetings. These people's parties had new com-

[1]Procopius is telling here of the famine areas he visited in earlier years before he left Italy with Belisarius. The plague and famine conditions returned in '58.

plaints, that food supplies were being requisitioned by imperial officials and siphoned off to Constantinople. Wealthy magnates, the spokesmen declared, suffered no such calamity as ordinary people; they hoarded grain and meat, guarding their stocks with hired soldiery.

Anxiety increased because the emperor, now so aged and obsessed with his Scriptures, did not appear to be aware of the crisis. Yet he would make no change in his ideas or the government. Gradually the popular misgivings increased to the point where miracles were looked for, to give some aid in the crisis. And something very startling happened in Constantinople itself.

After an earthquake tremor, the dome of the Great Church fell in.

A palace official, sleeping near Justinian, was killed by the fall of a marble slab. Those who came to look at the body remarked that the earthquake had selected for death only this one person, notably evil in life. "I doubt," said Agathias, one of the observers, "if an earthquake can pick out the evil individuals from the good. If it could, it would be a very desirable thing."

When Justinian visited his edifice, he found the round base of the dome open to the sky and the altar exposed to the rain. There were murmurs among his attendants that this sign had been given to punish the pride of the builders who, as at the tower of Babel, had tried to raise an edifice against the will of God.

Anthemius, who had designed the dome, was dead. But Isidore, the master of masonry, survived. After inspecting the ruin with his architects, he confessed that the dome had been too flat in form, exerting such outward thrust that its center had given way under the strain of the earthquake. If the dome were rebuilt more in the round, with its base immobilized forever by giant outer buttresses——

Justinian ordered the new dome to be built in this way,

to endure. "It is not the anger of the Lord but the fault of the builders that destroyed the dome," he announced.

Perhaps the rumor of disorder and earthquake in the Queen City passed northward, beyond the forts of the Danube; perhaps the distant Avars, pressing closer upon them, drove them south; more likely, they heard from merchants of the wealth accumulating in the city, and the lack of armed forces to defend it; whatever stirred them into action, the Huns crossed the frozen Danube that winter of '58 and drove at Constantinople.

These Kutrigur Huns of the steppes were more dreaded than the Herules of the borders. This time they came on in thousands, led by their khan. They did not follow the highways; they avoided the castles and walled towns, to circle like wolf packs through the countryside, sweeping up horses, herds, captives, and loot.

For a while, when the ice melted in the streams and mud clogged the trails, the Kutrigur Huns paused in their advance. This gave Constantinople hope that they would turn back with their loot, as they had done before, grazing on the new grass, to return to the steppes. But when the roads hardened and the crops stood in the fields, the Huns divided. One army turned west, into Justinian's old homeland, to make a descent on Greece; a second force occupied the mountains of Thrace. The main army of the khan headed south, past Hadrian's City, toward Constantinople. Seven thousand riders followed the khan and they came fast.

"Meeting no resistance," Agathias, a witness, relates, "they overran the countryside, plundering it mercilessly. Well-born women were carried off. Those who happened to be pregnant bore children on the march. Unable to hide their throes or to take up and swaddle the babies, they were hauled along in spite of their suffering. The wretched infants were left where they fell, for dogs and carrion birds to find."

It seemed to Belisarius, weighing the news from the north,

that this was an invasion. The Huns were taking routes where no garrison forces had been posted; they were also trying to build boats of branches and logs along the rivers. The two columns in the west might be gathering in plunder, but the force under the khan had Constantinople for its objective.

"There was nothing to drive back the barbarians," Agathias relates. "No military garrison, no engines of defense, nor trained men to work them. For the Roman armies had dwindled to a small number, insufficient for the size of the State. The whole force should have been six hundred and forty-five thousand fighting men. Actually it amounted to no more than one hundred and fifty thousand. And of these, some were in Italy, others in Africa, others in Spain, others in Colchis, others at Alexandria and along the Nile, with a few on the Persian frontier (where only a few were needed on account of the peace)."

There remained the barrier of the Long Wall across the peninsula, and the great triple Land Walls of the city itself. With so many thousands of men in the streets, surely these defenses could be held. For generations no enemy had actually reached the gates of the city, protected by God——

At first Justinian did not believe the news that came in from the northern road. The Roman army waiting on this road had been overrun and annihilated. Nothing more could be learned of the garrison contingents, the excubitors and Blue and Green volunteer militia that had formed it. The commander, Sergius, Master of the Armed Forces, was a prisoner. After chasing the fugitives, the Huns were advancing toward the city.

The Long Wall did not check them. The dreaded horsemen simply rode through gaps made by the earthquakes and rounded up the peasants and students of the military academy who had marched out at Justinian's order to defend it. After that no barrier remained between them and the city.

Slowly at first, panic spread through the streets. The trickle of refugees coming into the gates became solid streams of families with loaded carts, driving cherished cattle, weighed down with their household gear. The villages of the suburbs were emptying into the city. With them the refugees brought tales of deaths and burning that grew more fearful in the telling. They sat with their carts in the Mesé and crowded into the scarred Great Church. Becoming more afraid, they sought for a protector and began to cry Belisarius' name.

Before long a throng of senators and officers gathered in the Chalké entrance, calling for the emperor to appear. When he failed to do so they sought out the silentiaries, to send in messages. All these messages had one prayer—the Caesar should summon Belisarius to take command and defend the city.

This Justinian was not willing to do. In spite of his retirement the First Citizen was still the hero of the city. Probably the seventy-seven-year-old emperor had no suspicion of his brilliant general, but he resented him. Justinian still had his hidden vanity. From his window he watched the press of anxious people in the Augusteon climbing up on the purple marble base of the colossal brazen statue of their emperor—to beg him to send Belisarius to them. It seemed as if they expected no aid from the Caesar himself, who had directed wars for thirty years.

Stubbornly Justinian ignored the increasing appeal of his patricians and officers. He ordered that the treasures of all churches in the suburbs, from the Golden Horn to the Euxine shore, should be brought into the city and shipped over to the Asia side.

This was a mistake. At the first sign of vessels leaving the harbors a rush began toward the waterfront. A rumor got around that the palace was being evacuated. In the Augusteon a cry went up: "Send Belisarius to us. Thrice August, let Belisarius give the orders."

In its panic the crowd remembered only that their First Citizen had proved himself the master of barbarians on every front. Refugees who had abandoned their homes in the path of the Huns felt more bitterness than the city dwellers, who had suffered no harm as yet. What protection did this emperor give them, they demanded—this emperor of the Romans who shut himself up in his palace with his gold and bodyguards, while he prepared to sail away on his fleet?

That was unjust to the aged man who had prepared to do no such thing. But he was dealing, here, with panic. He tried to make it clear that he kept no armed force about him, by ordering that a new army of defense be mustered to save the city. To man the walls he called on senators, and all of patrician rank to join his palace attendants. Yet his order failed to quiet the crowds. The people had no confidence in guards and senators as fighting men.

From the housetops a haze of smoke could be made out, rising along the seashore miles distant. The smoke spread along the horizon in the northwest. The Huns were close to the city, burning villages they had ransacked. They were making camp at Melantiadum, at the edge of the sea.

After the news reached him, Justinian sent for Belisarius. Wearing diadem and shoulder band of jewels, the aged man spoke to his champion, as if from the throne. "You are still our Count of the Stables. In this emergency, until our armies can arrive from across the water, we order you to do what you can to protect the city."

The words were cautious, jealously pondered, giving only a certain authority for a limited time, by the will of the Caesar. Belisarius accepted them as he had done for thirty years, as an order to be carried out.

The veteran commander could not, of course, muster an army in a day; the last militia had been lost out on the Long Wall. Then, too, the city armories had been stripped of reserve weapons. Going out of the palace, he paid no attention to the nervous crowd of patricians who formed in a sort of line in obedience to the emperor's summons. Instead he told announcers to run through the streets calling, "Belisarius is going out with the standards; he asks for all who have served under him."

Such veterans were to meet at once in the Strategium square. In addition all horses were to be seized, from carts and litters, and even from the inviolate stables of the Hippodrome chariots. Belisarius wanted swords from the houses, spears from the theaters—every bit of armor hung in the halls, especially the helmets with the plumes of his old comitatus. Above all he wanted casting weapons, javelins, and bows. Planks from the shipyards, poles, axes, sailors and peasants from the countryside, he wanted all of those.

Although close to sixty years of age, he still made a fine figure in helmet and cuirass, under the faded red mantle. When he rode to the Strategium he had the standards with him. From the alleys men hurried after him, shedding cobblers' aprons and porters' shoulder pads. Out of the taverns they staggered, their heads dripping from rinsing in water butts; they galloped in on stolen horses.

Belisarius hardly remembered many of their faces, and the veterans identified themselves by familiar names—by the pits of Daras, the Ten Mile mark, and the Milvian Bridge. Walking among them, he sorted them out, talking with them casually, telling them that this business of driving off Huns needed the old army.

There was a pallid and massive merchant who held his head still, with his hand on the shoulder of an anxious boy. "Illustrious," this one called out, hearing his leader's voice, "Photas, flank man of the first Illyrians."

Studying the soldier's face, Belisarius passed his hand before the other's eyes and noticed that they did not move. Judging the man Photas to be blind, he shook his head at the officers following him, responding quickly, "Then you are the Photas who was wounded coming out of the aqueduct at Ariminum. Wait here. I want you to tell the recruits about that."

He seemed to be making a jest of his rounds among the biscuit eaters. Quick to catch his mood, they flung back jokes. "The biscuits are maggoty. . . . Master, this chariot steed will go nowhere but around a post. . . . If we frighten the Huns, we'll never catch 'em. . . . Have we cooks or will we eat out of the khan's pots?"

To his officers he explained that he desired implements to make both fire and noise. One of them who still had his uniform intact hazarded the guess that they would face odds of five to one, as at Tricamaron.

"No," Belisarius said, "this will be like the Euphrates crossing where we threw javelins and chased hares."

At no time would he speak of tactics or plans. Apparently he was preparing for a new kind of game, with seven thousand Huns joining in the sport. In reality, he understood the hopelessness of mustering in a force to make any stand against the Huns, and he encouraged his motley command to think it would do something novel and unexpected. So by costumes and jests he put together the semblance of an army.

By the next day he had three hundred of his veterans armed and mounted well enough to resemble a regiment; five hundred more had horses, spears, and swords, and were capable of riding after him. About as many more, on foot, could use javelins and bows, and might carry out orders. The sturdier peasants and seamen were given axes and clappers made out of boards, with anything left over. Although nothing but a mob, these last might be taken for soldiers at a distance.

At the head of his new comitatus the First Citizen rode out the Golden Gate, by the shore of Marmora. He did not waste thought on any attempt to hold the triple city wall with civilians—the Land Walls stretched all of four and a half miles to the harbor. With flutes playing, he went out to meet the Huns in open country.

Beyond the first milestones, he had his following make camp and barricade themselves in with branches and beams at the village of Chettus. Some clear fields extended around the village to wooded land through which the highway ran. At night he had a great number of fires lighted and saw to it that his new cohorts kept moving around the fires as long as the light lasted. He did not post scouts outside the camp until the first daylight.

Belisarius at Chettus had only one advantage. Knowing the Huns from long experience, he believed they might turn and race away if surprised. Their instinct drove them like animals, at the scent of danger. Since his semblance of an army could not stand firm against either the arrows or the charge of the horsemen of the steppes, he intended to set a false trap for them. It would have to be a very makeshift trap.

By then he was certain that scouts had arrived from the Huns to look over his exhibition camp. But he could not be certain what the sharp eyes of the nomads had noticed or what conclusions they had reached. (Actually the scouts returned to Zabergan, khan of the Kutrigur, with the report that a small and weak Roman army waited, encamped, on the highroad; the Hun chieftain sent a third of his column ahead to clear the road.)

After daybreak Belisarius sent his missile throwers in two groups to either side the road within the woods. "Whatever you do after the first shafts are thrown," he warned the officers of the two detachments, "make a noise and keep moving."

With his advance parties screened by the tree growth, Belisarius set his stage in front of the village, moving out his three hundred biscuit eaters leisurely, keeping the other riders behind them, with the mob in the rear. Seen from the forest road, this array would resemble the first lines of a greater force. In any event, it would catch the eye of the foremost riders coming along the road——

That happened as he had hoped. The advance detachment of Huns in their dark leather and mail came on cautiously, waiting for the remainder of the column. The Roman cavalry at a halt offered no visible menace, and the whole scene appeared to puzzle rather than rouse the Huns, who had become contemptuous of Roman soldiery. Then the sudden discharge of javelins and arrows from the brush on either side drove the flank riders down into the road.

In some confusion, the Huns took to their bows. Around them the woods rang with exultant shouting. Belisarius chose this minute to charge with his three hundred dependables. Behind them other horsemen galloped, stirring up dust, while the rabble sounded its wooden clappers and trumpets.

The Hippodrome racing steeds, mad with excitement, turned into the wood as if rounding the Spina.

There was a moment when anything might have happened. The veterans, once in motion, drove in their charge, while the Huns, trying instinctively to circle out, were caught in the tree growth and scarred by the Roman javelins. The forest seemed to become a trap, with the enemy triumphant.

The Huns turned to race back along the road and lost heavily in doing so. The veterans pursued at the best speed of their cart and chariot horses.

Belisarius' luck they called it. The flight of his advance column disturbed the Kutrigur khan, who suspected a trap and the presence of a trained Roman army—which he had no desire to meet. Hastily he evacuated his camp and retired with his horsemen to the north.

Luck had played no part whatever in this. A battle is like an epidemic of fear; at some moment, somewhere, a few men who happened to be less afraid than the others facing them with weapons will push forward, and the others will turn to run to safety. Two days before, a hundred thousand men in Constantinople had been so afraid that most of them were searching for boats to escape across the Bosphorus. Belisarius had mocked them, and jested and hinted, until the multitudes had begun to think of other matters than running from the city. Then he had gambled on the courage of three hundred over-age soldiers in armor, pressed in a narrow way against two thousand savage tribesmen. There had been no fake about that. The three hundred had pushed ahead, the two thousand had turned, to seek safety.

Once they started to retreat, the Huns kept on going. They carried off loot enough to satisfy them, and to Zabergan Khan at least it now appeared too painful a business to try to rush the walls of the imperial city. To that extent the civilized fighter had outguessed the more powerful barbarian.

Once in pursuit, Belisarius forged ahead easily. Fugitives in hill resorts and forests ran in to join the advancing standards. Detachments of the dispersed Blue and Green militia turned up again, now that the road was safe and the Hun camp at Melantiadum waited to be ransacked. It was both safe and exhilarating to be following up a fleeing enemy.

Knowing that enemy, Belisarius arranged the pursuit with only less care than he had taken in staging the scene of the trap at Chettus. (It was ridiculous to think of catching up with the Huns on their swift mustangs; the last thing he wanted was for his rabble to come within reach of the bows of the nomads.) Since Zabergan's scouts in the rear would be watching the highway, he reshaped his restless contingents to make them appear like advance patrols of a disciplined command. Compact squads climbed to ridges along the road; trumpets sounded calls back and forth. Massive silver plates, snatched up by the prowling soldiers, were held up to flash against the sun; along the road the mob moved in tight groups, like closed-up regiments . . . the Hun observers were impressed by what they discerned coming after them.

At Melantiadum, with his back to the sea, Belisarius had something like an army ready to make a stand—as long as the Huns kept moving away from it. There Belisarius sent out swift sailing craft to summon in passing galleys and transports, to add to the effect of a general mobilization.

Presently he got more help than he had expected from the sea because vessels arrived with troops from Salonika-way, where the second Hunnic army had been driven off, after making the mistake of trying to go out in its log boats against the imperial galleys. When the regulars landed at Melantiadum, his biscuit eaters had their big moment. Displaying the souvenirs they had picked up in the Hun camp, they asked the regulars what the Roman army had been doing while they—the veterans—took time off to defeat the Kutrigur Huns.

After a week of this the First Citizen prepared in earnest to follow up the invaders toward the Danube. Then a command from the emperor halted him. With the danger over, Justinian did not want Belisarius to have all the glory of the victory. Unexpectedly, he marched out himself to the battle zone.

Robed for ceremony and riding a white horse, followed by his nobles and excubitors, Justinian traveled the forty miles out to the Long Wall. Encamped in a village not far from Chettus, he took command of the campaign. He held Belisarius at Melantiadum; he ordered a multitude to begin repairing the gaps in the Long Wall, and he watched it done. He ordered out naval vessels to hasten around to the Danube, to ascend the river and cut off the retreat of the Huns there. And, secretly, he sent gold to his nephew Justin, in command along the Danube, instructing him to use it to ransom Sergius, the captive Master of the Armed Forces, and the others, and by no means to risk any lives by attempting to stop the Huns when they began to cross back over the Danube. They would do that, Justinian believed, when they became alarmed by the appearance of his fleet in the river. And it all happened as he anticipated.

Then, with his campaign ended, Justinian rode back to his city as a conqueror. Early one August morning he passed in splendor through the Golden Gate. Curious crowds thronged the Mesé to watch him. The tired old emperor really made a fine figure on his white horse. The crowds shouted: "Hail, Justinian! Live long, our emperor, given by God."

Again Justinian did something unexpected. Turning aside to his old home at the house of Theodora, he dismounted at the church of the Apostles. Entering there afoot without his diadem, he lighted the two candles at the tomb of Theodora and knelt by it awhile.

Belisarius, however, had his triumph. It was hardly planned. He simply came back along the coast road at the head of his mock army. But when he rode through the towers of the Golden Gate, past his palace, to turn into the familiar main street of the Mesé, he found the sidewalks packed, with refugees standing in their carts and women waving along the housetops. Students of the university square climbed the monuments; bishops in robes stepped down from the doors of their churches to bless him, while children hurled flowers and ran beside his horse. The roar of the street crowd was like an ovation . . . "Belisarius, thou hast conquered!"

The crowd was hysterical with relief and joy at being still alive, with homes and property safe.

Belisarius did not go into the Hippodrome this time. At the palace Justinian was not to be seen, being absorbed in his affairs. By the statue of the Gorgon, where bakers tossed fresh bread to the returning veterans, Belisarius left the Mesé and ended the route march in the Strategium square. There must have been an odd moment when he sat his saddle and the survivors of his three hundred waited, stiff with unaccustomed aches, to be dismissed as usual. Perhaps they all laughed. The jest was over; they could go home.

Consider them for that moment with our present-day understanding. They were no longer the Roman army of the legions; they were free men-at-arms defending a city. Belisarius, no longer the Magister Militum, was the Constable, or head of the defense, of a king. After little more than two centuries a Christian Frank, a Roland, would serve his king,

Charlemagne, in very much that fashion, and after that the plumes and cloak of Belisarius would be worn by a Chevalier Bayard, who combined skill in swordsmanship with a peculiar sense of honor.

For the time being, however, the machinery of the empire functioned well enough to end the menace of the Kutrigur Huns. The first, and probably the strongest, column of those enterprising barbarians, feeling its way toward the cities of Greece, was stopped at the famous mountain pass of Thermopylae. Of all people, Alexander the Scissors commanded at this new Thermopylae, or at least arranged for the battle. Thereafter, to forestall another invasion, Justinian and his Economist went to work with the foreign office to stir up a diversion in the steppes by sending information to the rival khan of the Utigurs, across the Fetid Sea, that his archfoes the Kutrigurs had taken gold from the empire that had been earmarked for him. It was a trick to play on unreasoning, barbaric minds. This time it worked. The two segments of Huns got into conflict over the loot that the Kutrigurs had carried back across the Danube.

Even in his study, however, Justinian could not escape the realization that Belisarius had become more of a hero with the populace than before. There was danger that the city might intrude its champion upon the palace. It needed little to wrest the imperial purple from Justinian's aged body and bestow it upon the popular soldier. Belisarius had vanquished the Huns while Justinian remained merely the ruler who refused to dispense with the taxation that had to be paid in coin or in kind every year.

After a year or two the contrast between the two leaders became more marked, in popular opinion. The soldier could be approached any day in the streets; he gave away money to anyone in need; every veteran who had served under him found a meal and a bed in his palace. On the other hand, the emperor lurked in his palace like another Cyclops, making the most worthy notables crawl across his reception floor to kiss his scarlet boot. Thus, in welcoming Belisarius as a champion, many people began to conceive of Justinian as an enemy.

"Now with the Romans at peace with the whole world, by reason of his lust for blood and not knowing what else to do with himself, Justinian kept bringing all the barbarians into collision with one another. He kept handing over huge gifts of money to the leaders of the Huns . . . so they sent bands to ravage the Roman lands, in order to sell a peace again to this man who always foolishly wanted to buy one . . . who paid out huge amounts of gold to Chosroes [Khusrau] for peace . . . who thought of many devices to spill more blood over the earth, and to plunder more money from his subjects."

This gossip came from the secret writing of the well-known Procopius, now dead after enjoying a comfortable pension from Justinian. These notes—*Anecdota* the Greeks called them—Procopius had kept hidden, allowing only intimate friends to peer at them, as a favor. Since Procopius had been the companion of the First Citizen, Belisarius, and since he claimed to have known Theodora intimately, his secret notes were read eagerly.

". . . Justinian, who never ceased to be a barbarian, uncouth in speech as well as dress, brought calamities upon all his people . . . he was not the son of Sabbatius or of any other man, but of a demon . . . so he displayed a curious interest about the nature of God . . . those who sat with him late at night seemed to see a sort of demon appear in place of him; then he would rise and walk up and down, and the head of Justinian would disappear while the rest of him walked on . . . impelled by this demon who reigned in place of Justinian."

After his death, the envy of Procopius besmirched the sovereigns who had never been aware of his rare ability. In that way he managed to identify himself with them forever. He was really a brilliant writer.

At eighty years of age Justinian had only a remnant of his great vitality. "He grew very weary," relates Agathias—a plain writer but an honest one—who had taken up the task of Procopius, "and adverse from waging war."

His convictions, however, had not changed in other matters. Aware of the popular unrest and dislike of him, he issued again the edicts of reform of thirty years before. There were more than a hundred of them by now, and they were little heeded except as nuisances. Agathias himself complains of the tax collectors, who held back percentages of the soldiers' pay "by the rascally science of arithmetic."

There were cliques in the city who listened to the stories about the Demon Emperor, and debated realistically the advantages of assassinating him. Unlike the plot of the disgruntled Armenian and Artabanes, these back-chamber intrigues might have been dangerous. Inevitably the intelligence agents of the palace got wind of them, and in time brought evidence before Justinian, who only reluctantly turned his attention to their documents. But when he came across Belisarius' name he studied the evidence carefully.

The conspirators had been caught with weapons hidden on them in the Sacred Palace.

A certain Paul, steward of the First Citizen, had been seen in talk with the alleged conspirators. Under questioning—and Justinian knew that torture had aided the questioning by the police—Paul had confessed that Belisarius had been advised of the plot and had not objected.

Here was Justinian's opportunity to rid himself of the man who might seize his throne. And every detail of ceremony at that throne had become precious to the aged emperor. Like Anastasius before him, he refused to speak the name of an heir to succeed him.

At the same time a twist of memory recalled that Belisarius had been accused before, without cause. There was no real evidence against the soldier, now as then. It had been Theodora's desire to humble him——

Justinian did something unusual. Calling a meeting of the senate, which had had little notice from him of late, he laid the evidence of conspiracy before that ancient body. When the senators, weighing the politics of the question, decided tentatively that everyone named in the documents *seemed to be* guilty, Justinian passed a long time in meditation. He was apt to drowse now, in trying to think out a problem. There was the much more vital question of the creed of the churches . . . the substantial or unsubstantial nature of Christ . . .

Justinian did as Theodora had done. He suspended Belisarius, as it were, in his displeasure, by confiscating his wealth and palaces, and revoking his only title, that of Constable. The name of First Citizen, not being a rank under imperial protocol, could not well be abrogated.

Belisarius made no protest. As before, he moved out of his palace. He had his horse and he seemed to be comfortably at home on the benches of the Strategium, or in fact wherever he chose to pass the night. All doors in the city were open to the victor of Chettus. If he appeared in the streets old servicemen were sure to accost him with offers of a fresh catch of swordfish or an invitation to hunt across the Bosphorus.

Justinian realized that there was no way of disgracing the soldier. And as for property, the careless Belisarius had never cared particularly for it, except to make gifts. Antonina had been the one to crave the slaves at the gateposts and the imitation garden courtyards. Penniless, Belisarius remained every inch a patrician. (There is no truth at all in the legend that grew up in the course of time, of Belisarius in his last year blinded by the inexorable emperor, begging for food in the streets from the soldiers who had served under him.)

After seven months of this, Justinian, with a sort of exasperation, restored his wealth to him as Theodora had done. It seemed not to matter to the soldier, who merely resumed sleeping in his own chamber overlooking the Golden Gate. The realities of Belisarius' life lay far behind him, in distant places. His memory fought over again the breaking of the barrier on the Tiber, when Totila had looked on, and he himself had turned back—or the ride over the causeway to Ravenna. Those realities could not be changed now.

Without being called upon to serve again, or to hear other charges against him, Belisarius died in the year 565. He had no following except those who had served under him, and his end caused no stir in the palace. He had made mistakes and had never been able to understand the higher strategy of the empire he served. He had simply carried out orders, but perhaps no one ever improvised so brilliantly against such odds. His name stood for something intangible, that defied defeat.

One of his soldiers said, "The army will get along well enough, but what will the emperor do without Belisarius?"

Justinian seemed to feel the loss of the man he had disliked and envied and relied upon. Without being satisfied thereby, he claimed Belisarius' rich possessions for his own. Yet he never set foot in the other's palace.

Belisarius had been the last but one of the fellowship that had surrounded the son of Sabbatius—Theodora, Tribonian, John of Cappadocia, and Anthemius the Architect. Narses survived in Italy, ruling like an animated mummy untouched by years, and refusing to return to the palace as a Grand Chamberlain. With no one to question his commands, Narses bickered and bartered with the Franks, hanged a khan of the Herules—which Justinian would not have allowed—and sat at ease on the old throne of Theodoric at Ravenna.

In those years Justinian seldom thought of Narses because the adroit eunuch took pains not to trouble him. The two aged men remained fixed and unchanging as the mosaic portraits in their entrance halls. Justinian, who had tried to be an architect of destiny, was content at last with the routine of his days.

For the first time in the many years of his rule he made plans to journey out of his city. He meant to journey as a pilgrim to a shrine in Galatia where he could set eyes on a most holy relic of Christ. But in the streets of his city the Blue and Green factions were rioting again. And he did not make his one journey.

Sleepless at dawn, he heard the passing of the Grand Janitor, and he stirred to bring the white silentiaries to his couch to aid him into his robe to go to the chapel of the Daphne to pray before the ikon.

When the water clock turned the third hour, he was led out to the throne, behind the veil, there to sit while officials prostrated themselves and told him of the execution of his commands through the empire.

Sitting so in the great hall, with the veil drawn back from his presence, while distant music sounded and incense drifted up, he exacted a submission never known before.

"He was the first of the princes of Constantinople," Agathias observes, "to show himself to be an absolute sovereign in fact as well as in name."

No one of those who listened to him thought of him any longer as Flavius Justinian, Caesar and victor. They spoke of him more as the Autocrat.

When he signed the lasting peace of fifty years with Khusrau—by which for a heavy payment in gold he demilitarized the eastern frontier, secured some careful trade privileges, and protected the Christians under Persian rule—he read with delight the words of the Persian salutation to him: "Divine Khusrau, King of kings from ancient days . . . to Justinian Caesar, our brother."

It seemed to Justinian, then, that he had become the equal of his mighty antagonist, the oriental despot who traced his throne back for eleven centuries. As men would speak of

Khusrau the Great, they would also mention Justinian the Great.

He hardly heeded other details. On the Syrian coast the silk culture had begun, from the first worms smuggled out of the Land of Silk. But Justinian was more intent on his argument with the patriarch of Constantinople, who dared to question his edict to the churches.

For Justinian and his elderly theologians had worked out a formula for a universal creed, to answer all the questions as to what had been human, or divine, in Christ. By the doctrine of the *Aphthartodocetae*—incorruptibility of the flesh upon the Cross—the whole problem was made clear. So they believed. This final solution Justinian made ready to impose upon the churches by his authority. He had rationalized the unknowable. Yet in east and west the bishops murmured and popes and partriarchs objected. They seemed to prefer to believe in what they had been unable to understand.

At times, poring over the words he had written in his dragging hand, Justinian wondered if he had indeed discovered an eternal truth.

Eagerly he sought for confirmation. Aspects around him had new significance . . . the dome stood completed over the Great Church . . . he had watched the baptism of a khan of the pagan Herules . . . as far as the Caucasus, pagan Lazgians and Iberians had been baptized by the thousands, to bring those wild people to Christian salvation.

In Ethiopia, he had established the Christian Church.

Vaguely he remembered that the envoys of the savage Avars had been different—slant-eyed, animallike beings with hair braided down their shoulders, clad in horseskins with manes hanging down . . . he had made great gifts to the Avars for peace in the steppes, and the barbarians had wasted their gold by buying up weapons in the city markets—weapons that his nephew Justin had prudently taken back at the frontier, in spite of the anger of the Avars. No, they had not been baptized. . . .

Lying motionless, looking up at the gleaming stars in the blue mosaic ceiling of his chamber, Justinian watched the sun glow strengthen on the alabaster screen of his window, while he waited for the steps of the Grand Janitor . . . at his birthplace, now Justiniana Prima, he had finished the improvements and dignified his old home by making it an archbishopric. There were twenty cities bearing his name now, but Prima Justiniana would be the foremost, because it had in it the house of his father, of whom he had never spoken in Constantinople, being ashamed to claim a peasant farmer as father.

He wanted to rise up and go to the ikon. His new edict to the churches waited to be signed. But the silentiaries waited in the shadows where he could not see them . . . there was something else that needed doing, and had been finished now. He did not speak of that, either, except to the goldsmiths who worked on it . . . the sarcophagus of pure gold upon bronze, ornamented with a massive cross, in readiness for his death.

Justinian waited, thinking that he would like to go out on the roof of the Daphne—he could not venture now to the imperial box in the Hippodrome—and look down on the Augusteon where stood the statue with hand upraised of Justinian the Great.

He waited and heard the steps of the Grand Janitor passing, and it troubled him that this should be evening instead of morning, with the silentiaries lighting the candles instead of lamps. There were two candles, of the kind they put in churches, and close to him some priest was repeating the Trisagion.

Watching the two candles placed by his head, Justinian wanted to speak to the silentiaries, to ask for his robes instead. He wanted to rise from his couch and be helped out of the sleeping chamber, away from the candles.

His death was that night, eight months after Belisarius, on the fourteenth of November, 565.

In the hall of the Delphax the patriarch had been waiting with the Count of the Excubitors and the most influential senators, and they had agreed who must succeed the eighty-two-year-old emperor, in his dotage. They sent an announcer to rouse Justin II, nephew of Justinian, who had been kept in readiness near the palace.

Into the chamber of the dead man where the silentiaries stood on duty by the candles came a woman flushed and breathless, with purple silk over her arm. Bending her knee as she approached the couch, she prepared to put the purple silk robe over the body. It had on it, beautifully embroidered in gold thread, the symbols of his victories and rank.

As they went over to help her, the silentiaries noticed that she had the dark hair and eyes of Theodora. She had that family resemblance, being Sophia the daughter of Comito, the actress who had married the patrician Sittas.

The silentiaries understood that the great personages in the Delphax chamber had taken thought of Sophia. It helped Justin that his wife should be the niece of Theodora, the pious Augusta.

IX

Emergence of Byzantium

Failure of a Plan

JUSTINIAN I HAD NOT BEEN LONG IN HIS SELF-DESIGNED SARcophagus of gold before his attempt to turn back the course of history failed. Nor did his successors give to him the only title that he had not awarded himself. They did not call him Justinian the Great.

His nephew, Justin II, endeavored to carry out the defense of the recovered empire, while restoring its economy, and then went quietly insane.

Within the city, however, Justinian's handiwork wrought a change. Byzantium became *the* city of the known world, fabulous both in its splendor and in its activity. During the ensuing dark ages it remained a storehouse of scientific knowledge and a powerhouse of endeavor. Generations later a visitor noted with surprise that "in Byzantium everybody works."

For a while after the mental breakdown of her husband, the Empress Sophia—the niece of Theodora—ruled with the aid of the Count of the Excubitors, Tiberius, who was more of a soldier than an economist. When Sophia accused him of emptying the treasury, Tiberius retorted, "Our treasury will never be empty so long as the poor get alms and captives are brought back." Yet this was the end of Old Justin's family dynasty; Tiberius was followed by military men who tried to meet the desperate need of the empire for defense. The dream of a universal Christian Roman Empire yielded to the necessity of saving the city itself.

Physical Collapse of the Empire

Justinian's reconquest of the west had consequences not anticipated by him. In Spain and Provence the Visigothic kings pushed the Byzantine governors and merchants back from Cordova to the seaports; in Africa, more slowly, the native Berbers did the same, confining the imperial posts to the coast. Since the islands were safe for the time being, the empire held firmly to Sicily and Carthage—Belisarius' first captures. The Middle Sea had been, in Justinian's imagination, a means to an end. Its mastery was to be the chief gain of his military endeavor.

Promptly the energetic Lombards migrated down into the Italian peninsula—whence the aged Narses was recalled by the exasperated Sophia. There was no longer a buffer kingdom of Goths along the Po to stop them. The Longbeards settled pretty much where they chose down the peninsula. The Byzantines held to ports like Ravenna, and to the south below Naples. Thus both the Gothic kingdom of Theodoric and the imperial province sought by Justinian failed to materialize, and Italy became—as it was to remain for a long time—divided, the north separated from the south, with its centers of culture, and papal Rome from both. In ruined Rome the remnant of the old population came to beg from pilgrims who braved the malarial Campagna to visit its shrines. In time it was to regain close contact with the outer peoples more through the northwest, toward the Catholic Franks rather than toward the city in the east. Gregory the Great, not the Byzantine emperors, renewed touch with Britain by his missionary, Augustine.

The Danube frontier that Germanus had manipulated so long almost disappeared. There the weakening of the "Romanized" barbarians like the Herules and Bulgars left a vacuum into which the dreaded Avars descended, pressing as far as the gates of Constantinople in 591. At the same time the seemingly indestructible Slavs infiltrated farther within Justinian's old homeland of Macedonia, Greece proper, and the Balkans at large. They seldom adhered together; they appeared to follow the invasions of the steppe nomads as coyotes trail the path of a wolf pack.

In the steppes farther east, Justinian's last defensive endeavor—inciting the Kutrigur and Utigur Huns to mutual extermination—cleared the plains north of the Euxine (Black) Sea for the advance of a new power from the east, the Turks of the Oxus River region. (The first embassy of the Turks had appeared in the Queen City in 563, to marvel at the apparition of the emperor on the world throne set in unearthly splendor.) This new contact to the eastward had two vital consequences. First, when the Persian war broke out in full force, the Byzantine emperors sought the alliance of the formidable Turks, while the Persian shahinshahs—Khusrau the Just died at a ripe old age, in 579, toward the end of the great Sassanian renaissance—sought the aid of Hunnic elements. For the first time the two culture centers, Constantinople and Ctesiphon, availed themselves of the power factors of eastern nomadic groups, thereby extending the war into the northern steppes. Second, Justinian's missionary activity among the steppe peoples (and this was Justinian's, not Theodora's, endeavor) began to open the boulevard toward the northeast, through which Byzantine culture and trade passed outward, beyond the Balkans and the Black Sea. It penetrated by river and trade routes above the Crimean peninsula and the future Kiev on the river Dnieper, to influence the vast hinterlands of Eurasia. (While the religious and cultural influence of papal Rome stemmed northwest, toward the terminal points of England and Scandinavia. The outlines began to take shape of a Latin-speaking Roman Catholic western Europe, and a Greek-writing Eastern Orthodox eastern Europe.)

But the great crisis came with the renewal of the Persian war. Justin II opened it up again, although Tiberius the military dictator tried to hold to Justinian's unheroic policy of peace at a price with the powerful Persians. The later soldier-emperors sought a decision in the age-old conflict and thereby brought the empire to the brink of disaster. The war extended outward again into the Caucasus land bridge, and this time into the steppes. In this maelstrom of conflict the old eastern frontiers vanished. For the first time the Persians pierced the heart of the empire, Asia Minor, and appeared at Chalcedon, across the strait from Constantinople itself.

In this emergency the popular demes took a hand, with the clergy of the city. While the parties of the Blues and Greens never regained the power they had held before the Nika revolt, the populace and the patriarch remained the final arbiters of the destiny of the empire. The last of the three soldier-successors to the throne, the objectionable Phocas—"Gorgon's-head Phocas"—was assassinated (610) and the command and responsibility alike were given to a newcomer from the African coast, Heraclius, son of the exarch of Africa who arrived in the city with a relieving fleet. (Heraclius I began a new family dynasty which is usually described as the first to face east, the truly Byzantine emperors.)

The disaster mounted rapidly, as the Persians swept south, over rebuilt Antioch, down the Syrian coast, into Jerusalem itself, as Khusrau had predicted. They carried off the traditional Cross, with most of the inhabitants, to Khusrau's "New Rome" on the river Tigris. They reached the Nile, and in so doing occupied the regions—Asia Minor, Syria, Egypt—that Theodora had believed to be the true heart of the empire.

With the Persians at Hieron, and the Avars advancing

again along the path of the Kutrigur Huns to the Long Wall, there appeared to be no hope for the empire except in its small fleet. This fleet held the water barrier of the Bosphorus, preventing the Avars from joining forces with the Persian army. Heraclius prepared to evacuate the city, to migrate by sea to Africa, but the will of the unpredictable populace and the persuasion of the patriarch Sergius held him in Constantinople.

There, religious enthusiasm took hold of the people. When, apparently, only a miracle could save their city, they looked for a miracle. They took slaves into the army for the first time, and enlisted or conscripted themselves with the devotion of crusaders. More than that, they sent the new army away from the city, by land and sea to the Caucasus front, to strike at Ctesiphon, the heart of the Sassanian domain.

With the army and Heraclius gone, the city seemed lost. Slavs joined the besieging Avars; the Persians held the Asia shore. "Not a bird," announced the khan of the Avars, "can escape from the walls now."

In this year (626) the danger to the city and the supremacy of the Avars alike reached its highest point. The triple walls of Theodosius held firm; Heraclius won his famous campaign through Asia and sealed a victorious peace with the Persians.

By then Constantinople had been converted into a vast mechanism of defense, with fifteen thousand slaves enlisted, the citizenry conscripted, and military authority replacing civilian rule—Justinian's governors would soon be superseded by military "strategists." In the rival Persian dominion Khusrau's descendants had been overthrown by revolution—Khusrau the Second taking refuge for a time in Constantinople—and the great age of the Sassanians had ended. Both empires were exhausted by war.

But there was no peace. The Arabs emerged from their deserts to sweep over the cities and battlefields of the two empires. The new faith of Muhammad the Prophet created an Islam (Submission) that, more than the fanatical armies of nomadic horsemen, overcame resistance. The eastern peoples, wearied by the long wars and taxation of the two empires, had no will to resist the throngs of Islam. Muhammad's faith in a single God had drawn much from the Magi, and was close to Nestorian Christianity. It offered kinship and refuge to the dissenting Christians of the east, such as the Nestorians and Jacobites. In Egypt and Syria—Theodora's chosen lands—it was welcomed as bringing security and peace, rather than resisted.

The Arab armies led by the Companions of Muhammad defeated Byzantine forces in Palestine and Sassanian chivalry in the Tigris Valley almost simultaneously. Incredibly, Jerusalem fell to them; they rode through Armenia and all of Persia. Alexandria yielded to them in 643. They thrust outward along the African coast and, taking to the sea, accomplished the unbelievable by defeating a Byzantine fleet.

Their invasion of the sea endangered the great arterial of the empire. The wealth of Syria and Egypt that had strengthened the empire so long was gone, and the granary of Africa was soon to go, with the ports of Spain. In this crisis Constans the Second, grandson of Heraclius, followed the counsel of desperation and moved his army and court back to Sicily and Italy in an effort to stem the Arab expansion. His retreat to the west was futile. The Lombards held firmly to the Italian peninsula, while Arab armies penetrated Asia Minor in the east. The emperor's troops mutinied. Constans was killed, and his court returned to the patriarch and the populace of Constantinople. It returned to the menace of the Slavs on the north and the Arabian imperium in the south.

Justinian had been dead then a century and three years.

So the city emerged from its birth throes under Justinian as the Byzantium we know. The roads that led out from the Golden Milestone in the Augusteon did not extend far. Yet the Great Church marked the center of a strong religious and cultural dominion. It was an outpost of the darkening and diminishing west. Guarding our heritage of Greek and Roman culture, it faced the aggressive forces of the east.

It became the impregnable center of Christianity. Its waterways and triple walls were rendered impregnable by the will of its people to defend them.

It became the desire of the world. The splendid buildings above the Golden Horn held the treasures sought by successive waves of barbarians. Vikings, coming over the long ways of the sea, would know it as Mickligarth, the Great Enclosure; Slavs of the steppes would call it Tsargrad, Caesar's City.

It would endure in a continual state of siege. But the people would never betray and never surrender their city.

The Riddle of Justinian

Justinian's name has become proverbial. We remember him by his code of laws and his majestic church. But the man himself remains a paradox. A Macedonian peasant, he undertakes to restore classic Rome; a favored aspirant for the throne, he takes a wife from the gutter; a man vain enough to name twenty-odd cities after himself, he lives as abstemiously as a monk; working harder than any slave, he conceives of himself as above all laws; afraid to step out of his gate to face physical violence, he ignores later conspiracies against his life; innately suspicious, he refrains from punishing an antagonist; a stubborn stickler at trifles, he enlarges even our present-day notions as to what a human being may set out to do and accomplish.

The son of Sabbatius has never been evaluated, as to personality. Ernest Stein,[1] remarking that he never lost control

[1]The last work of this great scholar, the *Geschichte des spätrömischen Reiches,* deals with Justinian's epoch, and has been published first in French translation, *L'histoire du Bas-Empire,* by Ernest Stein: Desclée de Brouwer, Bruges (Belgium), 1949.

of himself, concludes that he personified the "Janus-head" complexity of his time. Nicolai Iorga[2] says that instead of being the last Roman emperor in the east Justinian was the first Byzantine, and the circumstances of his life made him so. (Stein calls him a proto-Byzantine.) Perhaps the riddle of his personality is stated most clearly by the elder scholar, Dr. E. L. Woodward.

"Was Justinian a narrow-minded official, unable from his exalted station to see the problems of his empire, deluded by a subservient court into believing that the world would obey his word? Was he in all his life the theological fanatic whom Procopius describes as neglecting practical affairs to sit through long nights of controversy with old priests? Or did that fierce ascetic nature fret itself away until only imagination was left—the gigantic imagination of an age which built the Church of the Divine Wisdom and looked into the very eyes of the angels of famine and earthquake, fire and pestilence?"[3]

Perhaps he was all that. He never emerged, as it were, from the bureaus through which he governed. Deeply religious, he felt to the full his obligation as Basileus of Byzantium to carry out the work of God on earth. (More than any other people before or since, these Roman-Byzantines separated the things that were Caesar's from the things that were God's.)

The truth, however, may be that in Justinian's case we are confronted not by a dual personality but by two personalities. Without Justinian there could have been no Theodora, and without Theodora there would have been no Justinian. Paul the Silentiary praises the wife as the co-

[2]N. Iorga, *Histoire de la vie byzantine: empire et civilisation*, Vol. I, *L'Empire Oecumenique* (*527–641*), Bucharest (*édition de l'auteur*), 1934. His work emphasizes the birth of Constantinople rather than the death of Rome; it brings out the function of the city as a melting pot of people and the character of its society as *nouveau riche*.

[3]E. L. Woodward, *Christianity and Nationalism in the Later Roman Empire*, London, 1916.

worker of the husband. Among historians the wisest have formed almost a habit of adding to an enterprise of Justinian—"although it might have been inspired by Theodora." Often enough their strong wills pulled in opposite directions but only once did an open breach occur between them, over the exile of Anthimius.

The picture of his early personality is clear. As a student and favored nephew of Old Justin, he was an orthodox churchman and a good party man of the Blues. After his marriage we perceive a new Justinian. After her death, the pattern of his identity becomes clear again, as a pontifical bureaucrat solacing himself with theological studies.

No, we are dealing here with an inseparable pair who might well have remained obscure as individuals but together accomplished amazing things. Justinian and Theodora are the first notable man and wife of modern history.

We have their portraits from life set in the mosaics of St. Vitale in Ravenna. There they stand apart but in balance, emperor and empress, flanked by their courts, making similar offerings to God. His face, fleshy, with tired eyes, shows vitality and anxiety; hers, thin and tense, appears like a mask of pain relieved by eloquent dark eyes. (These mosaics were made in the last years before her death.)

Theodora's Reputation

The character of the daughter of the bear keeper has been attacked and defended for fourteen centuries. They say this imp of the circus was the first feminist of the modern world. Other empresses had great influence before her—Ariadne and the Athenian. Theodora got things done with a reckless and resistless determination. Others had been religious; she got religion in the stews, and fought to protect her spiritual fathers. She craved the imperial purple and she had it for her shroud in the church designed for her. In the eyes of the western clergy she was a destructive schemer; the eastern clergy claimed her as a revered protectress.

Literature—in the privately printed editions of Procopius' *Anecdota*—has commemorated her as the harlot empress. The pontifical Gibbon (*Decline and Fall of the Roman Empire*), with his knack of setting down the right facts and wrong inferences, declares that "those who believe that the female mind is totally depraved by the loss of chastity will eagerly listen to all the invectives . . . which have dissembled the virtues of Theodora, exaggerated her vices, and condemned with rigor the . . . sins of the youthfull harlot."

And he adds, "From a motive of shame or contempt, she often declined the servile homage of the multitude, escaped from the odious light of the capital . . . [to] the palaces and gardens which were pleasantly seated on the sea coast of the Bosphorus."

Gibbon sounds as if he championed the poor girl, but actually he attacked her. (In his mind eastern Christianity was one of the causes of the decline and fall of his beloved ancient Rome.) Theodora was not depraved; nor does a study of her actions reveal any contempt for the multitudes. In her famous stand during the crisis of the Nika revolt she said only that she would stay behind in the palace, if it meant her death. The attack of Belisarius and Mundus on the crowd in the Hippodrome followed Theodora's refusal to leave, but she did not ask for it. As to the garden palace at Hieron, it served as an escape for her but hardly because she was ashamed to face the people in the Sacred Palace. It can be safely said that Theodora had no guilt complex.

Gibbon's "youthful harlot" echoes Procopius' strange hatred of the empress. The girl nymphomaniac of the little chronicler's secret history never existed. If Theodora had been that, she could hardly have carried out her intensive work as ruler for more than twenty years. Nor would popular opinion have allowed her to remain on the throne for a month. Even Procopius admits that "no senator thought of objecting to the marriage; no priest was seriously concerned." The muted opposition to her marriage came from the women of society, and was expressed by Euphemia. Dr. Woodward finds that the chronicles of the clergy of the time condemned or praised the actress-empress on religious, not personal, grounds.[4]

John of Ephesus, who admired Theodora, makes no bones about saying she was a woman from a brothel. By that he does not mean a house of prostitutes so much as the stage itself—the two were alike, in Constantinople: he calls the Hippodrome the "Church of Satan"—and he thinks of her marriage as we would think of a show girl wedding a man of society. Theodora did grow up in the *mise en scène* of the Hippodrome and make exhibitions of herself there; she did belong to men and follow one of them, Hecebolus, to Africa; before meeting Justinian she gave birth to her daughter. Out of such reality Procopius conjured up the image of the harlot-empress.

There is an element of the fantastic in her later life as Basilissa of the empire. Her light touch enters the somber writing of the Corpus Juris; her temper and indomitable will flash out intermittently as heat lightning; her mockery and legerdemain alter the course of intrigues throughout the empire. Certainly she caused damage enough—witness the fall of the objectionable but necessary John of Cappadocia—but she never harmed Justinian. Zonaras says she influenced him too much. Of the modern masters of history, Stein terms her influence on her husband *nefaste*—by which he may mean either unfortunate or baneful.

[4]"Liberatus can only say of Theodora that she was an impious enemy of the Church. Victor Tonnennensis expiates on the heresy of the empress, but not on her past wickedness . . . Malalas and Theophanes record little of Theodora except actions of goodness and piety . . . Evagrius is very hostile to the morals of Byzantine society, but he finds nothing to say against Theodora."

Professor A. A. Vasiliev[5] observes that "After her marriage to Justinian, Theodora broke entirely with her turbulent and equivocal past and became a faithful wife. . . . She brought to the throne her boundless ambition, her greed for wealth, her sympathy with the monophysites, with whom she had become acquainted during her wanderings in the Near East . . . and her own practical mind." As to her authority, Vasiliev adds that it was "almost superior" to Justinian's. I do not believe Theodora was greedy for wealth, as such. Procopius says she was, when he tries to stigmatize Justinian as rapacious; yet the actress-empress was entitled to the large revenues of a Basilissa of the empire, and Justinian's devotion increased them. Many large donations by her, as in the relief of Antioch, appear in the records; she was generous to petitioners.

R. M. French[6] declares, "There are those who think that from the political point of view she sensed the future more clearly than Justinian . . . the eyes of the empress were fixed upon the east."

Perhaps Charles Diehl[7] has given most thought to Theodora as an empress who was also a woman. "While Justinian," he points out, "entranced by the grandeur of memories of Rome . . . a theologian in spirit, occupied himself with religious questions for the empty satisfaction of dogmatising, Theodora was of the fellowship [*famille*] of the great emperors of Byzantium who, under the shifting semblance of theological disputes, have always been able to observe the enduring base of political problems."

[5]A. A. Vasiliev, *Justin the First: an Introduction to the Epoch of Justinian the Great,* Harvard University Press, 1950. The study of Justin's reign by the master of Byzantine research.

[6]Rev. R. M. French, *The Eastern Orthodox Church,* London, 1951.

[7]Charles Diehl, *Figures byzantines,* Paris, 1925. Professor Diehl's works on Byzantine art and on the lives of Justinian and Theodora result from a lifetime of study and have brought the obscure medieval east into focus with the west. Unfortunately only his brief summary of Byzantine history entire seems to have been translated into English.

Procopius' Portrait of His Time

As a war correspondent Procopius of Caesarea has made an everlasting name, and he deserves it. Like reporters of this present age of war, he lived with the troops; he noticed when commanders—except for Belisarius—got drunk, when foul biscuits bred dysentery, and when the men were too frightened to do anything but run away. And he understood, or he found out, why such things happened.

In his fourteen small volumes he pictured the wars, the peoples, the buildings, and geography of his world as he knew it—and much that he did not know at first hand, such as the ferrying of the dead souls across the Channel to "Britta." For Procopius could seldom resist an omen, an alleged miracle, or a good yarn. It all helps in visualizing the mentality of his time.

Then he wrote—the majority of scholars believe that no other man wrote it—the famous *Historia Arcana*, the *Secret History*, or *Anecdota*, in which he avenged himself on his superiors for the flattering tone of his official writings. Sandwiched in between the vitriol and exaggerations of the *Anecdota* Procopius set down the facts that he had stored up until he could write as he pleased The *Anecdota* were not to be published until after his death. European scholars did not discover its text until long afterward, and they have been occupied ever since in trying to isolate its facts from Procopian fiction.

For Theodora was not the only victim of Procopius' wrath. He reduces his hero Belisarius to a spineless husband, with a hint of cowardice; Justinian becomes avid for gold while taking a fiendish delight in slaughter. After reading the *Secret History*, Voltaire observed that Justinian, like Belisarius, was "a silly cuckold." Procopius got his revenge.

It is a baffling although fascinating task to try to pick out the places where this shrewd writer makes use of his poisoned pen. Rarely does he contradict himself. He puts the blame for the murder of Amalasuntha on Theodora in the secret book but explains in the official history that her cousin Amalung arranged the death of the unfortunate Gothic queen. In building up the rapacity of his pseudo-Justinian, Procopius asserts that he squandered the gold reserve of 324,000 pieces left by Anastasius. John of Ephesus declares that at Justinian's death this particular reserve was intact. As to bloodthirstiness, Procopius' own careful casualty lists of the wars show that both Justinian and Belisarius were niggardly of the lives of their irreplaceable fighting men. Unfortunately, almost the only appeal from Procopius drunk is to Procopius sober.

So skillfully did this Boswell of the Byzantines use facts to lead to wrong inferences in the *Anecdota* that some careful historians have been misled. For a long time Justin I appeared in the pages of history as an ignoramus, because Procopius described the stencil of goldwork which he used to sign his name. Obviously the stencil existed, or there would be no sense in Procopius claiming it was used. But *why* was it used? Busy executives of today avail themselves of rubber stamps and automatic signatures. The Byzantine emperors also had gadgets at hand. Procopius was intent on belittling Justinian's family at that moment. The most modern authority on Justin's reign, Vasiliev, brushes the ignoramus legend aside with the observation that no illiterate man could have been the head of such a government.

There is another Procopian legend that sprang from reality. Or at least from a reality in popular opinion. It is the Demon Emperor pacing the corridors—with or without his head—listening to no voice but that of a spectral companion. All that reflects the popular impression of Justinian obsessed by his plans, heedless of his surroundings. It is interesting to trace the growth of the legend, especially after Theodora's death. There have been modern examples of the same phenomenon.

Perhaps the greatest miscarriage of ideas scored by the *Secret History* was not anticipated by Procopius. His harping on the small vanities and lusts of great personages has distorted the memory of the age in which they lived. Invaluable as are the incidents he presents, in reading his pages we come to picture the epoch as a composite of such incidents and to make Voltaire's mistake of setting it down as a "silly era." Greed and adultery and inconsequence become high-lighted; we look for amusing morsels of immorality or treachery, and are ready to believe that the moods and spites of a few people shaped events. To this Procopian distortion Gibbon joined his condemnation, making the tale of the emperors of Constantinople one of—in his own words—"weakness and misery."

Largely because of this twofold defamation and our own ignorance of happenings east of the Tiber, we came to visualize the first Byzantines as a species of treacherous puppets ensconced on gilded thrones, remote and hieratic through an age of long stagnation. We came to think of them as the ghosts of Rome. We assumed that they endured in that fashion for a thousand years without effort on their part.

Now these first Byzantines are being evaluated anew. The outlines are taking shape of a very different time and people.

The World of Justinian and Theodora

"Here is the great turning point in the history of the Mediterranean lands."[8] Constantine and those who followed him tried to build a new empire around a city that would be a powerhouse—St. Augustine's City of God, prepared to

[8]Norman H. Baynes, after Wilamowitz-Moellendorf, in *Byzantium: an Introduction to East Roman Civilization:* edited by Norman H. Baynes and H. St. L. B. Moss, Oxford, 1949. This volume of the Legacy Series offers a new evaluation of Byzantium.

defend itself on earth. They went to work like pioneers and labored like supermen.

The generation of Justinian and Theodora marks an uplift of achievement. Emergency is routine, and danger endemic. The people have stored up the scientific knowledge of the past, and make use of it to meet their needs. The days pass in unceasing activity. The sports of the Hippodrome provide rest from the strain.

The spirit of the age is humane. After the Nika revolt the death penalty is not invoked. Offenders may lose their property or go into exile; conspirators are sent to the cloisters; conquered kings are retired as country gentlemen. Hermits who castigate the sovereigns earn rewards; no Fra Savonarola goes to the burning stake. On the other hand, most conspirators do not seek to put themselves in power; they aim to remove those who seem to be injuring the state.

The spirit is gay, except during disasters. Great personages earn nicknames for themselves . . . Theodora could play the tricks of the stage in her throne room. Boccaccio would have laughed at the chatter of the actress-empress and her ladies when they plagued a worldly-wise man. How often hidden music sounded for them, from viols, flutes, and organs! It sounded for Theodora walking to her bath and for the intonation of Romanus, who composed a thousand hymns. A vestige of that music survives in the "Gregorian" chants of the dark ages in the west.

Poets sang their verses, which told of hunting, of the old Greek myths, and the wanderings of Alexander the Great.

The spirit, in short, was one of a renaissance. It resembled the Quatrocento, in which human beings sought to apply new creative skill to ancient knowledge. John of Cappadocia might have been an eastern Cosimo de' Medici; Procopius had a distant kinship with Niccolò Machiavelli.

The Emperor's Assistants

Probably Justinian would have accomplished less than a Theodosius or Heraclius if he had not had an instinct for picking men who could get things done. He took John of Cappadocia from a tax clerk's desk, and Belisarius from a frontier garrison.

These prime movers of an empire were by no means personal favorites. But once selected, Justinian had a way of keeping them at their tasks for a lifetime. If credit must be given for the manifold achievements of his reign, it should go to his chosen assistants. They were men of supreme ability, in a dynamic age. And probably most of Justinian's concrete ideas originated with them. Certainly John of Cappadocia suggested the most trenchant edicts of reform; after his dismissal Justinian's novellae diminished in number and force. Did not that fantastic genius, Anthemius of Tralles, put before him the design of the Sancta Sophia?

Once they started their labors, however, the demiurge of an emperor drove them to further accomplishment. The famous Code of Law was no sooner completed than Tribonian and his jurists had to tackle the Digest, and after that the explanatory Institutions. Belisarius hardly consolidated a victory before he was pulled out to begin a new operation He was used mercilessly until physically disabled Probably Narses was the only eunuch and Grand Chamberlain of history ever to be sent to recruit an army of Huns

Apparently all these members of Justinian's work-family were allowed to accumulate fortunes in reward. It seems also as if the son of Sabbatius had a gift for conciliating them There is no indication that personal affection for Justinian drove them to such tremendous tasks; rather he seemed to inspire a loyalty to something else—as if in aiding him along the path of his imagination, they served a cause. At times he called on men who were in the act of conspiring against him.

Unquestionably Justinian had the ability of a commander who could force others to carry out duties even when they hated him. For thirty-eight years the responsibilities of the Christian world centered upon him. Vasiliev says that his great undertakings gave the empire a new age of flowering.

But in the final analysis, Justinian and Theodora and their assistants were no more than the catalysts of a dynamic age.

The Preservation of Education

Schooling was maintained at a high level in Constantinople during the sixth century. The Roman-Byzantines seemed to realize that they depended upon mental resources to survive. Belisarius graduated from the city's military academy, Procopius from the famous law school at Beritus. Barbarian migrants were "Romanized" by schooling and indoctrination rather than by police action—for the barbarian peoples of the empire's fringe always had supremacy in physical force.

In well-to-do families children had their religious lessons, grammar, and rhetoric, from slave pedagogues; at the state-supported university they studied such sciences as mathematics, astronomy, music. Professional tutors hired themselves out, to women as well as men. Often they professed to teach the sciences of the Egyptians and Chaldeans. One family sought for a tutor in Persia, to find a man who would not instill in the children a fondness for hunting and sports!

Libraries seemed to serve more than colleges in educating the people at large. The famous museum at Alexandria, although deteriorating, still preserved its wealth of Hellenistic literature in carefully copied manuscripts. At Caesarea the library owned twenty thousand volumes. At such places the scientific work of Ptolemy the Geographer was probably

more dangerous Avars. For the remainder of the sixth century Byzantine naval strength kept Lombards and Avars from building and launching fleets. The challenge of the Arab attack by sea resulted in the construction of the fine Byzantine fleets of later centuries.

Yet Constantinople, unlike the Italian merchant cities, never developed a strong merchant marine. Venice, growing into a sea power, built merchant craft of a uniform design that could be converted into war craft. In time the Byzantines made the mistake of relying on the Venetian fleets for transport and defense. In 1204 Venetian fleets detoured wandering forces of crusaders to besiege Constantinople and to break through its defenses for the first time along the sea wall. In their capture of the Queen City they devastated it, crippling the Byzantine imperium, leaving little more than a half-populated shell of Constantinople for the Osmanli Turks to enter in 1453.

Secret of the Sancta Sophia

Why does Justinian's Great Church produce such an effect on a person entering it? It has been called incomparable, and it has never been exactly imitated. In some way those two geniuses from Asia Minor, Anthemius and Isidore, created an interior that seems to have a *presence* of its own. We can say just what Procopius did, that size alone does not account for it, nor the money spent on it; human spirit went into it; we are amazed, and our eyes wander without knowing what to look for.

Ornament plays no part in this impression, because the walls are bare now. I have gone back to the Sancta Sophia many times, and wondered at it. Perhaps the coloring has an unusual effect; around you, below, the matched marble surfaces are dark, sea-green, reddish purple, tawny, or faintly blue; up toward the supporting half domes the coloring lightens; within the dome itself sunlight quickens the golden yellow. You have the impression of radiance coming from above that no artificial lighting could give.

An explanation is offered by Walter Lowrie, who quotes Auguste Choisy.[10] "It is not merely the feeling of unity one experiences in viewing a Byzantine interior, but also a sort of tranquillity which is simply the satisfaction of the spirit . . . the eye embraces in one glance the dome which covers the edifice and the elements which support it. This is the clarity of Greek art . . . the main lines produce a simple impression, the details make the size evident. They are needed to furnish a scale and to spare St. Sophia the strange praise bestowed upon St. Peter's, that there is nothing to indicate how big it is."

The Art of the Byzantines

"But St. Sophia is by no means the only creation of what has aptly been called the first Golden Age of Byzantine Art. . . . Never has Christian art been at one and the same time more varied, more creative, scientific and daring," Charles Diehl explains.[11] "In all these buildings we find the same in-

[10]Walter Lowrie, *Art in the Early Church*, New York, 1948.

[11]*Byzantium: an Introduction to East Roman Civilization*, Baynes and Moss. Professor Diehl adds that the same fine design is found in aqueducts and cisterns and bridges of the period In *L'Art chrétien primitif et l'art byzantin*, Paris, 1928, he reminds us that the wellsprings of this early Christian art were Koptic imagery, Alexandrian tradition, and the artistry of the Syrian coast. Even Persian motifs of floral patterns and stylized figures appear, with all the wealth of oriental coloring, in this renaissance of Constantinople. Anthemius and Isidore learned their trade on the Anatolian coast. (Such origins, however, are still disputed, and Dr. Lowrie does not share Professor Diehl's convictions.)

Byzantine mastery of techniques extended to the minor arts. Their skill with *pietra dura* and marble mosaics could not be equaled in later ages. The finest cloth-of-gold, brocades, enamelwork, and ivory carvings came from Byzantium throughout the medieval period. They remained the masters of manuscript illumination until the time of Giotto, who was a disciple of Byzantine painting. The Metropolitan Museum of New York has a collection of their ornamentation of gold-glass.

ventive power, the same skill in the solution of the most delicate problems of construction, the same alert activity, and in each of the churches there was, as in St. Sophia, the same wealth of decoration in the form of carved marble capitals, polychrome marble facings—and, above all, in the play of light upon the mosaics."

The art of this early Christian renaissance took its imagery from the east, its creators from the Nile and the Syrian coast, and developed within the studios of Justinian's city. Joyousness rather than suffering infuses the pictured scenes. In this imagery Christ remains a shepherd, and the Apostles appear as human beings. The darker imagery of crucifixion, martyrdom, and the torments of hell was to develop later in the west. To these early Byzantine artists St. George remained a human Christian soldier, without horse and armor and dragon; the favored archangels, Michael and Gabriel, do not appear as in Dürer's drawing, flying over dying humanity. Christ in judgment sits alone, lacking entirely the compelling horror of falling bodies in Michelangelo's mural of the Last Judgment in the Sistine Chapel.

Look where you will at the remains of this art, combined of Syrian realism and Hellenic simplicity, and you will find nothing hieratic or morbid. It is a fragile art, lacking perspective in its mosaic murals, avoiding sculpture in the round, but it appeals with more than naïveté. Little of the deft goldsmiths' work or the rare silk brocades or carved ivory furnishings have survived because they disappeared almost entire in the centuries of plundering. We can find today few of the lovely things that surrounded Justinian and Theodora. There is a carved ivory chair in Ravenna, unequaled in craftsmanship, that escaped destruction because it happened to be a bishop's chair.

In the carvings of that chair and along the walls of St. Vitale bright scenes appear, of the story of Joseph, the visitation of the three angels, and the three Magi. In the mosaics of St. Apollinare Nuovo at Ravenna the three Magi run eagerly, holding up their gifts; the procession of the twenty virgin martyrs—and only Byzantines depicted a group of women within a church at that time—appear as women of flesh and blood, although they hold wreaths and palms.

In Venice you approach St. Mark's across a busy piazza. This is the church copied from that of the Apostles, rebuilt for Theodora by Anthemius. The façade, with miniature archways and tinted domes, appears gay enough in the sun. It hides the shape of the building, that of the Greek cross.

Entering, you step into another world where the mosaics reflect in dimness. You feel that you have come into something withdrawn that will never change. Close as you are to the reality of the pictured happenings on these walls, they remain remote from all familiar things.

Author's Note

All characters in this narrative are taken from the historical record. That applies to such minor figures as Porphyrius the charioteer and the blind dog of the Hippodrome. The events are actual and the incidents taken from sources of the time. Conversations between *two* persons have been invented for the most part, while based upon known particulars or viewpoints. Communications, letters, and episodes in the court and Hippodrome come from the record established by such scholars as J. B. Bury.

This book attempts to give the story of Justinian and Theodora in relation to the fellowship that served them, and to the people of Constantinople. The story is laid against the background of the time, as I could understand it. It relies on visualization rather than analysis, and seeks only to make more real, and perhaps closer to ourselves, the epoch of this husband and wife.

Names are given in their most familiar form, whether Greek, Latin, Iranian, or Gothic. Thus, for whatever reason, most texts dealing with sixth-century Constantinople adhere to Belisarius, Justinian, Vitigis, and Isidore rather than Bielisar, Justinianus, Wittich, and Isidoros. Rivers appear under their modern names. The Euxine Sea retains its Greek christening; it was not yet called the Black. Why the Pleasant Sea should become known as *Charnomore,* the Black Sea, remains one of the mysteries of geographical nomenclature. Evidently the Greeks regarded it as mild and agreeable because it was free from the sudden storms of the

Mediterranean, while the Slavs noticed that, by some peculiarity of lighting, its waters appeared darker than the other seas.

The army had changed entirely in our time from the hard-marching legions of classic Rome to the cavalry formations of the Parthians. (That is, the shock troops had been mounted and formed on the Persian pattern, equipped with Persian linkmail and bows as well as the old Roman breastplate. The infantry served more as garrison troops.) There were many and confusing units of palace guards and city militia, mentioned in this book simply as the excubitors and militia. Modern terms such as "general" and "regiments" are given for *drungarius,* and *tagmata* and so forth. The *buccellarii* were the personal or household mercenaries of commanders like Belisarius, and the word means "biscuit eaters." The high-ranking commanders, known as *Magister Militum,* were, like our General of the Army, at the head of all defense forces of an area.

I am indebted for the gleanings from Procopius to the superb and best translation in the Loeb Classical Library—*Procopius with an English Translation* by H. B. Dewing, London and New York, 1914–40. For details of Justin's election and reign, I have relied on the definitive study of A. A. Vasiliev—*Justin the First: an Introduction to the Epoch of Justinian the Great,* Harvard University Press, 1950. My guide from first to last has been the work of Ernest Stein—(in its French translation)—*L'Histoire du Bas-Empire,* Tome II, *De la disparition de l'Empire d'Occident à la mort de Justinien,* Desclée de Brouwer, Paris, Bruxelles, Amsterdam, 1949.

We have so many books that tell of the classic Rome of Julius Caesar and Trajan, and so many that pick up the continuity of the past with the medieval legendry beginning with the King Arthur cycle, the deeds of a Cid or a Roland. There was a long gap in between them, a sort of misty mid-region, peopled in the imagination of a layman like myself with galloping Huns, obscure Byzantines, and St. Benedict. The great Frenchmen, Charles Diehl and Louis Bréhier,[1] helped to fill in the gap with thoughts and details; Nicolai Iorga brought out this period as something alive.

[1]Louis Bréhier, *Le Monde byzantin: vie et mort de Byzance* (3 vols.), Paris, 1947.

The father and son, Henri and Jacques Pirenne,[2] brought happenings in the east into balance with the west. In England also there were rebels like Steven Runciman who believe that history did not tail off, after Gibbon's dictum, from the ruins of Rome, and that Nestorians and Armenians were, in this transition period, as significant as western Angles and Saxons or Goths.

An incident of twenty-four years ago started me on the attempt to tell this story. It was a startling surprise, after landing in Venice for the first time to begin a narrative of the crusades. Being too excited to stay in the hotel the first evening, I walked back to the Piazza San Marco and the Ducal Palace. In a dim corner, light picked out a group of porphyry figures. Four of them stood shoulder to shoulder, armed, wearing old flat helmets. It seemed like a good omen to come face to face with such a band of crusading knights, as I thought them to be.

Very quickly, in the full light of the next day, I learned that the dark impassive group were not crusaders but Byzantine soldiers. They had been shaped out of their purple stone in Constantinople, and carried away by Venetians. In the years since then I have come across other Byzantine remains, as far off as the African coast, or Yugoslovia. Their paintings turned up in the great church of Kiev. At each encounter they gave the impression of being apart from their surroundings—like the men-at-arms of San Marco—and significant.

I kept wondering why Byzantine remnants should be different from others, and why they were like that, and why they seemed to be filled with a meaning that was hard to understand.

[2]Henri Pirenne, *Mahomet et Charlemagne*, Paris, 1937. Jacques Pirenne, *Les Grands Courants de l'histoire universelle* (3 vols.), Paris, 1950.

Index